PRAISE
PAGANS IN THE PEWS

This is a landmark book, prophetic, stating for our times what Machen did for his. It is essential reading for every pastor, elder and serious Christian.

JAY ADAMS
NATIONAL ASSOCIATION OF NOUTHETIC COUNSELORS

This sobering assessment of contemporary society is a wake-up call for the Church to re-arm itself with God's Word. Retailers should aggressively promote this title.

CHRISTIAN BOOKSELLERS ASSOCIATION
TRADE JOURNAL

Dr. Peter Jones sounds a wake-up call: The ancient gods are back. The book bursts with quotations and vignettes of contemporary leaders and research on the Gnostics of the past.

EDMUND CLOWNEY
WESTMINSTER THEOLOGICAL SEMINARY

Pagans in the Pews is one of the five most important books I have ever read.

EDWARD S. CROOK
PRESBYTERIAN PASTOR
BRISTOL, TENNESSEE

Every pastor, elder and alert Christian should be informed of this work.

BRUCE DEMAREST
PROFESSOR OF SYSTEMATIC THEOLOGY, DENVER SEMINARY
DENVER, COLORADO

Pagans in the Pews is one of the most stimulating and encouraging contemporary books I have read in the last 10 years.

ANDREA FERRARI
BAPTIST PASTOR
ROME, ITALY

Warning: Don't read this book! Don't read it IF you like things the way they are. Don't read it IF you don't like to think. Don't read it IF you are complacent and apathetic (and want to stay that way). Why? Because this book will tell you the way things currently are—and you aren't going to like it. This book will not permit you to sit on the sidelines. And it will cause you to be unusually discerning. So, I warn you . . . proceed with caution!

DR. JIM GARLOW
SENIOR PASTOR, SKYLINE CHURCH
SAN DIEGO, CALIFORNIA

A stunning profile of prevailing apostasy.

GEORGE GRANT
WORLD

With grace and erudition, and a welcome leavening of humor, Dr. Jones illustrates that the contemporary culture wars . . . are symptomatic of a deeper conflict between . . . two views of God and man.

WILL GRIGG
THE NEW AMERICAN

If you want to understand why our culture is in chaos, read *Pagans in the Pews*.

LINDA HARVEY
MISSION AMERICA

Peter Jones's book is a warning label on our times! It is not a despairing critique but a discerning analysis of the cleverly intellectualized, spiritually homogenized religion of blindness, bondage and decadence vying for the soul of this generation.

JACK W. HAYFORD
CHANCELLOR, THE KING'S COLLEGE AND SEMINARY
VAN NUYS, CALIFORNIA

An obvious triumph! What an important and impressive book!

MICHAEL HORTON
CHRISTIANS UNITED FOR REFORMATION

The Gnostic Empire Strikes Back whistled across the bow of the good ship *Church*. *Pagans in the Pews* is a defensive missile system aimed at sophisticated invaders. You must read this book.

WILLIAM KOOIENGA
CHRISTIAN REFORMED PASTOR, CANADA

This book is awesome. After 10 years in radio, you gave me language for finally understanding this culture.

MICHAEL LAW
"THE GRAPEVINE," KPRZ

Pagans in the Pews is on my "book of the decade" list.

PAUL LONG
PROFESSOR OF MISSIONS, REFORMED THEOLOGICAL SEMINARY
JACKSON, MISSISSIPPI

In this courageous book, Peter Jones rips the masks off the most powerful spiritual influences assaulting our society. No wild-eyed conspiracy theorist, Jones is a scholar who makes his case in a carefully reasoned fashion. Clearly written and powerfully persuasive, *Pagans in the Pews* is essential reading.

John MacArthur
PRESIDENT, THE MASTER'S COLLEGE AND SEMINARY
PASTOR, GRACE COMMUNITY CHURCH
SUN VALLEY, CALIFORNIA

Opinion-makers and ministry leaders should devour this book.

Marlin Maddoux
"POINT OF VIEW", USA RADIO

Essential reading for the church, *Pagans in the Pews* deserves a wide audience.

Jerome Marroquin
PRESBYTERIAN CHURCH U.S.A. PASTOR
FALLBROOK, CALIFORNIA

I devoured this wonderful, scholarly but easy-to-read book. Believe me, it will set you on your ear. Get this book, please. Every Christian needs to read it.

Duane Miller
KKHP RADIO
HOUSTON, TEXAS

Like Paul in the Areopagus, Peter Jones uncovers for us what the culture is really saying.

Janet Parshall
HOST, "JANET PARSHALL'S AMERICA"
WASHINGTON, D.C.

A book for which I have the greatest conceivable appreciation.

Paige Patterson
PRESIDENT, SOUTHEASTERN BAPTIST THEOLOGICAL SEMINARY

Jones asserts that American gnosticism has begun to serve as the theological underpinning of cultural and even political liberalism.

JOHN J. REILLY
CULTURE WARS

There have been many great recent books—William Bennett's *Book of Virtues*, and Judge Robert Bork's *Slouching Toward Gomorrah*—but this is the greatest wake-up-call book I have ever seen. Reading *Pagans in the Pews* is like getting a sudden slap in the face while in a deep sleep. Lord, what has happened?!

CRAIG ROBERTS
HOST, "LIFE LINE"
SAN FRANCISCO, CALIFORNIA

An example of good, classical, living theology, after the fashion of Irenaeus and Augustine.

ROUSAS RUSHDOONY
CHALCEDON

A thought-provoking and accurate book about today's culture.

BARBARA SIMPSON
"HOT TALK," KSFO, SAN FRANCISCO

Reading this book will be life-changing . . . an incredible, convincing, brilliant conclusion.

JOHN SMED
CHURCH-PLANTING COORDINATOR, PRESBYTERIAN CHURCH IN AMERICA

Peter Jones has emerged as a skilled knight in the culture wars.
He lays his theological axe at the root of the tree, cutting to the naked core
of neo-paganism. *Pagans in the Pews* is a must read.

R. C. SPROUL

HOST, "RENEWING YOUR MIND"
PRESIDENT, LIGONIER MINISTRIES
ORLANDO, FLORIDA

A sobering and stimulating read.

DICK STAUB

HOST, "THE DICK STAUB SHOW"
CHICAGO, ILLINOIS
SAN DIEGO

Pagans in the Pews goes beyond *Slouching Toward Gomorrah* to the spiritual
roots of the problems besetting our culture.

PAT SWINDOLL

FORMER MEMBER, HOUSE OF REPRESENTATIVES
ATLANTA, GEORGIA

The preface of *Pagans in the Pews* is worth the cost of the entire book.
Peter Jones eloquently, with anointing, sets the stage for our understanding of
the eternal cosmic collision. He uses the hard hammer of truth to crumble the
disguise of false deity and exposes hidden battlefields we are losing simply
because they go unnoticed in spiritual camouflage.

TOMMY TENNEY

GODCHASERS.NETWORK
BEST-SELLING AUTHOR, *THE GOD CHASERS* AND *GOD'S DREAM TEAM*

PAGANS
IN THE PEWS

PETER JONES

Regal

A Division of Gospel Light
Ventura, California, U.S.A.

Published by Regal Books
A division of Gospel Light
Ventura, California, U.S.A.
Printed in the U.S.A.

Regal Books is a ministry of Gospel Light, an evangelical Christian publisher dedicated to serving the local church. We believe God's vision for Gospel Light is to provide church leaders with biblical, user-friendly materials that will help them evangelize, disciple and minister to children, youth and families.

It is our prayer that this Regal book will help you discover biblical truth for your own life and help you meet the needs of others. May God richly bless you.

For a free catalog of resources from Regal Books/Gospel Light, please call your Christian supplier or contact us at 1-800-4-GOSPEL *or* www.regalbooks.com.

Cover and Internal Design by Robert Williams
Edited by Rebecca Jones and Rose Decaen

Library of Congress Cataloging-in-Publication Data
Jones, Peter, 1940-
    Pagans in the pews / Peter Jones.
        p.c.
    Includes bibliographical references and index
    ISBN 0-8307-2798-1 (trade paper)
        1. Liberalism (Religion) 2. United States—Religion—1960— 3. Liberalism (Religion)—United States. 4. Apologetics I. Title

BR1617 .J66 2001
239'.93—dc21   2001048286

1 2 3 4 5 6 7 8 9 10 11 12 13 14 15 / 09 08 07 06 05 04 03 02 01

Rights for publishing this book in other languages are contracted by Gospel Literature International (GLINT). GLINT also provides technical help for the adaptation, translation and publishing of Bible study resources and books in scores of languages worldwide. For further information, write to GLINT, P.O. Box 4060, Ontario, CA 91761-1003, U.S.A. You may also send e-mail to Glintint@aol.com, or visit the GLINT website at www.glint.org.

To that wonderful group of people

affectionately known

as the Jones Tribe:

Eowyn, Stasie, Julien, Myriam, Tessa,

Zoé and Toby

CONTENTS

PART I
THE ORIGIN AND PURPOSE OF THE NEW SPIRITUALITY

PART II
ANATOMY OF AN APOSTASY

ACKNOWLEDGMENTS

I wish to thank:

my students, who have stimulated my thinking about Gnosticism and its lessons for today;

my colleagues at Westminster Theological Seminary in California, who have constantly encouraged and inspired me; I especially acknowledge the help of Professors Dennis Johnson and Steven Baugh, who, by teaching my courses for a semester, enabled me to give my complete attention to research;

Dr. Mark Futato, who has sharpened my thinking about the Bible's teaching on creation, ecology and sexuality;

the library staff, for their competent help;

my secretary, Mrs. Jackie Vanden Bos, for her invaluable assistance, which went beyond the call of duty;

John DeFelice for his original translations from the Coptic of the Gnostic texts cited in this volume;

my wife, Rebecca, who, as expert editor, stylistic critic, astute theologian, constant encourager, friend and helper, has allowed this project to progress from endless unworked paragraphs and notes into a finished, readable text.

The twentieth century . . . is to witness a gigantic conflict of spirits. . . . More serious and fiercer than ever before, the conflict is between the old and new worldview.

HERMANN BAVINCK
CHRISTIAN THEOLOGIAN, 1901

There was some primary warfare going on . . . an archetypal battle between principalities and powers . . . and I willed to go all the way in this death battle.

MARY DALY
ECO-FEMINIST PAGAN WITCH AND FORMER ROMAN CATHOLIC NUN, 1968

We women are going to bring an end to God.

NAOMI R. GOLDENBERG
JEWISH FEMINIST, 1979

I call out for protection of the goddess's people from the wrath of right-wing fundamentalists and their God.

WENDY HUNTER ROBERTS
PAGAN PRIESTESS, 1993

The Goddess has returned: Magic is afoot.

CALIFORNIA BUMPER STICKER, 1995

The western notion of God is in desperate need of transformation . . . The . . . Goddess embodies the requisite transformation.

RICHARD GRIGG, ROMAN CATHOLIC THEOLOGIAN, 1995

The loving care of Mother Earth is . . . replacing the former sense of obedience to the Heavenly Father.

LLOYD GERRING, THEOLOGIAN, 1999
FROM THE PUBLISHING ARM OF THE JESUS SEMINAR

FACE-OFF

John Lennon was an old school chum. Simple fellows, with little intellectual sophistication, we never spoke about religion or philosophy. Instead, we listened to Bill Haley and the Comets over fish and chips in a greasy spoon "chippy" on Penny Lane—strictly against the rules of traditionalist Quaker Bank High School for Boys, where we enjoyed education for all the wrong reasons. At age 16, John left Quarry Bank to go to the Liverpool Arts School. I stayed on for "A levels" and went to university. We never met again.

History is funny. As everybody knows, John became a megastar and converted to New Age Hinduism. Hardly anyone knows that I became a committed orthodox Christian and taught New Testament Greek in French to future pastors of the old Huguenot Church in the south of France for 18 years. But our lives once again became strangely intertwined.

In 1991, with great reluctance, I left my adopted land and church to accept a teaching post in Southern California. The culture shock shook a few synapses loose in my brain. When they came together again, I made the connection that Lennon had made years earlier between ancient Gnosticism and New Age spirituality. In "The Mysterious Smell of Roses," a chapter in *Skywriting by Word of Mouth*, an anthology of his writings published after his death, Lennon made a most unusual affirmation for someone not trained in theology or philosophy: "It seems to me that the only true Christians are the Gnostics, who believe in self-knowledge, i.e., becoming Christ themselves, reaching the Christ within."[1]

As jocular high-school pals sitting together at a two-seater desk, we never imagined that divergent interpretations of an obscure Christian heresy would put us on opposing sides in the war of the worlds. Were Lennon alive today, he might well have been a leader of the neo-pagan, pseudo-Christian camp this book seeks to describe and unmask. I discovered Gnosticism as part of my graduate studies. But how did Lennon, with no formal training beyond a two-year technical school, come to know about such arcane matters of ancient Christian history? There is clearly more to life than meets the eye!

IS THERE A PROBLEM?

Most Americans do not have a personal vendetta against Christians, in spite of a media elite that brands committed believers as bigots and homophobes. Tolerance, dialogue and civil exchange are the order of the day. The terminology of spiritual battle has gone the way of "Onward Christians Soldiers" in our politically correct churches of peace and love. Relativity, compromise and civility without principle have replaced the antithetical, black-and-white thinking of Scripture. But, like it or not, warfare has existed from the beginning, as God declared to the serpent and the woman concerning their opposing historical progeny: "I will place enmity between . . . your seed and her seed."[2] In our time, that warfare has broken cover, but most of America remains disturbingly uninformed.

From behind the oak doors of impeccable suburban homes and the surgically sterile partitions of abortion clinics, the blood of unborn children cries out. The battle for the soul of this nation and of Western civilization rages unchecked. This is no video game of the mind that returns the player to reality when the quarter runs out. Homes and marriages, like unborn babies, are torn to shreds in a culture heralded as the epitome of enlightened civilization. America, defender of the great values of Western Christian culture, is staggering, critically wounded by a radical ideology of "empowering" pro-choice personal autonomy.

At the beginning of the third millennium, two radically opposed ways of understanding human nature and the universe vie for our allegiance. One defends the truth, the other the diabolical lie. One follows the God of the Bible; the other follows the goddess of paganism.

Like two hockey players poised over a puck, ready to force it in one direction or the other, two religious faiths—the only two—battle for the spirit and the mind of the modern world. The game no longer pits the dark forces of atheistic humanism and godless materialism against the spirituality of the "Christian" West. The present contest is between two powerful spiritualities: Christian theism (God the Father) and pagan monism (the Mother goddess).

If the teams in this "face-off of the soul" wore different-colored uniforms, the game would be easier to follow. Alas, one team seeks to win by making all the uniforms gray and, in the confusion, steals the puck to score the winning goal. Only a closer look shows that the teams differ in style of play and direction. Choose sides, for the puck is our souls and the game is a spiritual battle to the death.

INTRODUCTION

PAGANS IN THE PEWS AND PULPITS

The title of this book can be taken in two ways.

In one way, we should long to see our churches full of unconverted people, flocking to hear the preaching of the gospel. Though they might squirm in their seats, as they hear the truth about their lost state, by the grace of God, those under the sound of the gospel will turn and be saved. We need to pray that pagans will be found in great numbers in our pews. This not the subject of this book.

In another way, there are far too many comfortable pews in churches where the gospel is no longer heard. According to recent polls, only 33 percent of the American Catholics, Lutherans and Methodists, and 28 percent of the Episcopalians agreed with the statement that Christ was without sin. Thus they no longer believe in the divinity of Christ and therefore do not understand the gospel. A mere 17 percent of the Catholics, 18 percent Methodists, 20 percent Episcopalians, 21 percent Lutherans and 22 percent of the Presbyterians actually believe Satan is real.[1] And the trend is a downward one. Says Mary Ann Lundy, deputy director of the World Council of Churches and a well-known worshiper of the Goddess Sophia: "We are learning that to be ecumenical is to move beyond the boundaries of Christianity . . . yesterday's heresies are becoming tomorrow's Book of [Church]Order."[2]

One has to wonder if the prophecies and predictions of occult seers are not coming true in our time. Alice Bailey, a leader in the Theosophical Society, declared in the 1950s: "[Thanks to the] the efforts of the UN a new church of God, gathered out of all the religions and spiritual groups, will unitedly bring to an end the great heresy of separation."[3]

Marilyn Ferguson, New Age popularizer of Helen Schucman's *A Course in Miracles*, is certain she is a true Christian. She writes: "Many Christian churches are seeing that direct spiritual experience offers a revitalization for modern Christianity."[4] Her description of what is happening in "many Christian churches" is not frivolous; spirits are at work. Ken Carey, the author of *Starseed: The Third Millennium: Living in the Posthistoric World* and a "channel" for "spirit beings in the eternal fields of light" makes a similar statement. "Associate only with congregations whose atmosphere encourages love . . . enjoy the rich diversity of truth's multiple expressions."[5] In other words, appropriate churches are those that have rejected biblical ethics, scriptural demands for holiness and the Christian doctrine of redemption in a space/time incarnation of the eternal Son. The spirits love churches like these.

Alas, pagans are more and more comfortable in pews like these, because there are far too many pagans in the pulpits. It is to this subject we now turn.

PART I

THE ORIGIN AND PURPOSE OF THE NEW SPIRITUALITY

CHAPTER ONE

THE BIRTH OF THE RELIGIOUS LEFT

The sixties ended before the turn of the decade, but the seeds of change had been planted.[1]

MARILYN FERGUSON
AUTHOR, THE AQUARIAN CONSPIRACY

The social movements of the 1960s and 1970s represent the rising culture, which is now ready for passage into the solar culture.[2]

FRITJOF CAPRA
NEW AGE PHYSICIST AND PROFESSOR AT
UC BERKELEY

On November 3, 1992, the people of the United States voted into the most powerful position on Earth a man who had smoked pot, dodged the draft and espoused the sexual morals of the hippie revolution. The antiestablishment, flower-power children of the '60s entered the halls of political power in the '90s. Politics would never be the same again.

With short hair and three-piece suits, hippies squatted in the White House—legally.[3] In the last decade of the twentieth century, America witnessed the second coming of the '60s[4] and the birth of the Religious Left.

Conceived in the '60s, Born in the '90s

Mystics like Marilyn Ferguson analyzed the impact of the '60s with chilling accuracy: "The values that had powered the movement of the '60s could not be institutionalized without a shift in cultural assumptions. *As consciousness changes, the world changes.*"[5]

The change has occurred. Americans not only tolerate but have also institutionalized divorce, abortion, homosexuality and feminism. This has happened because the religious consciousness of America has changed. Calls to strengthen the family, clear the streets of crime, make sex safe and abortion rare and beef up educational standards go unheeded. Patriotic optimists who hope that a sensible nation will pull itself together one more time may be the most disappointed. The new consciousness cannot hear calls for reform, because it is deaf to anything but revolutionary spiritual and social change. How has this metamorphosis of the American psyche come about?

More prophet than comedian, one journalist observed that the mix of piety and popular culture in the Clinton inaugural celebration convinced her that she was present at "the birth of the Religious Left."[6] Everyone knows the Religious Right. But the Religious Left?

"This is our time," proclaimed President and Mrs. Clinton as they entered the White House. But just whose time was it? The new-look first couple symbolized not so much a political party as the maturing fruit of the '60s counterculture revolution. Here was a new kind of religious commitment that would in the same breath—or at least in the same week—sing gospel songs with genuine tears and promote the new morality of abortion and homosexual practices. Southern Baptist presidential tears also spilled in spiritual communion with Buddhist Dalai Lama, whom Clinton found "a most remarkable man."

"Our time" was Marianne Williamson, who wrote the best-selling book *A Return to Love: Reflections on the Principles of "A Course in Miracles."*[7] Williamson, a hard-core New Age believer, wrote the laudatory preface to Ken Carey's *The Third Millennium.* Carey wrote under the influence of a voice from "a spirit-being in the eternal fields of light." It was "as if something enormous were looking through my eyes," says Carey.[8] His "revelations" are radically anti-Christian, but Williamson heartily approves. This was her time. One of the spiritual advisers of Hillary Clinton, with whom she often lunched, Williamson dined at the White House and slept in the Lincoln Bedroom.

"Our time" was Jean Houston, who is recognized as a leading New Age feminist guru (author of *Godseed, The Hero and the Goddess* and *The Passion of Isis and Osiris*) and cofounder of the Foundation for Mind Research. She is a board member of the Temple of Understanding, which promotes a one-world religion. Houston was a leading participant at the Parliament of the World's Religions in Chicago in 1993, of which the occultic Theosophical Society was a sponsor. Her lecture, which I attended, described in globalist terms a new day "being called forth by an evolution in . . . spiritual practice." She went on to say, "We are on the brink of the planetary person, who represents a whole new order of capacities and consciousness necessary for sacred stewardship of the earth."[9]

Such new spiritual capacities intrigue old-style social-gospel liberals from mainline denominations. White House spokesman Neil Lattimore denied that they were séances; but official sources have acknowledged that Jean Houston led Mrs. Clinton, a United Methodist, in "imaginary conversations" with figures of the past, such as Eleanor Roosevelt and Hindu peace activist Mahatma Gandhi. "We have to draw strength from wherever we can, to make it from day to day," said the White House chief of staff, underplaying the enormity of these revelations. Nancy Reagan's dalliance with astrology pales to insignificance compared with Hillary Clinton's "reaching out and searching hard" away from her Christian roots into the pagan core of the new Religious Left's occult spirituality.[10]

"Our time" was the appointment of 150 practicing homosexuals to the Clinton administration[11] and, behind them, the rise to power of the homosexual lobby in every area of society, including mainline churches.

"Our time" was the pro-choice abortion-rights forces that influenced the president to veto the 1996 bill outlawing the horrendous procedure known as partial-birth abortion. These powerful forces outweighed the fact that this legislation was supported by the vast majority of both houses of Congress and that the veto was condemned by all 11 living past presidents of the Southern Baptist Conference, President Clinton's denomination.

"Our time" was the radical feminists who surrounded the First Lady while Clinton was in office. They monopolized the American representation both at the United Nations Conference on World Population in Cairo in 1993 and at the Beijing Conference on Women in 1995. Radical alumnae from Mrs. Clinton's alma mater, Wellesley College, were a major force in Beijing and in the formulation of the Platform for Action, the conference agenda that refused to recognize the normativity of heterosexuality and of the two-parent heterosexual family. Such women believe they are "a critical mass," called to spread this ideology throughout the globe, to accomplish what is "truly Wellesley's mission."[12]

THE DESTRUCTIVE GENERATION: FROM BERKELEY TO WASHINGTON

Today's Berkeley seems stuck in a 40-year time warp. Streakers, hippies, saffron-robed Hari Krishna bands, junkies, pot-pushers, esoteric bookstores and health-food stores lead the visitor on a magical mystery tour of yesteryear—a living museum of a social experiment now faded into memory. It is all so quaint and reassuring.

But do not be misled. Most of the '60s revolutionaries cleaned up their act and are no longer in the Berkeley backwater.[13] Some even moved to Washington, into pretty nice digs. The Baby Boomers have had babies themselves and have reached 50 and beyond. Their ideas are alive and well and have made phenomenal progress.

David Horowitz and Peter Collier were members of the revolution's inner circle. Editors of *Ramparts* magazine, the unofficial voice of radical politics, they were friends with everybody in the radical scene, from Huey Newton and Jerry Rubin to Tom Hayden and Jane Fonda. Having helped foment the rebellion, they now have troubled consciences. Not based on religious or Christian convictions, the mature assessment from these leaders of the rebellion on what they call the "destructive generation" is most telling:

> The stones we threw into the water of our world in those days caused ripples that continue to lap on our shores today—for better and more often for worse.[14]

What was destroyed? Nothing less, I believe, than Western Christendom and civilization.

The "spirit entity" that channeled messages through Ken Carey underlined the importance of the '60s for the coming of the new religion:

> Our communications during these closing years of the seventies are reaching past the social fringe of your culture that was contacted during the sixties. This time, we are reaching deep into the heart of global civilization. . . . We are not in much contact yet with government officials, nor with world banks or international financiers. Our first contacts with them will occur during the more powerful transmissions of 1987 to 1989. Those who [sic] we are contacting now, nonetheless, are critical enough in the maintenance of your social systems to ensure that the world will make some incredible leaps in consciousness during the next decade. . . . By the time of the eighties revelations, knowledge of our existence will be widespread.[15]

If the spirit entities consider the '60s rebellion such an important moment for the coming of the new religion, perhaps Christians should pause and listen. The rejection of authority and of biblical sexual morals, as well as the search for a new spirituality were not artifacts of a failed revolution, but the weapons used to destroy Western civilization.

The revolution succeeded beyond the wildest dreams of the long-haired revolutionaries. While most thought the revolution had failed, its leaders undertook the long march through the institutions. Tenured radicals now rule those institutions.[16] As one repentant hippie said, "Those who loved the '60s own the '90s."[17]

"Western Civ Has Got to Go"

The New Left radicals of the '60s wanted to bring the system down. History will show that they did just that—by taking it over. Rejection of landlords, university senates, police and the federal government was transformed into the rejection of Western civilization *in toto*. Radical students today chant, "Hey ho, wha d'ya know? Western Civ has got to go." They silence dead white male authors like Plato, Shakespeare and Jonathan Edwards, bringing in instead the chorus of contemporary intellectuals (including many orthodox Christians) who call for the dismantling of patriarchy.[18]

Betty Friedan's *The Feminist Mystique* attacked patriarchy and defended the autonomous woman. The plaint of the lonely housewife became a deafening battle cry, as a phalanx of formidable feminists stormed the walls of Judeo-Christian civilization. But destroying fatherly authority and the responsible, representative role of men dismantles the traditional family unit. There is no use calling for the defense of the traditional family if you do not see this.

The document "Project for the Republican Future" notes that the Supreme Court's rulings on abortion, which eliminate the decision-making responsibility of fathers, have "affected a fundamental alteration in the meaning of the American democratic experiment—that of the radically autonomous individual and the coercive state . . . in which the community of husband and wife is no longer of constitutional or legal account."[19] This mortal, though muted, attack on the pillars of our society goes mostly unnoticed.

The rejection of patriarchy is but one example of the power of the deconstructionist movement that began in the '60s. Reacting in part against *modernity*—the proud Enlightenment belief that mankind's problems could be solved by human reason, apart from God's revelation—postmodern deconstruction destroys everything in its path. Jesus told of a house swept clean of one demon, into which rush seven more. A world cleansed of rationalistic, atheistic humanism now welcomes new, very "spiritual" tenants.

Deconstruction sees all rational discourse, all attempts to explain the world, as the naked use of power.[20] Claims to absolute truth are only impositions of the ideology of those in power upon those who have no power. Truth is considered ideological harassment of minority victims. The Equal Employment Opportunity Commission wants to eliminate religion from the workplace so that no one may be "harassed" by religious ideas at work. The time is coming when it will be illegal to play "Silent Night" in the shopping mall. The word "Christmas," even on Bing Crosby's lips, will soon disappear as well.

The Sexual Revolution as Government Policy

As a bare-chested revolutionary in the '60s, Jerry Rubin said, "We've combined youth, music, sex, drugs and rebellion with treason—that's a hard combination to beat!"[21] The balding, besuited entrepreneur Rubin lost his youth, his revolutionary zeal and, unfortunately, his life (in a traffic accident in Los Angeles), but music, sex and drugs have had greater effects than anything Rubin may have imagined.

Sexual liberation in the '60s was "anything goes" heterosexual love.[22] Michael Lerner was the leader of the Berkeley Students for a Democratic Society, and another of Hillary Clinton's spiritual gurus. On his first wedding cake were the words: "Smash Monogamy."[23] The manifesto succeeded. Lerner weathered a number of marriages, and all over America divorce rates and cohabitation skyrocketed. Today's sexual revolution goes beyond extramarital, premarital and multiple-partner heterosexual activity. "Anything goes" has become the mass-media promotion not only of boundless immoral heterosexuality, but also of sadomasochism, bisexuality, homosexuality and pornography. Pedophilia[24] and bestiality are already in the wings for those who surf the web.

A biblical text thousands of years old captures this sliding morality. Leviticus 20 prohibits the following: adultery, the sacrificial killing of children, the consulting of mediums, homosexual behavior and bestiality. Such abominations were the root cause of the destruction of the ancient pagan nations.[25] Can this nation avoid a similar fate? Gary Bauer, reacting to the government policy for the promotion of condoms in pornographic television ads, said:

> For the first time in our nation's history, a generation of young Americans is being told by government leaders that if they will just use condoms, promiscuity is perfectly safe and, in fact, no big deal.[26]

The '60s revolutionaries who now head government agencies have made free love into official government policy.

MAGICAL MYSTERY TOUR: THE SEARCH FOR A NEW SPIRITUALITY

The '60s counterculture revolution was a spiritual movement.[27] Woodstock, a spiritual happening, was a drug-trip search for the Garden of Eden.[28] Richard Alpert's soul journey exemplifies the spiritual maturation of the '60s. Professor of psychology at Harvard and colleague of Timothy Leary, Alpert broke with Freudian reductionism and, with the help of LSD, discovered that there was life beyond the id.

The chemically inspired mind-and-soul expansion of consciousness that gave Alpert unity with the universe sent him on a religious quest to India, where he practiced Hinduism for many years. He returned to the United States as Ram Dass, a Westernized Hindu guru who tours the lucrative lecture circuit, replete with hip humor, a male lover and a spirit guide named Emmanuel. His midriff corpulence brings to mind the fattened Buddha rather than bony Eastern holy men on the streets of Calcutta. Ram Dass, a practitioner of New Age spirituality, claims to have finally rediscovered his Judaism. The "rainbow" trajectory of Ram Dass is reflected in the musings of a "death of God" theologian at the beginning of the '70s:

> It may be that this need to recall an old symbol system [polytheism] for new purposes may be behind the recent interest in the occult, in magic, in extraterrestrial life, in Hindu India and Buddhist Japan, in multi-daemoned China, in sorcery, in new forms of multiple-family life, in communes, in the "new religions," and many other alternative lifestyles and meaning systems which have been hitherto foreign.[29]

The revolutionaries said it; we just didn't believe them. The Beatles went East, while the gurus came West. Chemically inspired highs of acidheads and predictions of polytheists have diversified into the multicultural spiritual highs of the new millennium. Just check your New Age advertiser, where you will find chakra meditation, yoga, witchcraft, channeling, astral travel, visualization, kundalini sex, Native American animism and all the gods and goddesses you can handle.

The movement has not lost its quest for spirituality. It has diversified and gone mainline, just as the Hindu mystic Swami Vivekananda prophesied at the first Parliament of the World's Religions in Chicago in 1893. His dream was the creation of "a society of Western science and socialism and Indian spirituality."[30] One century later, the 1993 Parliament in Chicago realized Vivekananda's dream and tasted of the global character and power of the syncretistic movement that had been just a tiny project in 1893.

INDICATORS OF SOCIAL DESTRUCTION

The "destructive generation" has done its work. Having promised freedom, peace and love, the revolution delivered the freedom of a derailed train and the peace of a beached whale.

The statistics speak. America leads the "civilized" world in fathers' absence from the home and in its permissive laws regulating abortion and divorce.[31] The *Atlantic Monthly* has called the last 25 years a vast experiment in family life. They could have said a vast destruction of family life.[32] Only about one in four American households is comprised of married parents with children, about the same percentage as those born to unwed mothers. In 1960, 243,000 children lived in single-parent homes. By 1993, the figure had climbed to 6.3 million, provoking a demographic expert to describe the trend as "astonishing." From 1970 to 1993 the number of unmarried adults in America nearly doubled, and the number of divorcees tripled.[33] Though the 2000 census shows slight changes in certain categories, it still presents a catastrophic picture of American family life.

Can anything stop the implosion of the American culture? The deconstruction of the Judeo-Christian family has created a voracious vacuum that is quickly being filled by alternate family lifestyles. Because these structures seem better than none, the public accepts them without examining the worldview of pagan spirituality that spawned them.

Destruction of the Christian Culture

The '60s movement did not rebel against religion. It rebelled against the *Christian* religion.[34] The dust of history has settled enough to see that the counterculture movement of the '60s did not seek secularization but a radically different spirituality.

Baby Boomers were "a generation of seekers."[35] Only 4 percent of them are atheists or agnostics. The rest follow some religion.[36] Our declining moral standards are not because we are no longer religious but because we have changed religions. The noble search for expanded consciousness and alternate spiritualities in the '60s led East, where seekers discovered mysticism and returned to spawn a relativistic religious hybrid: Western spiritual monism.

This new pagan monism joins the Eastern religious idea that "all is one and one is all" to Western technology, democratic self-determination and the ideal of autonomous egalitarianism. The whole is clothed in "Christian" dress for general Western consumption. The mix has created a potent elixir that fires the minds and hearts of social transformers in this new millennium.

REGENERATION FOR THE ME GENERATION

The '60s came of age in the '90s. In her book *Do You Believe in Magic? The Second Coming of the '60s Generation*, sociologist Annie Gottlieb posits that the rage of the '60s has been channeled into a new expression of spirituality. No longer hooked on the self, the "Me generation" developed a social conscience: "the politics of love," or "the politics of virtue or meaning." Rooted in the '60s revolution, the new consciousness has flowered in liberation theology, the women's liberation movement, the gay and lesbian quest for social and religious recognition, multiculturalism and political correctness. Gottlieb sees this second coming of the '60s as a new agenda for spiritual and religious transformation, not only of the self but also of the world.[37]

The real enemy of the Church's faith is no longer antireligious atheistic humanism but a revived pagan religion. It is not that we have *no* God but that we have *too many*. It is not a lack of spirituality but rather of spiritual syncretism. Many decry the dissolution of society, but few see the religious threat of the new spirituality. Hidden under its free-flowing robes of tolerance lies the skeleton of pagan monism.

CHAPTER TWO

THE CREED
OF THE
RELIGIOUS LEFT

*Do not forget that the fundamental contrast has always been,
is still, and always will be until the end: Christianity and
Paganism, the idols or the living God.*

ABRAHAM KUYPER
THE STONE LECTURES, PRINCETON SEMINARY, 1898

The disparate themes of our pro-choice culture have a central core.
Society's vaunted diversity hides the profound ideological coherence of
religious paganism—the worship of the earth and of the goddess behind it. The
apostle Paul would describe this religion as worship of the creature rather than
the Creator.[1] However, the term "paganism" is still imprecise, suggesting the
sum of unrelated, non-Christian religions. It is vitally important to see beyond
the external diversity and subtle distinctions to the inner coherence of paganism which is known as monism.

THE HEART OF AQUARIAN SPIRITUALITY: THE FIVE POINTS OF MONISM

"Ism" words frighten the average reader, but we had better understand this one. "Mono" means "one." In a monopoly, one company captures the market. Monism as a philosophy of life seeks to capture the Church in our day. Its tentacles, some secular and some Christian liberal, surround a sleepy Zion. They have drawn in most movements, claiming to deliver peace and prosperity for a renewed planet. Monism's symbol is the circle—its goal is to encircle the globe.

Five elements summarize monism in its contemporary expression.[2] It is essential to grasp them, in order to understand what is happening in our society.

1. All Is One and One Is All

This is the essence of monism, the idea that the universe is a mass of undifferentiated, related energy. God is not *outside* the universe; God *is* the universe. Christianity's Creator/creature distinction is eradicated. The big O of Monism is a circle—everything, including God, is within the circle. You cannot contain a watchmaker in his watch, but this is what monism does to God. The ancient symbol of the circle has reappeared in witchcraft (whose ceremony begins by "casting a sacred circle"), in Hinduism and in goddess worship. Even the symbol of the Parliament of the World's Religions was a circle.

This circular, all-is-one notion underlies New Age/Taoist physics, "deep ecology," the worship of Mother Earth and ultimately the use of female imagery for God. *Restoring the Goddess to Judaism and Christianity*, a recent politically correct publication, is a blatant attempt to reintroduce paganism into biblical faith. The mother is none other than the encircling, bewitching Mother Earth:

> She [is] . . . everywhere and encompasses everything: . . . She is everything and everybody and its opposite. . . . She shows for me that there is no disunity between something and its opposite. A totality includes all aspects. Linear and dualistic divisions do not exist.[3]

Break the spell. It is impossible to restore paganism to the Bible, for it was never there. But paganism, clothed in the emotive and seductive colors of tolerance and human rights, gradually changes perceptions of God. Its success would spell the end of Christianity, because the ultimate source of the new gospel is paganism.

In the movie *Star Wars*, Jedi warrior Obi-Wan Kenobi teaches young Luke Skywalker in monistic prose worthy of any pagan priest or priestess, ancient or modern:

> The Force is an energy field created by all living things. It surrounds us, penetrates us; it binds the galaxy together.

When Luke abandons himself to his intuitions and is in harmony with the Force, he is able to pilot a flying machine of unimaginable complexity in a pinpoint bombing of the headquarters of the evil Empire. Skeptical? Monism promises no less incredible results to its adherents.

2. Humanity Is One

If all is one, humanity is an expression of divine oneness. Humans are congealed cosmic energy who create their own reality. Belief that the human is divine, and thus essentially good, helps explain the burgeoning quest for personal spiritual discovery, to the detriment of doctrine and truth.[4] Mysticism has replaced true spirituality.[5]

Companies in the West, seeing commercial value in such optimism, are using these ideas to produce better sales personnel. Madison Avenue and New Age gurus may be an unstoppable, unholy alliance feeding the machine of political correctness. As an expression of divinity, they tell us, each self is a source of truth. Tolerance and relativity are necessary corollaries, since everybody's truth is different.

This monistic ideology defines the values clarification programs in the public schools. There is no such thing as right over wrong. Children must express their sexuality as they abandon themselves to their intuitions, untrammeled by moral considerations but protected by condoms. The individual is the final judge, and intuition is the path to oneself, to human freedom and to harmony with the Force.

3. All Religions Are One

In this great expanse of energy, divinity and truth, no religion can claim to have an exclusive claim on the truth. Because orthodox Christianity commits this unpardonable sin, it is the major obstacle to the religious and social harmony of the planet. Religions must blend into a global, unified syncretism.

Just below the surface of the apparent diversity of the world's religions, the various creeds are actually considered interchangeable, and spiritual experiences are believed to be in communion with the same deep reality. The Parliament of the World's Religions was a preprogrammed happening of monistic spirituality. Conferees were to discover behind their external differences a shared human experience of the divine within. Monistic syncretism is already the inspiration for many such gatherings, which will proliferate in the years ahead.

4. There Is One Problem

If all is one, the one great problem in the world is the splintering of reality into opposing camps—making distinctions between good and evil, right and wrong, truth and error, God and Satan, human and animal, male and female, homosexual and heterosexual, pagan and Christian, heresy and orthodoxy, reason and irrationality. Monists argue that such distinctions, typical of Western Christian culture, have numbed human beings into a spiritual amnesia in which they are no longer aware of belonging to the whole.[6] Evil is not tragic moral rebellion against the transcendent Creator; it is mere forgetfulness. The monistic circle must be unbroken, or the spell will be. A mystical experience of the whole is essential.

5. There Is One Means of Escape

Spiritual understanding acquired through intuition and meditation is the only way to salvation. Such insight is said to come through a nonrational, mystical experience of seeing oneself as the center of a circle that has no boundaries.[7] From the center of its own limitless universe the self necessarily reigns supreme!

The experience is engendered in the fast lane through drugs and in the safer slow lane, through time-honored (Hindu) meditation. When practiced correctly, meditation enables the mind and soul to be untethered from the limitations of the body. During the experience, the individual undergoes a liberating paradigm shift through which redemption of the self and the planet becomes possible. Though antithetical to the Creator's designs, and therefore ultimately noxious, the experience nevertheless produces a profound sense of release and liberation—

a bogus virtual redemption. In a triumph of mind over matter, the mind empties itself of all thought and the individual realizes his or her divinity.

Salvation through the redemptive, objective death of Christ on behalf of sinners has no function here. One is one's own savior. You see, this Eastern monism with a Western spin directly contradicts Christian theism and the civilization it has engendered. There is no neutral ground.

Monism and Theism: A Clash of Worldviews

Anyone with even a superficial knowledge of Christianity senses that these five points of religious monism are radically antithetical to orthodox Christianity (theism). While using terms like "God" and the "divine," this new spirituality is a form of atheism, because it denies the true God who created the heavens and the earth. Orthodox Christian theologians are not the only ones to understand the life-and-death nature of the conflict. Leaders of the new spirituality realize it, too. Though tolerance is considered by monists to be the ultimate virtue, one theological position, Christianity, simply cannot be tolerated.

The Parliament of the World's Religions scheduled no reasoned discussion of theism as a theological option. The organizers refused to recognize the conflict: Such recognition would only slow the worldwide uniting of religions. Faint echoes of the debate were banalized into conflict-resolution exercises by teams of professional "dialogue facilitators." Historic Christianity was absent, invoked only as the source of the planet's problems.[8]

In its global pretensions, this parliament of peace represented a more intolerant, totalitarian view of religious freedom than its favorite whipping boy, fundamentalism. Refusal to recognize the legitimacy of theism systematically characterizes the new liberal international gatherings and networks. In Chicago, theists and other outsiders were asked to leave whenever the practice of pagan spirituality began. Inclusiveness was extended to the orthodox Christian voice only as it was represented in a black choir, which was invited to sing gospel songs that nobody understood.

Theists are considered by monists to be nonpersons or heretics. Christianity's opponents do not use the word "theism"; they rely on the loaded word "fundamentalism." Theists are lumped together with violent extremists and racists, and they are generally branded as mindless bigots, impossible to convince.

THE CONFUSION GAP

The clash of worldviews has been called "culture wars," but the war goes much deeper than cultural preferences. The present clash of the irreconcilable worldviews of monism and theism creates total confusion and profound animosity. Who knows what the future will bring? One can only imagine what kind of spiritual hurricanes are lurking off our cultural coasts.

The forecast for this religious climate? Easy—100 percent chance of confusion. Jesus hailed the Pharisees as expert meteorologists who were unable to read the theological signs of their time.[9] In our day, spiritual confusion and moral schizophrenia reign. Here's a remedial course in reading the signs of the times today:

- A new Bible with pagan and Christian Scriptures. Monism and theism are served up together, creating confusion in the bookstore.
- A new Christ that blends the Bible's son of God with a monistic Jesus akin to Buddha, Gandhi and other spiritual leaders.
- New pagan churches of unity—offering Sunday celebrations led by male and female "reverends," Sunday Schools, nurseries, etc. Everything is picture-perfect, except that there is no guilt, no gospel, no Cross, no space-time Resurrection, no Christ of Scripture, no God of the Bible—and so, no salvation.
- A new, all-inclusive sexuality. An Episcopal seminary allows homosexual couples (including the professor of New Testament and her lover) in its campus housing but disallows cohabiting heterosexual students.
- Abortion: murder or health care? Abortions and births are performed in the same hospital by the same doctors, on preborn babies of the same age.[10] Killing a fetus in a gun or knife attack on a pregnant woman is a punishable crime, but when a mother and doctor team to attack a fetus, it is a heroic act of liberation.

Is anyone not confused? Contradictory views of reality are joined in the name of tolerance, the implacable progress of the democratic process and freedom of choice. But like oil and water, they cannot blend. The attempted blend has created a bewildering world, dislodging Christianity as the touchstone of morals and truth.

KISS CHAOS: A POSITIVE SPIN ON THE CONFUSION GAP

For some, confusion is part of the plan. Peter Russell, an expert in transcendental meditation and consultant for "the development of the learning process and creativity" for such multinational corporations as IBM and Shell—is a New Age channeler. Speaking through him, spirit entities reveal the immediate future of the earth:

> There is a new vibrational pattern descending upon your planet. . . . You are being offered an opportunity to enter a new reality. . . . Soon it will be the only reality to be seen. . . . Two worlds of consciousness will begin to form ever more distinctly: the world of Love and Life and the world of fear and death. There will continue to be some overlap of these worlds for several years to come, some going back and forth for certain individuals; but as the century draws to a close, the polarization will continue to intensify. The moment of birth will also be the moment of Last Judgment, the moment of final separation.[11]

This is heady wine for corporate global leaders who are thirsty for significance. The Charles Manson "family," to justify the mass murder of actress Sharon Tate and several friends in her Los Angeles home, wrote "Helter Skelter" in the blood of their victims on the refrigerator door. The term was taken from a Beatles's song describing the social destruction that would precede a new era of peace and love.[12]

New Age author Marilyn Ferguson sees the growing confusion gap as a positive sign. True, families are falling apart, education is in disarray, and many—especially the young—are plagued by gender confusion; but these are all *good* things, Ferguson says, for destruction must precede revolutionary reconstruction. The world is not falling apart; it is reconstituting itself. Ferguson appeals to modern science, which claims that "large perturbations of energy cause living systems to fall apart, then fall together again in a more elegant order." This is used to support her claims that the confusion caused by social experiments eventually brings about a better world, even if no one knows for sure where things are leading.[13] And so the 1996 Whole Earth Festival at the University of California, Davis, adopted as its theme "Kiss Chaos."

Few realize that the real game is religious warfare between truth and falsehood, with deep consequences for the spiritual and moral survival of the planet. Reality has been redefined: The "world of love and life" is the new religious monism, and the "world of fear and death" is Christian theism. Because few are acutely aware of the struggle, the program continues unopposed, taught to world business leaders, military personnel and schoolchildren and aided by the buzz words that ring everybody's bells—"freedom," "justice," "democratic rights" and "diversity."

THE SAME OLD ALTERNATIVES: CHRISTIANITY AND PAGANISM

This juxtaposition of antithetical worlds is not "business as usual." We live in a most uncommon time. Opposition to recent changes in Western society is not mere sentimental idealization of yesteryear, or the fear of change.[14] We are not faced with differences between miniskirts and maxiskirts, wide ties or narrow. Ours is a choice of civilization. It is not a question of turning back the clock to the rosy world of the '50s. It is the question of whether we opt for a Christian or pagan society.

Our society struggles at the brink of a new age, characterized by an unusual mixing of fundamentally antithetical views regarding the world and God. In the confusion of worldviews, monism and theism lock in a battle to the death. Which will emerge victorious to affect the future of the next generations? Though ultimate victory belongs to the Creator, the Church has never been promised every battle. As Professor Wilken of the University of Virginia has observed, with exceptional insight:

> The ferocity of the current assault on the legacy of Christian culture . . . has brought a new clarity of vision. The alternatives are set before us with unusual starkness: either there will be a genuine renewal of Christian culture—there is no serious alternative—or we will be enveloped by the darkness of paganism in which the worship of the true God is abandoned and forgotten. The sources of the cultural crisis, it turns out, are theological.[15]

THE GREATEST THREAT EVER TO THE CHRISTIAN CHURCH?

Does the average Christian know what is going on in our ostensibly civilized society? Pagan ideology, sometimes of the most radical and anti-Christian nature, is taught in university departments of religion, theological seminaries, mainline church agencies, feminist networks and Wicca covens across the land. It adopts the name of Christianity but will render our world unrecognizable. The political events that began in 1992 are the consequences of an ideological revolution promoted since the '60s in our halls of learning,[16] in our living rooms and home entertainment centers[17] and in our schools via the social engineers of the NEA and Planned Parenthood.[18]

If you doubt the success of this revolution, note the following statistic: 71 percent of Americans and 40 percent of those who, based upon their core beliefs, are considered Evangelicals, no longer believe in absolute truth.[19] Since the '60s, consciousness has changed.

The present hour is crucial. "The church faces a crisis of identity possibly unmatched since the second century. . . . We are back on Mount Carmel."[20] The threat has monumental implications for believers and especially for their children. What is the Church doing to prepare our children for survival in the Aquarian nightmare?

Writing in 1973 about the counterculture revolution of the '60s, Os Guinness remarked:

> The swing to the East has come at a time when Christianity is weak at just those points where it would need to be strong to withstand the East. Without this strength, the Eastern religions will be to Christianity a new and dangerous gnosticism.[21]

This insightful prophecy has become a woeful reality.

CHAPTER THREE

CHRISTIAN
LIBERALISM:
CRISIS AND
CONVERSION

*In polytheism man's free-thinking . . . has a proto-type . . .
the power to create for himself.*

NIETZSCHE[1]

The Religious Left has emerged like a phoenix from the ashes of liberalism. Old liberals are tired.[2] They are tired of orthodoxy as "televangelists" exploit it on radio and television for the aggrandizement of their personal empires. But they are also tired of the old critical liberalism, so concerned with "scientific" solutions to the Bible's supernaturalism. Like political Marxism, liberalism in the Church has given few answers to spiritual needs[3] and has not produced a gospel capable of meeting the global expectations of a unified planet. Liberalism needs a new lease on life.

MAINLINE'S DECLINE

For 30 years, the news, like British weather, has not been good. Sociological studies of the Methodists, Presbyterians, Congregationalists and Episcopalians
pronounce gloom and doom. After a period of growth in the '50s, mainline denominations began to shrink by the end of the '60s. The burgeoning liberalism of the
theological seminaries spread to the churches. By 1990, the loss of members had
reached staggering proportions—between one fifth and one third[4]—and the three
most liberal denominations declined the most.[5] Mainline churches have cut their
staff and moved their central offices to less imposing addresses in the heartland.[6]

A poll of Baby Boomers who were confirmed in the mainline church in the
'60s shows that 75 percent left church at age 21, half of them never to return.
Sixty-eight percent of those who did (middle-aged parents who traditionally wield
power in the Church) do not believe that a person can be saved only through Jesus
Christ.[7] The orthodoxy of their children will be even less robust.

The dropouts considered themselves religious, but felt that the mainline
church offered them conjectures, not commitment; a social agenda of "peace
and justice" but no spiritual power. The mainline church "lost the will or the
ability to teach the Christian faith . . . in such a way as to command . . . allegiance,"[8] thereby also losing the battle with competing secular or non-Christian
religious systems.

The study ends on a depressing note. "Perhaps some now unforeseen cultural shift will one day bring millions of baby boom dropouts back to the mainline churches. *But nothing we discovered suggests the likelihood of such a* shift."[9] Is New
Age liberal spirituality too big for these researchers to see?

RADICAL SKEPTICISM

Liberals are the most radical critics of liberal modernism. Confidence in the
power of human reason to solve human problems has evaporated in a century infamous for its bloody inhumanity. The collapse of secular humanism has
forced a repeal of its four spiritual laws: biological evolutionism (found to
have more holes than Swiss cheese and the ozone layer combined); existen-
tialism (among whose fruits are Nazism and the Cambodian genocide of Pol
Pot); Freudianism (which has produced more mental illness than it ever
cured); and Marxism (a massively embarrassing social and economic failure
that only survives, moribund, in China and Cuba).

Chafing under middle-class ethics and politics, radical scholars pushed modernity to its logical extreme. If truth is relative for the most essential questions of religious knowledge, as liberalism held, why is it not relative for all knowledge? This radical position is known as postmodern deconstructionism.

A New Day for Orthodoxy?

But the collapse of secular humanism is not necessarily good news for orthodox Christianity or society in general. Like a quick-change artist, liberalism now appears cloaked in the mantle of pagan spirituality. The misunderstood doctrine of separation of church and state has paralyzed Christianity, the religion most closely associated with America's history and culture. The call for more religion in the public square may favor a state-supported religious syncretism rather than a new day of Christian freedom.[10]

Liberals find deconstructionist philosophy a useful tool for shattering the Western Christian worldview, but the beast must not be allowed to turn on its handlers. It can be used to support sexual liberation and to undermine Judeo-Christian values, or employed to dislodge the classic forms of Bible interpretation. But no one can survive long in the same cage with radical skepticism. Brilliant ecofeminist authoress Charlene Spretnak says you *can* have it both ways:

> I agree with the deconstructive-postmodern project to stimulate awareness of processes by which conceptualizations are culturally constructed [she is thinking especially of patriarchy] . . . but I do not agree with their leap to conclude that there is nothing but cultural construction in human experience.[11]

Deconstruction has done its negative work. Now the pagans will reconstruct!

A Madman's Polytheism: Blueprint for a Liberated Future

Some readers remember the "Death of God" theology of the '60s. Twenty-five years after the Holocaust, certain radical scholars announced that the evolved humanity of the twentieth century could do without the God of the Bible. But as nature abhors a vacuum, mankind abhors atheism. So some of these theologians moved forward to the past of polytheism. Atheist theologian Friedrich Nietzsche

(1844-1900) became a prophet of this new age of human freedom. Son of a Lutheran pastor, Nietzsche believed that true human evolution would lead to the creation of a superman who would throw off Christianity, the faith of weaklings, and adopt a moral code of total freedom for strong, autonomous individuals. Nietzsche despised Christian humility, meekness and self-sacrifice, calling for the "transvaluation of values";[12] that is, for turning moral values on their head, making evil good and good evil. The best form of theism was not *mono*theism but *poly*-theism—a personal god for everybody and a multiple-choice pantheon for each state of mind. His influence on the later German notion of the pagan Aryan super race is a matter of debate, but his words ring with uncanny programmatic foresight for our own time of pro-choice ethics and religious pluralism:

> For the individual to set up his own ideal and derive from it his laws, his pleasures and his rights. . . . it was in the marvelous art and capacity for creating gods—in polytheism—that this impulse was permitted to discharge itself . . . . Monotheism. . . . the belief in a normal God, beside whom there are only false, spurious gods . . . has perhaps been the greatest danger of mankind in the past.[13]

Though Nietzsche died in 1900, one proponent of the death-of-God theology (now a major influence in religious higher education in America) said in 1974 of the above citation: "There is a bright, new future lurking in these lines, still waiting to be understood."[14] The future lay in the rebirth of polytheism; that is, the rebirth of the gods and goddesses.

The "bright, new future" would also come, according to one of the leaders in the modern study of religions, the Rumanian Mircea Eliade (1907-1986), from the contemporary meeting of East and West. Eliade believed that through this "the West will arrive at a deeper and broader knowledge of what it means to be human," and that this will bring about "transformations [of] human consciousness" to a new "global consciousness."[15]

A New Day for Liberalism: The Revival of Paganism

While orthodox theologians fought Kant, von Harnack and Bultmann on the cold German front of skeptical rationalism, the opposition cross-dressed into warm, spiritual, irrational mysticism. The future belongs to marginals such as Nietzsche, Mircea Eliade, Rudolf Otto, C. G. Jung and Joseph Campbell. The brush fire has jumped the interstate, and orthodoxy faces the threat of *mystical pagan polytheism* on the spiritual side of the theistic/atheistic divide.

THE GODDESS AND OTHER DEITIES

The bumper sticker "Honk if you love Jesus" has been replaced in California by "The goddess is back: magic is afoot." In 1970, the Leadership Conference of Women Religious (nuns) of the Roman Catholic church in America called for "autonomy and self-realization" rather than "corporate identity and self-sacrifice."[16] Who could have imagined autonomous Nietzschean nuns?

Charlene Spretnak entitled her book: *States of Grace: The Recovery of Meaning in the Postmodern Age.* How can a feminist deconstructionist philosopher speak of "grace" and the "recovery of meaning?" Are we on the verge of religious revival? Spretnak claims to recover meaning in spite of an intellectual context that mercilessly pours contempt on such a claim. How? By a "paradigm shift" consisting of:

> a radical reorientation that . . . is rooted in ecological sanity . . . an ecofeminist orientation [that feeds on] . . . the long-lost earth-based spirituality . . . of Mother Earth and other manifestations of the Goddess . . . the Dharma [of] Buddh[ism], the renewal movement within Judaism, . . . Native American spirituality . . . New Age spirituality.[17]

For those raised on biblical orthodoxy, this is truly amazing grace. *Meaning* derives from a neo-pagan Earth spirituality that finds God within—a lot of human effort and not much grace. In this new spirituality, contemporary liberals recover meaning.

I listened attentively as a Hindu swami with long black hair and a long yellow robe, gave an hour-long, rambling lecture in an accent that made me remember the wonderful curries I had enjoyed in the Taj Mahal in Manchester, England's Indian quarter. A featured speaker at the Parliament of the World's Religions, he sought to demonstrate rationally that the doctrines of Christianity were logically nonverifiable—that you could neither prove heaven nor the existence of the transcendent Christian God who lives there. At the end of the lecture, I asked him just what was verifiable in the religious domain, and with a typical Indian twinkle in his dark eyes he said, "The spiritual experience of the divine within." On this the world will be reconstructed.

LIFELINE FOR THE MAINLINE

Liberalism will live again, not just because orthodoxy does not seem to be posing a particular threat but because a "spiritual" revival is taking place in the liberal ranks. Hope is on the way. Mainline biblical scholars are finding ancient heretical Gnostic texts theologically reinvigorating. Contemporary skeptics, church dropouts and confused church members are getting religion from a similar source, namely New Age spirituality. Presbyterian Church (USA) minister Don Shriver, having given over the presidency of Union Seminary to a Unitarian, might find this infusion of new spiritual blood appropriate. In a public forum on "The Church: From Yesterday to Tomorrow" held at the Interchurch Center in New York, Shriver suggested that one way to keep the "church of tomorrow alive" would be to "develop partner relationships" with Eastern religions.[18] If this is Presbyterianism, John Calvin was a Buddhist!

The "unforeseen cultural shift" is actually shaking the Church's foundations. Already in 1980, Carl A. Raschke, professor of religious studies at the University of Denver, saw telltale cracks. In his prophetic book, *The Interruption of Eternity: Modern Gnosticism and the Origins of the New Religious Consciousness*, he argued that Westerners are becoming Gnostics. He singled out mainline churches that are regaining spirituality through the revival of Gnosticism without returning to Christian orthodoxy.[19] That's a deal. Old-time *religion* without old-time *theology and old-time morals*.

THE "NEW AGE" GOES TO CHURCH

Lynn Willeford, contributing editor of the *New Age Journal*, went back. She was raised in a "dignified Congregational church on the town green . . . where no one seemed to connect . . . (where) we spoke up to God and the minister spoke down to us . . . but was careful never to ask too much of us." In a long article in the *New Age Journal*, Willeford recounts how she has gone back to church after

30 years and rediscovered "Christianity" in a "freedom and justice" United Methodist church. "At times," she says, "it feels like my chest has been filled with a golden light." Never once is Jesus Christ as Savior mentioned as the source of her newfound spirituality. The following comment shows how far her experience strays from orthodox Christianity:

> A friend who follows some Eastern practices says I'm illuminating my heart chakra. I think I'm tapping into the Source, but whatever the name, I'm glad to be back. [20]

Meanwhile, the *New Age Journal* also plans to be back—in the "Christian" mainstream, adding a new-look form of Christianity to its potpourri of recommended spiritual techniques. A recent cover portrays a naked woman whose lower body is superimposed on that of a wolf. The title reads: "The Wild Woman." How can such a magazine also endorse Christianity?[21] Either the editors were converted, or their version of Christianity is not the one most people know.

NEW AGE SPIRITUALITY REVIVES MORIBUND CALVINISM

Some time ago a Dutch couple spent the night in our home. On tour with a Christian choir from Holland, they lustily sang the old hymns with contagious conviction. Over hot chocolate, after the concert, Rudi told us his story. Members of the liberal Dutch Reformed church, he and his wife had been burned by social gospel and radical causes. Their children had long since left the faith, something they too might have done with a little more courage. But their faith had recently revived. Their local Reformed church introduced them to a group studying *A Course in Miracles*, an extremely popular New Age counterfeit of Christianity. Rudi beamed as he spoke. "Since studying the *Course*," he exuded, "I have been walking on air."

The air is getting thicker, and anecdotes such as these suggest a significant trend in the mainline.[22] Thanks to New Age infiltration, social gospel liberalism is acquiring a dimension it has long lacked—spirituality. Famished Baby Boomers left the Church in search of the potent spirituality offered by drugs and Eastern religions. Now you can save the airfare to Katmandu. Such New Age spirituality can be found in many mainline churches.

NEW WINE FOR OLD WINESKINS

Confirmed by the following disparate sources, the above anecdotes should be taken with utmost seriousness:

The Sociologist

W. C. Roof, professor of sociology at the University of California, Santa Barbara, moves the discussion beyond anecdotes and hunches. His studies unveil a "new spirituality," wedded to a new social conscience, which transforms and reshapes those progressive churches "open to this new spiritual vision." "Religion," he argues, "was never the problem, only social forms of religion that stifle the human spirit."[23] Apparently, the particularly stifling form was orthodox Christian faith (theism), whose disappearance would presumably not bother Roof, Protestant though he may be.

The Seer

The analysis of the sociologist recalls the musings of Marilyn Ferguson, New Age popularizer of Helen Shucman's *A Course in Miracles*. Certain that she is a true Christian, she writes:

> My definition of Christianity has expanded over the years. After I became involved in meditation, for example, I experienced the vision of Christ more vividly than I ever had through sermons and dogma. . . .
> Many Christian churches are seeing that direct spiritual experience offers a revitalization for modern Christianity.[24]

Her description of what is happening in "many Christian churches" is not frivolous; spirits are at work.

The Spirit Guide

Ken Carey, the author of *Starseed: The Third Millennium: Living in the Posthistoric World*, makes a similar statement.[25] Ken Carey is but a "channel" for a "spirit being in the eternal fields of light," who, along with other "entities," dictated messages concerning humanity's origins and future state. The spirit entities reveal that the forthcoming planetary transformation will include various churches, great and small, and so the spirits exhort:

> Associate only with congregations whose atmosphere encourages love, whose atmosphere helps to dissolve the sense of separation among people, and between people and their God, congregations whose members welcome all without judgment, recognizing the eternal spirit of each one.

This religion is made for Aquarian Baby Boomers, heavily into self-discovery and self-expression. When sociologists, seers and spirit guides agree, we can suspect that something of great import for society is afoot. When Presbyterians are affected, you *know* something is afoot.

NEW AGE SPIRITUALITY: AN UPBEAT ASSESSMENT FOR PRESBYTERIANS

Presbyterians come from the tradition of no-nonsense Scottish piety and English Cromwellian politics. But even Presbyterians are getting "the spirit." Duncan Ferguson, Director of the Committee on Higher Education of the Presbyterian Church (U.S.A.), edited a book, *New Age Spirituality: An Assessment*,[26] meant to guide mainline Presbyterians in evaluating this religious phenomenon. The book contains no significant theological evaluation from a traditional Presbyterian position.[27] It is mainly an upbeat endorsement of New Age belief and practice. One contributor is David Spangler, a major figure in New Age circles, who shocked many Christians by his description of the coming of Christ as "Luciferic initiation."[28] In his contribution, he endorses the New Age redefinition of God. Moderate contributors depict the New Age as an opportunity for Christian renewal.[29]

The Presbyterian editor gives the final chapter of exhortation to Matthew Fox. This is asking a fox to give a lecture to chickens on the great spiritual values of life outside the chicken coop! Matthew Fox, a former Catholic priest dismissed from his Dominican order (surprising enough in our age of tolerance) collaborated with Miriam Starhawk, feminist pagan witch; Luisah Teish, Yoruba voodoo priestess; and former Senator Tom Hayden, '60s violent revolutionary, in his Institute in Culture and Creation Spirituality at Holy Name

College, Oakland, California. There he has taught a paganized, pantheistic, syncretistic Christianity at the opposite extreme from all Presbyterian standards
and confessions. Needless to say, Fox, though coyly and politically distancing
himself from certain frivolous expressions of New Age exotic,[30] calls upon
mainline believers to see the New Age spirituality as "an important movement
along the way of the in-depth transformation . . . (of) our species . . . (a part of)
the work of the Spirit calling us to a New Pentecost."[31]

Though presented in pious, semi-Christian language, the spirituality of
Fox's transformed species—pansexual promiscuity allied with the empowerment of animistic nature rites—is all that the Bible denounces as paganism.
This is the new spiritual fare now offered to Presbyterians, who certainly would
not want to be caught eating the toxic food of yesterday's orthodoxy. It is one
notable example of pagans in the pews.

TREATING THE MORTAL SICKNESS OF ORTHODOX CHRISTIANITY

Just as the demented Nietzsche's *Übermensch* (superman) promoted the aboli-
tion of Christianity and its moral values, Matthew Fox now dismisses orthodox Christianity as mental illness. Though more subtle than Nietzsche, Fox is
just as radical. Nietzsche knew only one form of Christianity—orthodoxy. Fox
identifies two. One, "pessimistic, very male and dualistic," emphasizes *original
sin*. The other, which is "holistic and cosmological and includes women's wisdom," emphasizes *original blessing* and is creation affirming, full of hope. For
the pessimistic kind, Fox does not hesitate to use the F word—"fundamentalism." From this Christianity, which is an enemy to life on this planet, one
needs to be "healed."[32] The secular press has already pegged orthodox
Christians as bigots living on the lunatic fringe. But from a so-called
Christian theologian, we learn that biblical Christianity is a mortal disease!
The ecological disasters, competitive economics and academics, and repres-
sive sexual norms of "heteropatriarchy"[33] are now presented as the rotting
fruit of jaded Christian fundamentalism. Christianity, argues Fox, will have to
change radically or, via the new theories of interpretation, say the very opposite of what it clearly affirms (see chapter 8). According to Fox, if there is no
change, Christianity will not survive in the third millennium. A new religious
paradigm is needed to solve the planet's problems and create a new age of

human liberation. Once again the future of human progress comes to the rescue.

In the days to come the enemy of true faith will no longer be the unbelieving skepticism of rationalistic liberalism and atheistic materialism. It is with the dazzling promises of utopian liberalism and its new-look spirituality that the Church will contend, and which we now must analyze in more detail. In the next chapter we ask: "Where is revived liberalism going?"

CHAPTER FOUR

THE NEW LIBERALISM: PAGAN CHRISTIANITY FOR THE THIRD MILLENNIUM

Postchristian (1975 ed.) adj.: occurring after definitive departure from christianity in all its religious and secular forms and simultaneously with entry into New Time/Space

MARY DALY[1]

America has never been more divided. Societal shifts suggest that the culture is imploding. Even during the Civil War, Confederate and Unionist generals and foot soldiers participated in the same prayer and Bible study groups. They differed in regional loyalties or on the place of slavery but not about worldview. Even those who never read the Bible probably held a begrudging jealousy for those who did. "Culture Wars"[2] may be an apt description of their time, but it does not do justice to ours. Today's conflicts are closer to *religious warfare—a war of two worlds.*[3] Imagine solving social problems with a Bible study in today's culture, where the Bible has been banned from public recognition and discourse.

New Agers speak of the "Christian interlude."[4] For them, Western civilization dominated by Christian values will be superseded in the third millennium by the neo-pagan religious world of the Age of Aquarius. The recent dechristianization of the West lends credence to this reading of history. New Age spirituality is not a fading fad from the freaky "left coast." It is the exotic tip of a religious iceberg—the syncretistic religion of the new liberalism—whose chilling progress may remodel life on this planet. Music, medicine, business, politics, sexuality, ecology and psychology; all areas of existence are affected by this utopian ideology.

Christian colleges and seminaries tend to discuss the New Age as the last chapter in a course on "the cults." But in proper perspective, the New Age is not a cult. Nor is it a heresy, which stresses one aspect of the truth to the exclusion of all others. New Age liberalism is apostasy. "Apo-stasis" means literally "a standing away from." The new liberalism stands away from biblical Christianity and the Judeo-Christian worldview, perhaps even more than the old liberalism. This apostasy is not a modification of Christianity but its obliteration. The hazy specter of New Age liberalism takes form before our eyes, recognizable as the very antithesis of biblical Christianity. The sleepy Church must awake and defend itself. Its enemy is busy defining it out of existence.

AQUARIAN ECCLESIOLOGY: A CHURCH OF RELIGIOUS SYNCRETISM

Although the paths to the summit may differ, from the top of the mountain one sees the same moon.[5] This Japanese proverb neatly expresses the agenda of much of contemporary theological liberalism. Classical liberalism denied the truth claims of Christian orthodoxy. Today's liberalism simply relativizes Christianity as one religious option among many, so that it can participate in the coming unification of the planet and of religion, advancing mankind along its evolutionary path.

According to the "Christian" theologian Knitter, professor of theology at Xavier University, Cincinnati, this stage of religious evolution is upon us.

The world's religions are evolving out of the *microphase* of religious history in which the various traditions grew and consolidated in relative isolation from each other. The direction today is towards a *macrophase* in which each religion will be able to grow and understand itself only through interrelating with other religions.[6]

"Christianity" forges ahead, leading the world into the third millennium, moving from "the Age of Monologue" through "the Age of Dialogue," which is its essence, into "the Age of Interrelation" and syncretistic assimilation. According to Knitter, only open-ended "dialogical" Christianity will survive, and in so doing will determine the shape of all the world's religions.[7]

The book *Christian Systematic Theology in a World Context*, by Ninian Smart and Steven Konstantine, should be read against this background. In the section entitled "Towards a World Theology," their statement of purpose is a jewel of syncretistic convergence:[8]

Our presentation of a *darsana* is more than the presentation of an intellectual construction. It is the putting forward of a *Tao*, a form of *bhakti* and *jnana* or "knowledge," a life clothed in sacramental *li*, a stimulus to *dhyana* and *karuna*, and invitation to eschew *shirk*, and to be called by the power of the *avatara*.[9]

This might be Aquarian liberalism. It is not what the dust jacket produced by the Lutheran publisher, Fortress Press, would have us believe, namely, a "fresh understanding of Christianity."

Syncretistic Fellowship in Chicago

Knitter was in Chicago for the Parliament of the World's Religions—along with 6,000 delegates, 250 religious leaders and 120 religions and sects—helping to promote unity through spiritual communion. It was not a parliament. Parliaments are representative bodies that debate, propose competing and contradictory ideas and vote. Not here. It was not representative, for historic Christianity was absent. The Chicago event was a religious festival, a consciousness-raising happening of shared pagan spirituality. Delegates were obliged to *practice* unity—in syncretistic "interfaith celebrations" that the apostle Paul would doubtless have called "fellowship with demons." Singing "Leaning on the Everlasting Arms," I suddenly stopped. The "everlasting arms of Jesus," had been amputated. The crowd now sang, "O what fellowship, O what joy divine, I can feel the friendship all around. . . . " Talking about the Chicago weather or the hard chairs in the cavernous hall, people around me were friendly, but their common bond was syncretistic convergence. Buddhist monks chanted, the high priestess to Venus gave a ponderous pagan blessing. Delegates danced round the hall to the beat of drums led by an American Indian shaman. Chicago demonstrated that liberal Christians, Hindus, Buddhists, worshipers of Isis and witches of the Covenant of the Goddess *do* have comparable Earth-based spiritual experiences. Human friendship had become the fellowship of humanistic, pagan spirituality.

Global Religious Vision

The syncretism evident in Chicago is reflected in the texts of the new liberal vision. It is part of the theory. Huston Smith, an expert on world religions, (whose influence on the new Jesus of the Jesus Seminar will be examined in chapter 6), in his book *Forgotten Truth* shows "how the great religious traditions of the world converge. . . . One finds remarkable unity underlying the surface differences. . . . It is as if an invisible geometry has everywhere been working to shape them into a single truth."[10] This is a significant statement by a syncretist, for it supports the Bible's affirmation that there are finally but two religious possibilities: pagan idols or the living God. Tertullian (A.D. 160-225) might have been in Chicago, rather than referring to the exclusionary "ecumenical" spirit of Gnosticism. How modern his comment now sounds:

> They maintain [ecclesiastical] harmony with all, making no distinction. As a matter of fact, it [harmony] exists among them although they hold different doctrines as long as they wage common warfare against one thing, the truth [orthodoxy].[11]

Following this logic, the "creation theologian" Matthew Fox, argues that the renewal of the Church must include the elimination of orthodoxy and the incorporation of the mystical practices of all the major religions, notably the spirit worship and initiatory rituals of Native American religion—hey, what could be more American?[12] He calls not merely for dialogue, but for "deep ecumenism," spiritual/mystical union. This includes sweat lodges, nocturnal dances, moon rituals, powwow dances, the Sun dance, pipe ceremonies and vision quests of Native American religion. According to Fox, "Christians" should therefore seek "mystical solidarity" with all the world's religions. Little wonder Fox's new-look "Christian" theology gets a thumbs-up sign from a pagan witch. Caitlín Matthews, priestess of the Fellowship of Isis, the Egyptian goddess of witchcraft, finds in Fox's "creation spirituality" a perfectly valid expression of her own pagan practice.[13]

Theologian Katherine Zappone accepts all kinds of empowering experiences, from liberation theology to witchcraft. "In journeying with other feminists," she observes, "I have found that the sacred stories of goddess religions affect my imagination in ways the story of Jesus never will."[14] More power to Zappone. Too bad for Jesus!

AQUARIAN ESCHATOLOGY: A PLANETARY REVOLUTION

The eschatology of New Age liberalism is upbeat. Matthew Fox announces the "Coming of the Cosmic Christ." But do not be taken in. This is not *Jesus* Christ.[15] This is the spiritual principle, the "over-soul" uniting all religions. The subtitle is revealing: "The Healing of Mother Earth and the Birth of a Global Renaissance." In other words, ecology leads us to this new religion of union with all creatures.

The idea of the rebirth of humanity in a new age of utopian progress appears in many places. A liberal, mainline theologian seeks to answer the challenge of this historic moment with a book *Towards a New Age in Christian Theology*.[16] What this "New Age" means is later explained. The redemptive work of Jesus includes reincarnation![17] A United Methodist theologian at Emory University in Atlanta offers a "bold hypothesis"—that we are experiencing a "paradigm shift in cultural consciousness" which will solve the problems in our present living patterns.[18]

Sister Madonna Kolbenschlag, a Roman Catholic nun and popular speaker at "Christian" feminist conferences, describes "an evolutionary process that is moving humanity, and the 'God-who-is-coming-to-be,' toward transformation in a 'New Faith.'" In the "Third Age of the Spirit" the Church will wither under the direct illumination of "a creative Spiritual Presence that comes from within . . . as well as from beyond."[19] Says another radical thinker: "A new God is being born in our hearts, to teach us to level the heavens and exalt the earth and create a new world."[20] At the same time, the "old" God, Creator of heaven and Earth, withers under this blistering attack from pagan eschatology and is cast away like a used paper napkin.

The Future According to the New Age Gurus

This new-look "Christian" eschatology is closer to secular New Age utopianism than to a scriptural view of the future. Theological liberals hastily disavow any connection with Shirley MacLaine or other get-rich-quick gurus. But ideological parallels are so close that the difference is often only one of style and vocabulary. The following examples of how hard-core New Agers see the future should suffice.

Marilyn Ferguson, famous New Age authoress of the best-selling *Aquarian Conspiracy*, declaring that the mainstream had gone New Age, points to the popularity of notions such as spaceship Earth, Gaia, planetary tribe, partnership, community and holism. These widely diffused concepts, she claims, "have potential to shape a planetary civilization."[21]

Chris Griscom, one-time guru of Shirley MacLaine, and in prose the literary equivalent of wispy New Age music, describes the coming religious and spiritual transformation with bewildering optimism. She exhorts her followers:

> Let us attune our frequencies . . . to mimic the pulsating formulas of ecstasy. This frequency, with its unlimited divine potential, can create an evolutionary mutation of our physical, emotional, and mental bodies, so that we become ecstatic light bodies of consciousness.[22]

This expectation of a human creation of heaven on Earth unites theological liberals and New Agers. In predicting the future of warfare, Ben Nova, a writer in *Omni* magazine, believes that after the bloodiest century in history (the twentieth), "the peoples of the world are slowly but steadily making their way to that new era [in which] . . . 'nation shall not lift up sword against nation, neither shall they learn war any more.'"[23] While understanding the deep desire for cosmic peace that is found in the human heart, one must not fail to see the hubris of such a utopian program. The Bible's vision is very different. Just as flesh and blood did not create the original heavens and the earth, so flesh and blood cannot inherit the kingdom of God and create the new heavens and the new earth. Both creations are God's work.

Just before he died in 1987, the mystical philosopher Joseph Campbell was asked by television commentator Bill Moyers if he still believed in what he had earlier written, that "we are at this moment participating in one of the very greatest leaps of the human spirit to a knowledge not only of outside nature but also of our own deep inward mystery." His answer was: "The greatest ever."[24] Campbell's response is not the fruit of scholarly analysis by a respected professor and serious public television commentator. It is religious prophecy.

The question is: Who inspired prophet Campbell, and will his prophecy be false? Such prophecy seems more fitting coming from the mouth of off-the-wall New Age channelers. Take Lazaris, whose weekend seminars cost $375-450 per person. Lazaris reveals that in the '90s we will witness the end of history—in the sense that human beings will no longer refer to the traditions and precedents of the past. Rather, man's dreams and fantasies concerning the future will determine his present.

This is the American dream gone bananas. The last Western frontier becomes the imagination, and if there are enough mainstream, wild-eyed optimists ready to believe it, then the idea becomes dangerous. If the future belongs to fantasy, then perhaps Hitler's fantasy of a 1,000-year *Reich* was not a bad idea after all. However, "the end of history" notwithstanding, if you stand on the roof and declare yourself a bird, when they scrape you off the sidewalk, they will *not* take you to a vet!

The Future of the Global, Syncretistic "Church"

Gurus bring the Church into the picture. In *Discipleship in the New Age*, her highly influential book written earlier this century, Alice Bailey, considered one of the leading New Age "foremothers," wrote about the start of an experimental effort by the "Hierarchy" (the Ascended Masters of the spirit world) to mobilize "Centers of Light." To her students, she wrote:

> If it is successful and if the spiritual momentum set up by all of you is adequate to the effort made, and if you can carry on with persistence . . . it may be possible to bring the experimental stage to an end;

the Hierarchy can then recognize (as effectively established upon earth) certain *focal points of energy which can constitute magnetic centers or rallying points for the new religion,* the new medicine, the new psychology and education and the new politics.[25]

Bear in mind that these words were first published around the end of the World War II!

The spirit entity speaking through the medium Ken Carey had no trouble getting a contract with Harper Collins. The reading public now knows the details of the immediate future:

> As you reorient toward the new way of being in the world, you will be drawn to centers where the vibrational atmosphere is more conducive to a healthy state of function. These centers will represent the focal points around which the organs of Planetary Being will form. They will be, in a sense, islands of the future in a sea of the past. Within their vibrational field, the New Age will blossom and spread organically to cover the Earth. These [centers] will be the first beachheads secured by the approaching forces, the points of entry through which the healing energies of transformation will be channeled. All of these centers will work together to prepare the human species for its collective awakening. . . . Many such places exist at this time. Many more will arise during the remaining decades of this transitional period. By the time the next generation reaches maturity [around the year 2000], there will be a widespread network of these islands.[26]

Stupefying technological advances have produced a small, interconnected planet. Our generation is the first to see live moving pictures in full color of planet Earth. Jim Irwin, one of the first astronauts to walk on the moon, describes the perspective he had, seeing Earth from space:

> From the moon, the earth looked just like a marble, the most beautiful marble you can imagine. The earth is uncommonly lovely. . . . I know that others will not have the opportunity to visit the moon . . . I went for everybody. . . . It was a human effort, and all human beings can feel proud that another human being made a trip to the moon and came back to earth.[27]

GLOBAL PERSPECTIVE

With that image engraved on our subconscious, it has become obvious that our problems—the relatedness of the world's economies, nuclear proliferation and environmental disasters that respect no boundaries—demand global solutions. Such a new "planetized" awareness creates favorable conditions for an ideology (monism) that affirms the interrelatedness of all things. The planetary circle fits the mystical, monistic circle.

But our planet may be too small for both monists and theists. Leaders in politics, business, academics, communications and the liberal hierarchies in many churches may find irresistible the temptation of this totalizing monistic ideology. We recall the words of Marilyn Ferguson: "As consciousness changes, the world changes." If our world has changed radically in the last generation, it is not merely because Hollywood has pumped its agenda into every living room in the land. Hollywood itself is a product of the new consciousness that dominates our culture. The Religious Left of revived liberalism has its hands on many of the levers of social control and its eyes on the world.

We see this happening, but can we stop it? Many are caught up in the movement, intrigued by one aspect of the agenda, but lacking the perspective of spiritual astronauts. Will we see the "full Earth," uncommonly lovely in the hand of its Creator? Or will we see a "new Earth," blackened into the oblivion of monistic space? If we can step far enough out of our culture to see the coherence of these various social and religious movements, we may step back in with some answers to the question, Where are we going? We might have to step back as far as the early centuries of the Church, but the insights gained are worth the trip.

CHAPTER FIVE

THE DEEP ROOTS
OF THE NEW
SPIRITUALITY

*Some years ago while trekking the wilds of the Soul Journey Jungle,
certain explorers stumbled upon the high-flying double-minded
Gnostic. Though they considered their discovery to be the dawn of
a New Age, research soon revealed that this was merely an
ape of ancient origin.*

WILDLIFE IN THE KINGDOM COME[1]

Why should orthodox Christians be concerned about "Christian" liberalism? Has such concern always been a dry debate between theologians, while true religion gets on with converting the world?

LIBERALISM: CARRIER OF THE PAGAN VIRUS INTO THE BODY OF THE CHURCH

Liberalism has "got religion." Gone is its skeptical reinterpretation of the gospel in terms of social involvement or Marxist theory. New liberalism has discovered a *spirituality* that will save the planet and fulfill the goals of an aspiring humanity. The liberal vision of an inclusive egalitarian culture of the future—"America as it was meant to be!"—conceives of a new world where the distinctions between the sexes, between right and wrong, between true and false are blurred; where Satan is but the creation of wild-eyed fundamentalists; where tolerance for all—except orthodox Christianity—is the highest good. This is not dry theory. The new liberals teach our children in schools and universities, influence the media by claiming to speak for the Church and for the best interests of the planet, and take positions of political leadership in our *very religious* country. And now they have spiritual power to back them up.

Theological liberalism, commendable for its attempt to express the faith in language that contemporaries understand, ultimately fails because it abandons the essence of that faith, and in so doing introduces into the pews the deadly virus of paganism. Throughout history, liberalism has rejected orthodoxy without daring to leave the familiar warmth of mother Church. Cut off from the lifeblood of Christian belief, liberals construct an intellectual version of Christianity that bears little resemblance to the original. Such a faith, when adopted by the average Christian in the pew, produces withered fruit. Just as soulless Marxism created both material and spiritual famine among the Russian people, so liberalism has failed to feed Christians. Human beings, including theological liberals, need spiritual reality. Today's liberals find their spirituality not in orthodoxy but in revived paganism. But "there is nothing new under the sun."[2] Modern liberals only imitate their long-lost cousins, the Gnostics, the first "Christian" liberals.

CHRISTIAN LIBERALISM AND ANCIENT GNOSTICISM: LONG-LOST COUSINS

Just when radical scholars are finding in the Gnostic texts a valid expression of "original Christianity," our world is awash in New Age spirituality. The liberal rehabilitation of these texts supports the thesis that the "new spirituality" adopted by "Christian" liberalism is Gnostic heresy in new dress.[3] In some profound sense, Gnosticism was the earliest expression of "Christian" liberalism, though liberals avoid such parallels.[4] Discovery of the Gnostic texts in 1945 produced a dramatic interest in Gnosticism, which led in turn to a recognition of the parallels between Gnosticism and modern times.[5] "Despite the vast cultural differences between North American Protestantism and ancient Gnosticism," says Philip Lee, "the parallels between the two . . . can no longer be ignored."[6]

Defining Gnosticism

Christians should read Church history, at least the history of Gnosticism, for it has a thoroughly modern message. Just as our culture offers a choice of non-Christian or Christian liberalism, so the second century allowed both non-Christian and Christian Gnosticism. A long and complex development of the political, social and religious megatrends of the pre-Christian Mediterranean world molded ancient Gnosticism. This pagan spirituality began when East met West in the fourth century B.C., and Alexander the Great took Greek (Western) culture to the Eastern ends of his far-flung empire. In that meeting, the rational culture of Greece was significantly modified by the great religions of the East (Hinduism, Manichaeism, Zoroastrianism, Babylonian astrology, the Egyptian goddess worship of Isis and Judaism, whether orthodox, mystical or apostate).[7] The blending of these great traditions produced the intellectual and religious syncretism of the so-called Hellenistic age (fourth century B.C. to fourth century A.D.). From this mix emerged Gnosticism.

Gnosticism was no abstract philosophy. Flesh-and-blood human beings adopted it, because it promised to change their social condition. Just as today, the New Age rejects both orthodox Christianity and secular humanism as tired, old and inappropriate for the challenges of the third millennium, Gnosticism criticized both "official" state paganism and "orthodox" Christianity. A recent, more sociological analysis of ancient Gnosticism describes "the rootless and the weary who had been cut adrift and were searching for a new life." Gnostic ideas found fertile soil in a newly mobile merchant and military community. Freed slaves, adepts of the transposable Mystery Religions and devotees of a form of feminism in the leisured classes all grasped at a spirituality that offered hope for a new understanding of individual freedom.[8]

Exploring the Importance of Gnosis

Prior to its "Christian" expression, Gnosticism was incubating in the Mystery Religions which in the ancient world represented the revival of spiritual paganism for the hungry of soul.[9] The Mystery Religions were secret societies which, through devotion to the god and often the goddess, offered gnosis, or spiritual illumination.[10] Though gnosis in Greek means knowledge of all kinds, in this context it means experience of occult powers through secret and mysterious initiation ceremonies, and of the divine self as the possessor of those powers.

Knowledge of the self as divine is the essential pillar of Gnosticism, however elaborate and "Christian" the outer dress. Gnosticism became a full-blown, appealing, religious system in the second century A.D. when certain so-called Christian thinkers (Marcion, Basilides, Valentinus, et al.) reinterpreted their faith to make it more palatable. They did what liberals have always done—blend the faith with the pagan philosophy of the day, claiming such an amalgam to be the truest form of Christianity. Unconvinced, the Church fathers saw in Gnosticism a Christianized form of paganism.

This sellout of authentic Christianity marked the high point of Gnosticism's development both intellectually and numerically. Perhaps a Christian veneer gave theological sophistication to the pagan Gnostic liberation movement. The pagan lie of the self as divine—the original diabolical temptation—is most believable when dressed in Christian language. The determined resistance to Christian Gnosticism by the Church fathers shows that it threatened the very existence of orthodox Christianity. Some of the finest theologians of the Christian Church devoted their lives to denouncing this heresy and to expunging its pernicious effects from Christian doctrine and practice. Today, the Christian faith is under similar attack, from outside the Church, but also from within.

GNOSTICISM: EARLY "LIBERAL" SPIRITUALITY

Spirit Wars rage in our day. Repeating the struggle between orthodoxy and heresy that marked the early centuries of the Church's history, the Religious Left attacks Christian orthodoxy in our time. In the second century, the gospel sustained prolonged frontal attack and subtle infiltration. But the Apostolic Faith survived, victorious. This will always be the case, because "Jesus Christ is the same yesterday and today and forever."[11] The gospel does not change over time, and it *will* triumph. But the liberal temptation to deform it does not change much either—hence the striking similarities between ancient Gnosticism and modern liberalism. The Roman Catholic journalist and authoress Donna Steichen observed that the "liberal consensus is a gnostic agnosticism."[12] The comparison becomes more striking as modern liberalism sloughs off the mantle of "scientific" atheism and dabbles in spirituality.

THE "FIRST PROTESTANT" OR THE "FIRSTBORN OF SATAN"?

It takes a liberal to spot one. In A.D. 150, Marcion, the first Gnostic, a "theologian" from Pontus in Asia Minor was excommunicated from the Church in Rome.[13] He dismissed God the Creator, the Old Testament, the Mosaic Law and three of the Gospels. From the few epistles of Paul that he accepted, he expunged Old Testament quotations and worshiped the "alien God" behind the God of Scripture. Because of Marcion's rejection of orthodoxy, Adolf von Harnack, the great nineteenth-century German liberal, hailed him as "the first Protestant"! By "Protestant" Harnack meant "liberal."[14]

Helmut Koester, a New Testament scholar teaching at Harvard Divinity School, calls Marcion "a textual critic, philologian and reformer."[15] Glowing appreciations like these could make you think that Marcion was the Early Church's equivalent of Martin Luther.[16]

What a difference 1700 years can make. The Church fathers expressed another opinion. Tertullian (A.D. 160-225) called Marcion

the Pontic mouse who has nibbled away the Gospels . . . abolished marriage, and . . . torn God almighty to bits with [his] blasphemies.[17]

Polycarp (A.D. 69-155), who knew the apostle John, called Marcion "the firstborn of Satan."[18]

Only contradictory understandings of the Christian faith can explain such divergent evaluations of Marcion. Orthodox Christianity maintains the antithesis separating all expressions of paganism, including "Christian" paganism, from biblical truth. Liberalism has always muddied the waters. Today, liberals claim that ancient Gnosticism is an alternate, authentic expression of early

Christianity. Is this estimation plausible? The Early Church fathers said no. Modern liberalism says yes.

What would a modern Gnostic, with no pretensions to Christianity either orthodox or liberal, say? Duncan Greenlees is just such a Gnostic, an adept of the theosophical/occult tradition. His independent evaluation of Gnosticism is most interesting:

> Gnosticism is a system of direct experiential knowledge of God . . . the Soul and the universe; therefore it has no fixed dogmas or creed. . . . In the early centuries of this era, amid a growing Christianity, it took on the form of the Christian faith, while rejecting most of its specific beliefs. Its wording is therefore largely Christian, while its spirit is that of the latest paganism of the West.[19]

Here is no claim that Gnosticism is a valid, alternate form of Christianity. Modern Gnostics and ancient Church fathers agree: Christianity and Gnosticism are different religions, though they may use common terminology. One religion is pagan humanism, the other divinely revealed truth.

CHRISTIANITY AND LIBERALISM: STILL TWO DIFFERENT RELIGIONS IN 1923

1923 was a gala year for Presbyterian golfers. All golfers know that in 1923 Bobby Jones won the first of his grand-slam tournaments, introducing the famous Calamity Jane putter that had been made in Presbyterian Scotland at the beginning of the century. All Presbyterians should know that in the same year, J. Gresham Machen, then professor of New Testament at Princeton Seminary, published *Christianity and Liberalism*. Machen made the same allegation regarding liberalism that the Church fathers had made concerning Gnosticism: that it was not Christianity, but a subtly disguised form of paganism taking over the Church. According to Machen:

> The great redemptive religion which has always been known as Christianity is battling against a totally diverse type of religious belief, . . . the movement designated as "liberalism.". . . But manifold as are the forms in which the movement appears, the root of the move-

ment is one; the many varieties of modern liberal religion are rooted in naturalism—that is, in the denial of any entrance of the creative power of God.[20]

By naturalism, Machen meant paganism. Machen tried to be both firm and fair, rightly distinguishing between liberalism as a system and liberals as individuals. His example still inspires:

> Whether or not liberals are Christians, it is at any rate perfectly clear that liberalism is not Christianity. . . . it proceeds from a totally differ-ent root, and it constitutes, in essentials, a unitary system of its own. That does not mean that all liberals hold all parts of the system, or that Christians who have been affected by liberal teaching at one point have been affected at all points. . . . it [liberalism] differs from Christianity in its view of God, of man, of the seat of authority and of the way of sal-vation. And it differs from Christianity not only in theology but in the whole of life. . . . Christianity is being attacked from within by a move-ment which is anti-Christian to the core.[21]

Two decades earlier, from the other side of the Reformation divide, Pope Pius X made all priests and seminary professors swear an antimodernist oath, declaring liberalism to be "the synthesis of all the heresies."[22] Machen and Pope Pius X make unusual bedfellows. Adamantly out of tune with the spirit of *our* times, they share a common perspective on liberalism. The evaluation that old-style liberalism overturned every Christian doctrine supports the present contention that overt, pagan New Age liberalism is a radical and open apostasy from the Christian faith.

THE MODERN HERESY: HERESY HUNTING

For most scholars and many priests in the Roman Catholic church, Pope Pius's oath became a pious sentiment, an artifact for the Vatican museum. Machen's allegations won few friends in the Presbyterian church he had faithfully served: he was defrocked for unacceptable behavior. Machen had committed the unpar-donable sin of calling a spade a spade, and heresy heresy.

Such an accusation may soon qualify not only as heresy but as a "hate crime" that disturbs the peace of a society high on tolerance, choice and love. Feminist scholars at the RE-Imagining Conference accused their critics, concerned for the orthodoxy of the Church's confession, of "hostility," "violence" and "harassment."[23] Bishop Earl G. Hunt of the United Methodist church warned that one symptom of the church's weakness was that its leaders "have declared ours to be a post-heresy age."[24] James Robinson, director of the translation project of the Nag Hammadi texts, reserves vitriol, not for the Gnostic distortions of the gospel, but for the Church fathers who denounced the Gnostics as heretics. Eight times in his 25-page introductory article to the Nag Hammadi texts he rails against the Church fathers, describing their polemical defense of orthodoxy against Gnosticism as the "myopic view of heresy hunters."[25]

One might expect such heated language from neo-pagan "Christians," "re-imagining" their way into positions of power in churches they refuse to leave, but why from the cool corridors of academia? Robinson loses his cool because naming a person or teaching as heretical has become *the* modern heresy. The former moderator of the Presbyterian Church U.S.A, David Lee Dobler, considers even the *use* of words like "pagan" and "heretic" by concerned conservatives in his denomination much more worrisome than the actual practice of heretical pagan rituals by appointed officials of his church's bureaucracy.[26] A British churchman has sized up this situation:

> It is Satan's sincerest wish that we should never make a negative judgment about those who set out to destroy the Church and its foundations, or who spread deadly heresy and false doctrine. Correspondingly, the real reason that human non-judgmentalism in any form is becoming so fashionable in this age is that it makes the concept of a judging, avenging God seem ridiculous, anachronistic and implausible.[27]

No Heresy—No Truth

There are limits to the modification of Christian doctrine—or of anything ("a" is still not "non-a," logicians will maintain)—before it is so disfigured that it becomes its own antithesis.

Steve Brown, a popular radio preacher, tells of the Jewish boy who asks his dad for a Honda as a bar mitzvah present. The father asks his orthodox rabbi what a Honda is, but he doesn't know. They both ask the conservative rabbi, who doesn't know either. All three then ask the liberal/reformed rabbi, who proudly informs them that a Honda is a motorcycle, a wonderful gift for the man's son. But as they leave, the liberal rabbi asks, "Excuse me. May I ask *you* a question? What's a bar mitzvah?"

The extremes of Judaism, indicated by this humorous story, illustrate our point about heresy. Philip Lee, hardly a right-wing fundamentalist, remarks: "At some given point, a teaching, an idea or an action which claims to be Christian is so utterly different from the 'faith which was once for all delivered to the saints' (Jude 3) that it becomes the opposite of Christianity."[28]

The formal, historical similarities between an ancient heresy and modern "Christian" liberalism suggest that such liberalism is not an authentic version of Christianity but its antithesis.

Liberalism has had a face-lift. Once associated with a religious rationalism and social-gospel activism, the new Religious Left has discovered spirituality—not the spirituality of the Bible but that of paganism.

As we move into Part II, we raise the following questions: What is the essence of this new Religious Left and of the spirituality that lies behind it? Beyond Culture Wars there are Spirit Wars: behind the pro-choice social agenda and the "politics of meaning" there is the defining component that comes from the Religious Left. Will this rediscovery of the religious dimension herald a new day for faith and the expansion of Christianity? Or will the revival of this new spirituality rather usher in ominous days of apostasy such that, were it possible, even the elect would be deceived?[29]

A Peek into the Future

The '60s revolution happened on the university campuses before entering today's mainstream. Present campus conflicts grant a vision of what the future holds for our children and grandchildren. At the May 1996 Whole Earth Festival at UC Davis, a handful of Christian students distributed literature in an overwhelmingly New Age, university-sponsored event. They were stopped by the "karma patrol." Their offense? Spreading bad karma by distributing Christian leaflets. To be forewarned is to be forearmed.

A Peek into the Past

In this new agenda there is deception, whether intended or not. The elements of ancient Gnosticism, presently proposed as a new lease on life for an aging planet, tend to emphasize the most moderate, least shocking parts of this hoary heresy. However, Gnosticism was a coherent system, and behind its seductive calls to spirituality, human freedom, fascinating diversity, inclusiveness and imagination lay an unimaginably revolutionary agenda whose ultimate aim and inevitable result was to cast the God of the Bible into hell. Is this also the ultimate intention of the contemporary karma patrols?

PART 2

ANATOMY OF AN
APOSTASY

Part I traced the recent history of the new spirituality and described the general monistic structure of its thought. Part II deals with key points of doctrine concerning the Bible, Bible study, the nature and person of God, and the important issues of sexuality and spirituality. The coherence as well as the great age of this extremely disparate movement becomes even clearer as these points of doctrine are compared with similar teaching in ancient Gnosticism. When Christians understand the coherence of error, they can better identify the battle lines in order to mount a compelling and creditable defense of the faith.

CHAPTER SIX

THE NEW BIBLE

A polytheistic theology, because it makes contact with the immediacy of life out of the depths, is itself a religion with no scripture, but with many stories.

DAVID MILLER[1]

We (the Nixon administration) would never have thought of rewriting the Bible. I found in one visit (with President Clinton) that he is bright and well-informed and so I assume he knows better. We're in real trouble when not even the Bible is safe from politically correct revisionism.

CHARLES COLSON[2]

For 2,000 years the Bible has been the most widely read book in the world. To change civilizations built on the Bible, *you must change the Bible.* In a new millennium, many dream of heaven on Earth, produced by an expected macro-jump in spiritual evolution. They happily pronounce obsolete the fuel that powered Christendom. There are cleaner energy sources. Pisces is a fish out of water as the Age of Aquarius dawns.

A New Bible for the New Spirituality

The Aquarian Age needs an Aquarian Bible, not the worn handbook of a dying civilization. Dissatisfied, a new ideology of social liberation clamors for a new Holy Scripture. Moderates agree with radicals that the Bible is "the founding document of patriarchal culture."[3] Since patriarchy is the great evil that must be eradicated, the future of its founding document looks bleak.

A leading New Testament scholar has said:

> The "orthodox" Bible today represents only a portion of the inspired books of the early Christian era and, at best, a partial explanation of Christ's teachings.[4]

Here we see the handwriting on the wall. The new liberalism intends to change the Bible. A New Age writer, defending abortion, speaks of "the bureaucratic priestly . . . patriarchal truth squad [who will] . . . go to any lengths to discourage independent thought, proclaim[ing] the heresy of certain 'lost' gospels and certify[ing] the infallible truth of their own translation of biblical documents."[5]

Nowhere do bold attacks on the Bible surface with such moral fervor as in the unholy alliance of feminism and radical biblical scholarship. Though liberals have always chafed under the orthodox canon of Scripture, they have rarely called for canonical revision. But feminist liberals believe they have found high moral ground and are willing to go all the way. Rosemary Radford Ruether, who elects to remain within the Church, states without nuance or apology:

> Feminist theology must create a new textual base, a new canon. . . . Feminist theology cannot be done from the existing base of the Christian Bible.[6]

Other feminists find the biblical texts "impossible" to read and feel the "need to write new ones."[7]

The Satanic Verses

Ruether's *Women-Church* exemplifies this approach. She sees parts of the Bible as demonic. In her "Ritual of Exorcism of Patriarchal Texts" (to the cry, "Out, demons, out!"), she eradicates or exorcises from feminist consciousness the following passages: Exodus 19:1, 7-9, 14-15; Leviticus 12:1-5 (purification after childbirth); Judges 19 (the Levite and his concubine); Ephesians 5:21-23 (the submission of a wife to her husband); 1 Timothy 2:11-15 (a woman saved through childbirth); and 1 Peter 2:1. Most of these texts express the biblical view of sexual role differentiation. At the end of the reading, the liturgist says:

> These texts have lost their power over our lives. We no longer need to apologize for them or try to interpret them as words of truth, but we cast out their oppressive message as expressions of evil and justifications of evil.[8]

On the other hand, Ruether gladly uses any text that agrees with the new orthodoxy. She also gives equal time to Gnostic texts like the *Gospel of Mary* (which founds the Church not on Peter but on Mary Magdalene), and she cites the apocryphal *Acts of Paul and Thecla* to defend her feminist view: "We remember Thecla, commissioned by Paul to preach the gospel and to baptize." For Ruether, the Gnostic texts give evidence of a "simpler, less hierarchical [original] Christianity," that she finds congenial for modern Christianity.[9]

Ashamed of the Bible

Some mainline biblical scholars are so ashamed of the Bible they are not sure they want their children to read it.[10] Others, like the editors of *The New Testament and Psalms: An Inclusive Version*, supposedly try to make it safe for children and other sensitive persons by eliminating all patriarchal language and any masculine terms for God or Christ. Claiming to be a work of scholarship, using "new manuscripts" and "new investigations into the meanings of words,"[11] this Bible is merely a verbatim reproduction of the *New Revised Standard Version* with the "offending" phrases reworked into something more politically correct. The imposition on the biblical text of an egalitarian philosophy so foreign to the Bible produces grotesque English and theological monstrosities. The editors, who boldly state their commitment to "accelerating changes in English usage towards inclusiveness,"[12] appear to have gone out of their way to improve on the new forms of English they claim are now accepted speech. Phrases such as: "Please contribute to the policeperson's ball" seem positively old fashioned compared to their rendering of John 13:31: "Now the Human One has been glorified, and in that one God has been glorified. If God has been glorified in the

Human One, God will also glorify that very one in Godself and will glorify that one at once." Did anyone understand? This egalitarian *newspeak* not only butchers English, it nullifies the Word of God by making it incomprehensible for the sake of the reigning ideology. The desire to be sexually inclusive produces a two-headed androgynous divinity that would be more at home in mythologies of ancient Greece than in the Bible. And so the Lord's Prayer begins: "Our Father/Mother in heaven, hallowed be your name." This is surely one of the most impressive attempts not to hallow God's name in the history of Christian thought, for the very heart of the revelation brought by Jesus concerning the Father is disfigured beyond recognition.[13] More devastating things will yet happen to Holy Scripture.[14]

"SCIENTIFIC" UNDERMINING OF BIBLICAL ORTHODOXY

When I began to specialize in New Testament studies over 30 years ago, orthodoxy was considered the original version of Christianity. To be sure, scholars suggested that Jesus did not consider himself the Messiah. They speculated that the Early Church had turned this Jewish prophet and the events surrounding his death into the object of faith and the essence of the gospel. But the "Easter faith" of those who wrote the New Testament was what explained the transition. It was the conviction of the *original* disciples, in their experience of the death and the resurrection of Jesus, that gave rise to the Church's gospel.

One generation later, New Testament scholars hail the Gnostic heresy (denounced by the New Testament and the Early Church) as the *original* teaching of Jesus and the propagators of that heresy as the earliest band of disciples after his death. The truly historical Jesus, they say, was a proto-Gnostic, politically correct, social revolutionary who bears little resemblance to the one worshiped as the Christ in the Bible.

DISMANTLING THE BIBLE

In 1985, as president of the Society of Biblical Literature, James M. Robinson issued a programmatic statement for the twenty-first century. He called upon his fellow Bible scholars to deconstruct their discipline in order to "lay bare [its]

... biblicistic presuppositions." The Bible would no longer serve as the ultimate source of authority to define true Christianity.[15] We were warned. Robinson's agenda fits the mood of the modern world; and he, along with his colleague Helmut Koester of Harvard Divinity School, has done seminal work to bring it about.[16] Robert Funk of the Jesus Seminar calls Robinson "the Secretary of State of the biblical guild . . . [an] academic counterpart . . . [to] Henry Kissinger."[17]

Both Koester and Robinson studied with Rudolf Bultmann, the German scholar who convinced New Testament science to look upon ancient Gnosticism and Hellenistic culture as the most important source of Christianity, rather than the Old Testament and Judaism. Both Koester and Robinson are committed to a clearly defined program: the "Dismantling and Reassembling of the Categories of New Testament Scholarship."[18] One category they have successfully dismantled is that of heresy and orthodoxy.[19]

They both argue that a radical pluralism existed in the earliest Church, causing Christian theology to develop along various "trajectories."[20] Orthodoxy was one trajectory, but the others are not heretical.[21] Koester contests that there is not "one gospel," as Paul said, but at least "four."

James Robinson put content to his manifesto. He founded and is director of the Institute for Antiquity and Christianity, which is devoted to the rehabilitation of texts and of a theology that the Early Church denounced as heresy. Within his institute, Robinson launched the Coptic Gnostic Library Project, which translates, publishes and promotes the Gnostic texts. Though it is a great service to the scholarly world, it is also a powerful tool for the neo-Gnostic theological agenda. The title "Secretary of State" is not an exaggeration. Robinson has been the leading force behind the Q Seminar (whose importance for the new understanding of Jesus we shall discuss below). He is an active member of the Jesus Seminar (founded by Robert Funk) and director of the Coptic Magical Texts Project, which rehabilitates heretical Gnostic and magical "Christianity."

Robinson rails against "myopic heresy hunters" because he believes the future lies with inclusion.[22] He argues that Gnosticism and Orthodoxy are two valid "trajectories" of early Christianity. What was a marginal position just a generation ago is now touted as majority conviction. Robinson encourages modern theology to extract values from both trajectories in order to produce a new formulation of Christianity for today.[23] Robinson's 1985 manifesto explodes the constraining limits of the orthodox biblical canon.

Helmut Koester, in the epilogue of a collection of essays in his honor,[24] gives his own prospective for the New Testament field. Early Christianity, he says, is "just one of several Hellenistic propaganda religions, competing with others who seriously believed in their god and who also imposed moral standards on their followers."[25]

He urges scholars to abandon New Testament canon "as part of a special book that is different from other early Christian writings." Koester issues this call in order to allow the other early "Christian" voices—"heretics, Marcionites, Gnosticism, Jewish Christians, perhaps also women . . . to be heard again."[26] Koester readily admits that this is not value-free, objective science. The old liberal historical-critical method was, he grants, "designed as a hermeneutical tool for the liberation from conservative prejudice and from the power of ecclesiastical and political institutions."[27] In the same way, future New Testament studies should have as their goal "political and religious renewal . . . inspired by the search for equality, freedom and justice" in the "comprehensive political perspective" of our modern world.[28] For Koester, the egalitarian, all-inclusive worldview of contemporary avant-garde thinking becomes *the* criterion of truth.

These two influential scholars apply the program of their mentor, Rudolf Bultmann, the "demythologization of the New Testament." This approach dismantles the theistic understanding of the New Testament in favor of a monistic, paganizing Gnostic one.[29] They are committed to the destruction of the canon and, consequently, to the undermining of orthodoxy.

CANON FODDER: HARASSED BY THE TRUTH

Everyone loves an underdog, especially if his opponents are establishment "fat cats" unfairly tyrannizing him. Today's heretics use sentimentality, political correctness and power politics to defend the downtrodden, theological "canon fodder."

Elaine Pagels, a student of Koester and colleague of Robinson, reads Early Church history this way. Gnosticism was suppressed because the bishops won, not because the Christian gospel of orthodox proclamation answered the needs of a reprobate empire, or because it was the true word of God. "It is the winners who write history—their way. No wonder, then," says Pagels, "that the viewpoint of the successful majority has dominated all traditional accounts of the origin of Christianity."[30] "It will be necessary," declares New Testament scholar Elizabeth Schlüssler Fiorenza, "to go beyond the limits of the New Testament canon since it is the product of the patristic church, that is, a theological document of the 'historical winners.'"[31]

This same power ideology rules in the Jesus Seminar. As one of the members says, in seeking to justify their inclusion of heretical gospels:

> Of course, history is written by the victors, in this case, by the orthodox authors known as the fathers of the church. From an objective historical perspective, however, "heresy" is a label for the rival religious currents that lost; they [the Gnostics] eventually ceased to be politically, socially, or intellectually sustainable alternatives to mainstream Christianity.[32]

The author goes on to call the heretical gospels "losers." "They lost out when the more powerful circles in Christianity imposed their own limits of doctrinal acceptability." Notice how this statement is full of value-laden terms. Heretical texts even receive the coveted status of "victim." The implicit emotional appeal says: "Is it not time to adopt these socially harassed literary orphans and give them a home at last in a church from which they were so unceremoniously and unchristianly dumped so many years ago by the evil, power-hungry patriarchs?" (Besides, they would be so useful for our contemporary new spiritual agenda!)

War of the Canons

Feminist biblical scholarship raises the level on the emotional Richter scale with a rumble of *patriarchal* power. The ultimate conspiracy theory, which has fiendish male plotters undermining the original egalitarian reality of the family, the Church and the society, works equally well for the history of the canon. Those who imposed the orthodox canon were Church *fathers*. The power lust behind the orthodox Bible is the desire for social control through the patriarchal suppression of women. Women now belong to the category of "losers." This is why "feminist theology must create . . . a new canon."[33]

Melanie Morrison, cofounder of CLOUT (Christian Lesbians Out Together) declared: "I know in my heart that the canon is not closed, it is open. I know this because the Bible does not reconcile me with the earth and the Bible does not reconcile me with my sexual self."[34] Has reconciliation with God and His holy law crossed Melanie Morrison's mind?

The Coming of Age of American New Testament Scholarship

In November 1995, at the annual meeting of the Society of Biblical Literature, victory was declared. Leading New Testament scholars rejoiced that the heretical Gnostic *Gospel of Thomas* had finally made it into the New Testament canon of Holy Scripture. Their elation was due, in part, to the publication of *The Five Gospels* in 1993, a volume that placed the *Gospel of Thomas* alongside the four canonical Gospels of Matthew, Mark, Luke and John. That year the Society celebrated the fiftieth anniversary of the finding of the *Nag Hammadi Library* of Gnostic texts. James Robinson, an ex-orthodox Calvinist, hailed the inclusion of the *Gospel of Thomas* as a canonical gospel as "the coming of age of American New Testament scholarship." How ironic. The great contribution of the sons of Christian America at the end of the twentieth century is the introduction of pagan heresy into the Church's Scriptures, destroying both the integrity of the canon and the theological coherence of biblical faith.

First Sightings of the New Aquarian Bible

A new "liberal" Bible, hoary with age but oh, so modern, has been waiting in the warm sands of Egypt, as if expecting this very moment. Perhaps the entire collection was placed in a large jar and hidden like a time capsule for future generations.[35] But for one reason or another, this Gnostic Bible emerged in 1945. It is now promoted in the Church by those who belong to the "incorruptible holy race" of the new Aquarian spirituality. Will this Gnostic Bible supplant the Bible of orthodox Christianity?

Some give this discovery an eschatological twist. Caitlín Matthews, theologian of the goddess Sophia and pagan priestess of Isis, sees the Nag Hammadi texts as the stimulus for present celebration of Sophia. For Matthews, a deeply religious and intelligent neo-pagan, the discovery of these texts "at the start of the New Age itself cannot be insignificant."[36]

A New Bible in Old Clay Pots

As he smashed the clay pot and pulled out an old papyrus, Mohammed Ali made it to the big time. In 1945, this Egyptian camel driver, with the same name as the international boxing star, unwittingly stepped into the ring of religious history. Ali was in Nag Hammadi, Egypt, 300 miles south of Cairo, poking around in the *sebakh*, the rich soil left when the Nile periodically overflows its banks. In the earthenware jar he found that day was the first of a 52-text library of ancient Gnostic scriptures. These documents describe a coherent, heretical account of Christian doctrine and offer a seductive picture of Jesus that will warm any New Age guru's heart.[37] Thanks to Mohammed Ali, the *Nag Hammadi Library* writings are shaking the Church's roots at the dawn of the Age of Aquarius.

This is eschatology with a malevolent twist. The irony is enormous. Precisely when New Age spirituality has emerged as the most dynamic religious force in the Western world, the firsthand documents of its long-lost spiritual cousin, Gnosticism,[38] have come to light. Thanks to James Robinson's well-orchestrated program of scholarly rehabilitation, they are now available in English for all to read. These texts fascinate liberals and New Agers alike—including contemporary New Age prophets. Shirley MacLaine states that "[Ancient] Christian Gnostics, operated with New Age knowledge."[39] New Age spokesman, Theodore Roszak, describes New Age spirituality as "the reclamation and renewal of the old Gnosis."[40] Roszak probably did not count on the help of prestigious New Testament scholars studying ancient texts from antiquity.

The battle of the Bibles is upon us. The attack on the Christian Bible comes from many sources, but the most pernicious comes from *"Christian" Bible scholars*. Today the attack is mounted on two fronts: the first is the rehabilitation of Gnostic texts; the second is the discovery of the supposedly lost gospel, Q.

The Complete Gospels

The Bible is incomplete, we are told. We need more texts—and radical New Testament scholarship is glad to be of service. Robert Funk, founder of the Jesus Seminar, also set up The Weststar Institute, "devoted to reducing biblical and religious illiteracy in America," and Polebridge Press, which published *The Complete Gospels*.[41] The canonical Gospels are completed by apocryphal gospels such as the *Infancy Gospel of James* and the *Infancy Gospel of Thomas* (a text dismissed even by liberal scholars as folk literature of little theological interest). Also included in this complete canon are a number of Gnostic gospels: the *Gospel of Thomas*, the *Apocryphon of James*, the *Dialogue of the Savior* and the *Gospel of Mary*, all of which witness to "the blending of Christianity and Gnosticism." We are asked to accept as "the religious convictions of sincere Christians" what the Early Church fought as diabolical heresy. There is no ambiguity here. The new definition of biblical literacy revives the Gnostic heresy and "scientifically" slips it into an emerging new Bible—all done in the name of academic objectivity and all-inclusive tolerance!

The Five Gospels

You thought there were only *four* Gospels. Rub your eyes and look again. "Progressive" scholars, with unprecedented feats of academic legerdemain, have slipped Gnostic texts into the canon. *The Five Gospels* uses a double-pronged attack on the orthodox Bible.[42]

First, it determines the authentic words of Jesus by using the critical criteria of classic liberals. Mimicking the popular Bibles that print Jesus' words in red, this publication makes red only those sayings considered authentic by the Jesus Seminar (pitifully few). Black indicates inauthentic sayings. Pink means "probably," and gray means "probably not." The Gospel of John has no red passages, only one pink and two grays. The Jesus Seminar has created a canon within the canon, dismissing much of what the Church has considered canonical as secondary accretion, at best.

Second, a heretical text, the *Gospel of Thomas*, is included alongside the four canonical gospels. Sprinkled with far more red and pink than the Gospel of John, it fares very well. *The Five Gospels* surreptitiously "canonizes" the Gnostic *Gospel of Thomas* by including it with Mark, Matthew, Luke and John as an (the most?) authentic source for the historical Jesus.[43]

Honey or Gall?

Today's radical Bible scholars attempt what their ancient cousins failed to achieve. In the second century, Irenaeus, defending the four canonical Gospels as "four pillars breathing out immortality on every side and vivifying our flesh,"[44] compares them to the four winds, the four zones of the world and the four faces of the cherubim.[45] Though his imagery might not impress modern readers, his intention was to oppose the Gnostic proliferation of gospels, insisting on only four true Gospels upon which the Church was founded—no other candidates need apply.

Line 67 of the second-century canonical list *The Muratorian Canon* specifically refuses to include the writings of the Gnostic teacher Valentinus, a book of psalms from the proto-Gnostic Marcion and the writings of Montanus. "Gall," the ancient author maintained, "cannot be mixed with honey."

Placing the *Gospel of Thomas* among the Bible's Gospels is not the triumphant progress of science over prejudice and reason over blind faith. It is the old Gnostic attempt to inject into the honey of the Gospels the gall of heresy. Today, as in the second century, two opposing versions of the gospel, two contradictory pictures of Jesus clash. Into the canonical record has crept the bittersweet, proto-Gnostic "Jesus," who came not to die for our sins but to reveal that we are all christs.[46]

If modern Gnostics succeed, it may not be long before a complete New Testament, with black leather binding and Indian paper, will include the *Gospel of Thomas* and exclude 1 and 2 Timothy and Titus or, at least, a selection of "satanic verses." An inclusive Bible that excludes what is politically incorrect is surely already in some publisher's files awaiting the propitious moment for publication.

Fair Play?

The addition of Gnostic scriptures to the Christian canon is called for in the name of diversity and fair play. But fairness demands that we keep them apart, for their internal coherence makes them mutually exclusive theologically. Even Bentley Layton, professor of ancient Christian history at Yale University, translator of many Gnostic texts and favorable to their message, recognizes that the Gnostic texts share "a coherent symbol system" that explains the texts themselves, the world and its origin and other people.[47]

With regard to coherence, one might argue that the interpretation of the first three chapters of Genesis reveals all of one's theology. The Gnostic writings are systematically suspicious of Genesis 1–3, denigrating not only the creation, but God the Creator who stands behind the Genesis text. Such suspicion permeates all that the Gnostic revealers and teachers say. The Christian Bible takes the opposite approach, honoring and glorifying God, the good and gracious Creator and Redeemer of heaven and Earth.

These two systems are fundamentally opposed. What one calls evil the other calls good, what one calls truth the other calls error. In the real world God created, one of them is false and one of them is true. But they cannot both be right. Only one can function as canon. It is, of course, the devil's work to spin a gray web of confusion from the black and white threads of truth and falsehood. In his world there is no canon.

Q: A SOURCE OF UNEXPECTED LIBERAL RICHES

How can a heretical Gnostic text like the *Gospel of Thomas* stand proudly beside the four canonical Gospels, the "four pillars, breathing out immortality on every side and vivifying our flesh," as Irenaeus, the redoubtable foe of Gnosticism, called them?[48] Modern reviews will be tolerant, not least because of the scholarship that such a volume claims. Part of that scholarship is the employment of Q.

James Robinson counters Irenaeus and orthodox Christians by elevating a hypothetical document, Q, as "surely the most important text we have."[49] What makes Q more important than Matthew, Mark, Luke or John, or the great epistles of Paul?

Q, from the German word *quelle*, meaning "source," is the name scholars have given to the material common to Matthew and Luke, a hypothesis first suggested by Johann Gottfried Eichhorn in 1794.[50] Since that time, Q has served as the most widely accepted theory about the sources used by Matthew and Luke. Known as the "Two-Source Theory," this argument suggests that Matthew and Luke had both Mark and Q before them when they composed their own Gospels.

Recently, scholars have begun to consider Q to be an independent document, offering its own theology and a window on the earliest Jesus movement.[51] Q functions in radical New Testament studies to rehabilitate the *Gospel of Thomas* and to reveal the radical "Christian" community in which Q was supposedly born.

Q and Thomas: A Dynamic Duo

The *Gospel of Thomas*, a collection of 114 sayings with no story of Jesus' life, is clearly Gnostic and so different from the canonical gospels that it is difficult to place it early in Christian history.[52] Enter Q, on cue.

The scholars argue that if Q existed, it was the earliest written document.[53] If it can be identified with the common material of Matthew and Luke, then it, too, is made up of sayings, has hardly any narrative and contains no accounts of, or reflections on, the death and resurrection of Jesus. And voilà, a literary and theological soul mate for the *Gospel of Thomas*. Q draws the *Gospel of Thomas* to the historical Jesus as a magnet attracts iron filings. According to Robinson, the hypothetical document Q shows that the *Gospel of Thomas* is among the earliest collections of Jesus' sayings.[54] "[The *Gospel of Thomas*]," says New Testament scholar Stevan Davies, "appears to be roughly as valuable a primary source for the teaching of Jesus as Q."[55] The *Gospel of Thomas* and Q share the same literary genre—a collection of sayings—and the same theology—Jesus as a wise teacher, not a savior from sin.

Q is absolutely essential to the new Bible. If one admits to Q, then the Gnostic *Gospel of Thomas* can be (somewhat) plausibly drawn into the orbit of the earliest community following the death of Jesus.[56] Without Q, the whole reconstruction falls to the ground like a house of cards.

Q—An Everchanging Hypothesis

Some of the best minds have sought to make the Q hypothesis stick. But many well-respected scholars have dissented from the standard view, even of Q as an existing source.[57] A British New Testament scholar, John Wenham, lecturer at Bristol University and warden of Latimer House, Oxford, gives the interesting judgment that since "no one knows for certain whether a Q document ever existed," it is still held as a working hypothesis "but with decreasing confidence."[58]

Already in 1955, A. M. Farrer argued there was no need for Q if Luke used Matthew. Everything that was common was the result of Luke incorporating Matthew into his Gospel.[59] The simplicity of this argument has convinced more than one contemporary scholar,[60] one of whom described Farrer's article as a "firecracker."[61] Farrer's argument still sparkles, awaiting a satisfactory refutation.[62]

GNOSTIC AGENDA

The scholarly program built around Q has theological fallout. The new radical Q scholarship agrees with the *Gospel of Thomas* in three significant areas:

- *The person of Jesus.* Jesus did not proclaim himself as the Messiah and the Son of God, the divine savior who was to die for the sins of the world;[63]

- *The work of Jesus.* The Jesus of Q [the hypothetical document supposedly embedded in Matthew and Luke—see below] is but a teacher of wisdom,[64] a sort of proto-Gnostic guru;
- *The nature of the Church.* The "Q people" (hypothetically reconstructed from the hypothetical document Q) did not focus "on the person of Jesus or his life and destiny. [Rather] they were engrossed with the social program that was called for by his teachings,"[65] including radical poverty, the lifestyle of the wandering beggar,[66] an attitude of political subversion,[67] and needless to say, an egalitarian, antipatriarchal feminism.[68]

The question is: Who is Jesus? Is He the Jesus of the ancient Gnostics and the Jesus Seminar or the Jesus of the New Testament and historic orthodoxy?

No Agenda . . . Except a New Pagan Christianity

Some in the Q movement may naively believe themselves "neutral" scholars, pursuing truth wherever it leads,[69] but most of the Jesus Seminar scholars have a religious commitment to some form of liberalism, and some have no Christian commitment at all. Another god than the God of Scripture seems to be using their science to promote his pernicious agenda.

The Complete Bible

The Jesus Seminar scholars are intentionally producing a new Bible which augments and completes the Bible we already have. Their *Scholars Bible* gives us texts such as the *Infancy Gospels of James* and *Gospel of Thomas*, which even liberal scholars in the past dismissed as pious legends and popular fiction, not worthy to be considered for a moment as part of authentic, early Christianity.[70]

The new Bible adds and takes away from Holy Scripture, spreading pagan monism in the Christian Church. Where will this lead?

A New Bible For a Global Religion

The new Bible and the Q community may be short-lived creations. But they will have deconstructed the Bible by relativizing the uniqueness of its claims[71] and by setting heretical writings alongside canonical ones. Q, *Gospel of Thomas* and other heretical texts, and eventually 1 Corinthians 13, will survive in a heady atmosphere, that of the next-generation all-world-religions Bible, already in process of production. We do well to recall here the prediction made in 1974 about the coming new polytheistic religion which, "because it makes contact with the immediacy of life out of the depths, *is itself a religion with no scripture, but with many stories.*"[72]

The production of a world Bible began with enthusiastic prompting by Robert Muller, New Age leader and assistant deputy secretary-general of the UN. In 1989 the United Nations launched the International Sacred Literature Trust. The purpose of this Trust is to make the world's sacred writings more accessible in the common language of English. This project is now headed by the Inter-Religious Federation for World Peace, a front organization of the Unification church.[73] At an IRFWP Symposium on World Scriptures, organized at the Parliament of the World's Religions, a number of well-known scholars, including Dr. Ursula King, a member of the Board of Advisors of IRFWP and professor of theology and religious studies at Bristol University, U.K., gave lectures on this exciting program. In her lecture, King announced that the International Sacred Literature Trust had agreed upon a publishing venture with Harper Collins, and she concluded that this series of ancient sacred traditions would "become a contemporary resource for shaping our future as a global community."[74]

A New, All-Faiths Bible

The new Bible will likely look something like the texts read at one of the plenary sessions of the Parliament of the World's Religions called "Voices of Spirit and Tradition." Texts from Hindu and Buddhist scriptures were read along with selections from the Koran and the Sufi masters, an American Indian animistic chant and a poem by a womanist claiming that humanity needs new revelations. The death-of-God theologian and polytheist, David Miller, professor of religion at Syracuse University and member of the Joseph Campbell Institute, called for the end of dogmas and doctrines that limit unity and for the discovery of a world soul through weaning and emptying. Miller read from Meister Eckhardt, a medieval mystic who prayed: "I pray God, free me of God." A representative of the "School of Spiritual Psychology" read from the Gnostic text *Pistis Sophia*, which revered the goddess and denounced the "lion-faced" prideful

Creator God of the Old Testament. There was one reading from the Bible, a text where God and Christ are absent. A New Age liberal Benedictine monk declared that as a representative of the Christian tradition, he was faced with an impossible choice. Unable to choose a passage that mentioned God, for fear of offending all the women present, or a passage mentioning Jesus Christ, since that would be too divisive, he solved his dilemma by reading from 1 Corinthians 13 as a text about love that speaks to the heart of every religion whose deep concern is to help humans become truly human in deep communion with plants and animals. I could not help noticing that this statement was enthusiastically received by all the witches on the platform.

In 1984, the year George Orwell made famous in his novel describing the ultimate form of totalitarianism, Harper Publishing brought us *The Other Bible*, a collection of "inspired" writings from the ancient Judeo-Christian world, including many Gnostic texts and material from the mystical Jewish Kabbala, that did not make it into the Christian canon. Its editor, Willis Barnstone, professor of comparative literature at Indiana University, makes the following statement as he introduces the collection: "Had events been otherwise and certain of these [noncanonical] texts been incorporated in our Bible, our understanding of religious thought would have been radically altered. Today, free of doctrinal strictures, we can read the 'greater bible' of the Judeo-Christian world."[75] The implication is that these books did not make it into the canon as the result of arbitrary dogmatism. But the accusation does not stick. Most of the material in *The Other Bible* (with the exception of the Dead Sea Scrolls) defends a monistic, anti-Christian worldview in fundamental contradiction to the Christian gospel.

A case in point. The contents of Gnostic *Apocryphon of John* are described in this publication as having to do with "Sophia, Mother of the monstrous Creator, Ialdabaoth, Jahweh." For a Christian this is unspeakable blasphemy since the New Testament presents God as the Father of our Lord Jesus Christ and the maker of heaven and Earth. If you claim *The Other Bible,* you adopt a non-Christian world and life view. You cannot have both Bibles, just as you cannot serve two masters. But that, of course, is the point. Harper San Francisco also brings us *The World's Wisdom: Sacred Texts of the World's Religions,*[76] calling it "Virtually a World Bible for an age of intercultural understanding." Penguin Books offers *The Portable World Bible* which includes selections from the "bibles" of the major world religions—the Upanishads and the Bhagavad-Gita of Hinduism, the Lotus of the True Law and The Tibetan Doctrine from Buddhism, The Gatas from Zoroastrianism, the

Koran from Islam, the Li Ki and the Book of Filial Piety from Confucianism, the Tao-Te Ching from Taoism, and "substantial selections from the Old and New Testaments" from Judaism and Christianity.[77]

The World Scriptures—a gender-and-religion-inclusive interfaith planetary Bible—is part of the brave new world of the Age of Aquarius awaiting us in the third millennium. Though not yet (to my knowledge) available in church pew editions, for use in "Christian" interfaith liturgies, the time is surely not far off when the *World Bible* will be a standard part of mainline Christianity. How important it is that Christians understand what is going on now, as liberals tinker with their Bible and seek to undermine the very objective basis of the Christian faith. How important that we preserve the Bible from such blatant attacks and continue to make it available for all to read, understand and obey.

CHAPTER SEVEN

THE ANCIENT GNOSTIC BIBLE

There was revealed in their hearts the living book of the living.

GOSPEL OF TRUTH

S trictly speaking, the Gnostics did not have a Bible.[1] A Bible only makes sense in a theistic universe in which the transcendent God, distinct from his creation, reveals himself in space and time, for the sake of redemption through the means of special revelation. Since the Gnostics redeemed themselves and were in touch with their divine selves, they had no need of revelation. God's intervention to save and to reveal were superfluous to those who possessed inner knowledge of their divinity. Spiritual gurus suggested wisdom from their own quest for personal transformation.

The Use and Misuse of the Scriptures

But Gnostics used Scripture when it suited them. They related to the Bible in three ways: (1) They quoted (and misquoted) the Christian Bible, (2) they produced bogus "scriptures," and (3) they used mystical sources for creating Gnostic wisdom from which they created a "canon" that looked nothing like the canon of the Church.

The Old Testament

One of the earliest Gnostics, Marcion, so detested the God of Creation and Law that he expunged the Old Testament from his "Christian" canon. The texts preached by the Apostles, the Scripture of the Early Church, were dismissed by second-century Gnostics as the disagreeable musings of an inferior God. Later Gnostics, like Valentinus, were more ingenious. As the chapter on Gnostic Bible study will show, the full-blown Gnostic systems commandeered the Old Testament for Gnostic purposes by turning the sacred text on its head. The Church father Tertullian (A.D. 160-225) captures the subtleties of this later approach when he compares Marcion and Valentinus:

> One man perverts Scripture with his hand, another with his exegesis. If Valentinus seems to have used the whole Bible, he laid violent hands upon the truth with just as much cunning as Marcion. Marcion openly and nakedly used the knife, not the pen, massacring Scripture to suit his own material. Valentinus spared the text, since he did not invent Scriptures to suit his matter, but matter to suit the Scriptures. Yet he took more away, and added more, by taking away the proper meanings of particular words, and by adding fantastic arguments.[2]

Generally, Gnostics disregarded the Old Testament. While numerous *Nag Hammadi* texts focus on Genesis 1–3, the rest of the Old Testament is virtually absent. The reason is simple. Gnosticism is a revolution of independence from the Creator God revealed in the Bible. Once the Creator is dethroned, the rest falls of its own weight. The Gnostics had no interest in the *history* of redemption, which is the unifying theme of the Old Testament. History has no status in a monistic world. Since the Old Testament Creator defines Himself as the Redeemer of Israel, He is of no interest whatsoever. Delivering the Law to His people sealed Yahweh's fate.

The New Testament

What befell the Old Testament also befell the New. It is interesting to compare the Gnostics with another ancient religious sect, the people of Qumran. The Dead Sea Scrolls of the Qumran Community were discovered just three years after the *Nag Hammadi Library*. They contain some commentaries on and full copies or fragments of every book in the Old Testament except Esther.[3] Though a marginal group in ancient Judaism, the Qumran community was clearly committed to the Old Testament Bible, even if their interpretations were at times idiosyncratic.

By contrast, the *Nag Hammadi Library*, the only extant collection of texts of this marginal Christian movement, witnesses to a profound disdain for the scriptures of its tradition. There is not one copy of a New Testament book. By their allusions to well-known phrases, Gnostic writings show familiarity with the apostolic writings. But they seemed deliberately to suppress the New Testament writings themselves. The Gnostics show apathy to Jesus as a person, and see no importance in His deeds, especially in His death and resurrection. The apostolic, eyewitness teaching on the person and ministry of Jesus is wrapped in Gnostic interpretation or changed to divert the original sense. An excellent case in point is the *Gospel of Thomas*.

Thomas and the Gospels

Scholarship associated with the Jesus Seminar regularly claims *Thomas* to be one of the earliest—if not the earliest—written gospel. But an earlier generation of specialists affirmed the contrary. Kurt Rudolf, whose work *Gnosis* was first published in 1977, sees in *Thomas* the typical Gnostic approach to other people's scripture, when he says:

> The *Gospel of Thomas* presents the ancient material of the sayings and parables of Jesus in a Gnostic interpretation and adds new material of the same sort . . . the Gnostic men of letters were frequently leaders in the production of such "gospels."[4]

Rudolf further observes that Gnosticism

> frequently draws its material from the most varied existing tradition, attaches itself to it, and at the same time sets it in a new frame. . . . the Gnostic view of the world . . . attaches itself . . . to old religious imagery, almost as a parasite prospers on the soil of host religions, it can also be described as parasitic. To this extent Gnosticism strictly speaking has no tradition of its own but only a borrowed one. Its mythology is a tradition consciously created from alien material.[5]

A wonderful example of this Gnostic method is saying 21:

> Mary said to Jesus, "What are your disciples like?" He said, "They are similar to children who have settled in a field which is not theirs. When the lords of the field come, they will say, 'Give our field back to us.' [The children will] disrobe before them in order to return their field and to give it back to them. Consequently I say, if the house owner is aware that a robber is coming, he will begin to keep guard before he comes and will not allow him to break into his house or his domain to seize all his goods. You then, be on your guard against the world. Equip yourselves with great fortitude lest the thieves find a way to get to you, for the distress you anticipate will take place. May there be in your midst a man of wisdom. When the crop ripened, he came promptly, sickle in hand, and reaped it. He who has ears to hear, let him hear."

Such a saying bears no hint of an individual author's creativity or literary artifice. This is clearly not the Gnostic author's purpose. Rather, numerous biblical allusions are combined with some Gnostic phrases in a collage of ideas that blunts the original scriptural intention and promotes obscure Gnostic teaching.[6] Scripture is not functioning here with canonical authority but as a mine of sayings and images to be used for other purposes and another agenda, while projecting a veneer of Christian truth. This is not serious exegesis. It appears distinctly like the self-serving, picking and choosing self, denounced by the Church father Irenaeus (A.D. 130-200). Here is his contemporary eyewitness report:

They try to adapt to their own sayings in a manner worthy of credence, either the Lord's parables, or the prophets' sayings, or the apostles' words, so that their fabrication might not appear to be without witness. They disregard the order and the connection of the Scriptures and, as much as in them lies, they disjoint the members of the truth. They transfer passages and rearrange them; and making one thing out of another, they deceive many by the badly composed fantasy of the Lord's words they adapt.[7]

This same Gnostic spirit is very much alive today. Rosemary Radford Ruether, while remaining in the Church and teaching at Garret-Evangelical Theological Seminary, Evanston, Illinois, in *Womanguides* recommends the use of any text, including Platonic, Gnostic or sectarian, that makes references to the divine female.[8] Personal agenda removes the canonical authority from Scripture and places it alongside any documents that further the theological program in question.

Another Gnostic specialist underlines the difference between Gnostic gospels and the Gospels of the Bible. With regard to the Gnostic *Gospel of Truth*, its editor says:

In spite of the title, this work is not a gospel of the same sort as the New Testament gospels: it does not focus upon the words and deeds of the historical Jesus. Yet the *Gospel of Truth* is "gospel" in the sense of "good news" about Jesus, about the eternal and divine Son, the word who reveals the Father and passes on knowledge, particularly self-knowledge . . . through this . . . the Gnostics . . . realize that they themselves are essentially sons of the Father.[9]

This is hardly good news if the truth about us is that we have all sinned and fallen short of the glory of God.[10]

The Gnostics used biblical texts, discarded others and imported material from any religious tradition to express the good news of their own divine nature. Theistic Old and New Testament Scriptures are brought under the yoke of that essential idea of Gnosticism. But since the Scriptures are theistic not monistic, they gave little support to the Gnostic program. Inevitably, the Gnostics were obliged to write their own texts and produce their own version of the Bible.

THE PRODUCTION OF
GNOSTIC SCRIPTURES

Gnostics claimed secret revelation that was kept from the Church in general and revealed only to the truly spiritual. Paying scant attention to what Jesus did and said on Earth, they emphasized the teaching of the "living" or resurrected Jesus who brought secret knowledge to His initiates after His time on Earth. The apocryphal *Acts of Peter* describes Peter entering a church where the congregation is reading from the gospel scroll. Peter rolls up the scroll and explains that only the deeper knowledge brings true gnosis: Jesus only appeared to take on flesh.[11]

This is the claim of the *Gospel of Thomas*, which begins: "These are the secret sayings which the living Jesus spoke and which Didymos Judas Thomas wrote down. . . . Whoever finds the interpretation of these sayings will not experience death." Thomas receives knowledge that goes beyond what is in the canonical Gospels, giving him the authority to reconfigure the gospel. The Gnostic gnosis defines the principle of the reconfiguration. Irenaeus recounts the vision of Marcus the magician who sees

> the Supreme Tetrad descended from invisible, unnameable places in the
> Pleroma in female form to reveal to him something never before revealed
> to God or man, who he really was and how he came into being.[12]

For the Gnostic, this knowledge lies beyond Scripture and gives to Scripture its true meaning.

Apocalypse Now

The New Testament contains one book entitled *Apocalypse*, and uses the term on many occasions. Behind the term is a verb which means "openly reveal, make known, disclose."[13] This word characterizes the gospel message of the New Testament as the revelation of God in the Old Testament, now fully and openly revealed in Jesus Christ and the writings of the apostolic witness. Gnosticism emphasizes the *Apocryphon*. Behind this noun stands a verb meaning "hide from sight, keep hidden, conceal."[14] This term characterizes the Gnostic view of Scripture: secret revelation to be kept away from prying eyes and to be revealed only to the inner circle. No New Testament book is entitled *Apocryphon*. The *Nag*

Hammadi collection contains two, the *Apocryphon of James* and the *Apocryphon of John*. *James* claims to be special, secret revelation, kept even from the twelve Apostles, and thus is considered superior to orthodoxy. James writes to a disciple and minister, a certain [...]thos:

> But because you are a servant of the salvation of the saints, strive diligently and take care not to relate this writing to many—this very one, which the Savior did not desire to tell even to all of us; his twelve disciples. But blessed will they become, namely, those who will be saved through the faith of this word [logos].

> And I also sent another *Apocryphon* to you ten months ago, which was revealed to me by the Savior. As the case may be, I consider that one revealed to me, James.[15]

At the conclusion of the *Apocryphon of John*, Jesus says to John:

> And I have I said [sic] you everything that you shall write it down and give it secretly to your brethren in the spirit, for this is the mystery of the generation which does not waiver.[16]

The difference between this heretical "Johannine" apocryphon and the canonical Gospel of John is most notable. At the conclusion of the canonical Gospel of John, the apostle declares: "Jesus did many other miraculous signs in the presence of his disciples, which are not recorded in this book. But these are written that you may believe that Jesus is the Christ, the son of the living God, and that by believing you may have life in his name."[17] The emphasis is on the astonishing deeds of Jesus, and the gospel is written to be spread in broad daylight, as Jesus prophesied: "But I, when I am lifted up from the earth, will draw all men to myself."[18] Where the Bible reveals, Gnosticism conceals.

It is true that there are five apocalypses in the recently discovered Gnostic texts, the *Apocalypse of Paul*, the *First Apocalypse of James*, the *Second Apocalypse of James*, the *Apocalypse of Adam* and the *Apocalypse of Peter*. When the term "apocalypse" (revelation) is used, however, it is in the sense of *secret* revelation for those in the inner circle. The *Apocalypse of Paul* is a classic statement of the ascent of the initiated one into deeper and deeper realms of gnosis. It goes beyond 2 Corinthians 12 and reveals what Paul in the New Testament said was unlawful to reveal, even to believers. According to the Gnostic text, Paul ascends through the third realm to the fourth, fifth, six and at the seventh is stopped by "an old man [. . . .] light [and] [whose clothing] was white, [His throne], which is in the seventh heaven, [was] [seven] times brighter than the sun." When the Spirit tells Paul to move on, "The old man answered me and said, 'How will you be able to escape from me? Look around and see the principalities and the authorities.' Then he spoke, namely the spirit, and said, 'Give him [the] token from your hand, and [he will] open for you.' And then I gave him the token. He (the old man, that is, Jahweh) turned his face down towards his creation." Then Paul goes to the Ogdoad, that is, the eighth mystical realm, then to the ninth and eventually the tenth heaven, where he is greeted by his fellow spirits.[19] This is secret knowledge of the mystical ascent, a classic type of pagan spirituality.

The *First Apocalypse of James*, says the editor, contains "the secret teachings of the Lord to James."[20] In the *Second Apocalypse of James*, James is "the escort guiding the Gnostic through the heavenly door."[21] The *Apocalypse of Adam* ends with the phrase: "This is the secret knowledge (*gnosis*) of Adam which he gave to Seth, which is the sacred baptism of the ones who know the everlasting knowledge (*gnosis*)."[22] The *Apocalypse of Peter* is the account of a revelation seen by Peter and interpreted by Jesus for an oppressed faithful remnant of Gnostics who are "summoned to knowledge."[23]

In Gnosticism, even its *Gospels* not to be preached on the rooftops, as in the New Testament.[24] The *Gospel of Thomas* describes its content as "the secret sayings" of the living Jesus.[25] The *Gospel of Truth* speaks of esoteric knowledge in a most (deliberately?) confusing way:

> This is the knowledge of the living book that he made manifest at the end to the Aeons . . . Every letter is an entire [thought], like a finished book, because they are written in unity, by the Father, for the Aeons, so that they may know the Father through his letters.[26]

These secret revelations claim divine origin. The *Gospel of the Egyptians* claims to be "the God-written, holy, secret book . . . of the great invisible Spirit."[27] *Zostrianos* makes the same claim: "Zostrianos: Words of truth of Zostrianos. God of Truth. Words of Zoroast[er].[28] *Trimorphic Protennoia* ends with the phrase "A sacred scripture written by the Father with perfect knowledge."[29] Though claiming divine inspiration, these books have another, different source.

THE ULTIMATE SOURCE OF THE GNOSTIC BIBLE

The source of the Gnostic Bible is not the transcendent God outside the universe he created. Gnostic "truth comes from within the circle of existence and from within the human heart." Says the *Gospel of Truth* about "the little children," that is, the Gnostic believers, "there was revealed in their hearts the living book of the living—the one written in the thought and mind of the Father."[30] Knowledge of the unknown God is found within oneself. But is there anything else out there that might determine what the human heart knows? The editor of the *Nag Hammadi* text *Zostrianos* argues that Zostrianos is directly related to Zoroaster, the founder of Persian Zoroastrian system and of "all sorts of philosophical, speculative and magical systems."[31]*Zostrianos* presents, says the modern editor, "a series of revelations made by exalted beings regarding the nature of the heavenly realm."[32]

One is reminded of the source of contemporary New Age revelations, the spirit entities, who speak through channels such as Ken Carey (*Starseed: The Third Millennium*) and Helen Shucman (*A Course in Miracles*). Others in the movement are claiming similar inspiration. Fritjof Capra, who teaches physics at UC Berkeley, speaks of "outside powers" so strong that "sometimes, while writing the *Tao of Physics*, I felt that it was being written through me, rather than by me. The subsequent events have confirmed these feelings."[33] David Miller, the death-of-God theologian and professor of religion at Syracuse University, speaks in almost "evangelical" terms of the process by which the gods and goddesses "in their reality and potency. . . . entered my life."[34] He describes bizarre occurrences during his lectures on Greek religion when these pagan deities would "take on a life of their own in the classroom." He would add details of his own to the Greek myths—as "the stories carried on with (or perhaps without) me—only to discover later, in further research, that these details were already in the ancient texts."

Christians are told to test the spirits.[35] Gnostic knowledge found within is occult knowledge. Its source is not only the human heart, as many so naively think, but also the forces of evil amassed against the truth of God as revealed in Scripture. It claims to be divine prophecy, but it is false prophecy from the father of lies.

The Gnostics effectively silenced the Bible in their communities by not recognizing its existence or power. The same is happening in our day, when two canons vie for ultimate authority. As yet, the Bible still occupies first place in pulpits and hearts across the land. But more and more an alternate bible is subtly introduced for the tolerant consideration of believers, so that one is forced to wonder if the day will ever come, as it did in the time of Gnosticism, when the Scriptures were eclipsed in many places by the esoteric writings of the heretics.

But this apostate movement, both in its ancient and modern forms, held and holds still another ace. If you cannot totally eliminate the Bible, you can so disfigure it by questionable interpretation and elimination of passages that irk, so that the Bible is turned to serve falsehood rather than truth. In our pews are some pagans with this agenda. They will be happy to lead a new variety of Bible study.

CHAPTER EIGHT

A NEW METHOD
OF BIBLE STUDY

*The scripture is the church's book. I think the church can do with
its scripture what it wants to do with its scripture.*

BURTON THROCKMORTON
MEMBER OF THE NATIONAL COUNCIL OF CHURCHES REVISION
COMMITTEE FOR THE *RSV* BIBLE[1]

Whisked through the clouds, Sherry Ruth Anderson, a Jewish feminist, is transported in a dream to a temple surrounded by snarling black dogs and defended by a ferocious guardian with bulging eyes. With uncharacteristic bravery she enters; the fearsome guards disappear as if made of fog. An old man, Melchizedek, with long robes and white beard leads her to the cabinet containing the holy Torah. He allows her to take the scroll, reserved for men, and cradle it like a baby.

"This is a very special Torah," says [Melchizedek]. Pulling out his dagger, he breaks the seal and rolls open the scrolls. They are blank. "The Torah is empty," he says, "because what you need to know now is not written in any book. You already contain that knowledge. It is to be unfolded from within you. . . .

Without speaking Melchizedek . . . places the [Torah] inside my body, from my shoulders to my knees."

The room fills with long-bearded patriarchs—including Moses, David, Solomon, Abraham, Isaac and Jacob—dressed in black coats and trousers, dancing in celebration of the emergence of spiritually responsible women. "But who will be our [women's] teachers?" she asks, and the answer comes: "You will be teachers for each other. You will come together in circles and speak your truth to each other." Finally the patriarchs give her their blessing, saying: "We have initiated you. . . . But we no longer know the way. Our ways do not work any more. You women must find a new way." [2]

READING THE BIBLE WITH POWER

In the postmodern world, the primacy of experience is not unique to feminism. Proponents of the new spirituality believe that experiencing themselves as divine constitutes saving knowledge (gnosis).[3] David Wells shows how evangelicalism follows society's intoxication with experience.[4] Some Christians read the Bible that way. "Whatever it says to me," regardless of the writer's intent, must be the Spirit's meaning. The reader's emotional needs dictate the meaning of the passage.[5] "Whatever it says to me" is reaching new levels of absurdity.

To affirm that feminism leads the way is not an expression of male prejudice. Feminists, male and female, proudly claim as much. Says a New Testament scholar in the movement: "The program of feminist biblical exegesis. . . . [is] one of the most important aspects of current biblical scholarship."[6] Others trumpet that feminism has brought a revolution in religious thought.

Such revolutionary and heart-felt convictions, when turned on the Bible, make it unrecognizable. Only an "empty Torah" has room for this world-changing agenda.

THE DECONSTRUCTION OF BIBLE STUDY

The most important event in our lifetime is not the bulldozing of the Berlin Wall or the fall of Communism in Eastern Europe and Russia. This event cannot be captured on TV news footage, for it is an idea: "deconstruction." Deconstruction was originally the product of hermeneutics, which is the theory of interpretation, associated with Jacques Derrida, a French philosopher and literary theorist.

Literary deconstruction doubts that any literary theory can truly describe written communication. By extension, it questions any explanation of anything. No general descriptions of why things are the way they are (called "metanarratives") are acceptable, since they are "totalizing discourses" that impose someone's or some group's ideas on the rest of us.[7] Deconstruction "is a worldview that denies all worldviews." Stanley Fish of Duke University, the leading deconstructionist in America, says: "Since all principles are preferences, they are nothing but masks for the will to power. . . . someone is always going to be restricted next, and it is your job to make sure that that someone is not you."[8]

David Wells measures the devastating effect of this intellectual movement:

> In literature, a whole generation of deconstructionists . . . now make their living by denying that words have any meaning at all. Words mean only whatever we wish them to mean.[9]

The disturbing development in deconstructionism is the identification of truth as power. If there is no absolute truth (which most people in the West now accept as true), then all truth claims are mere power plays. So everyone gets to play, but the game is deadly serious. In short order the Marxist belief that political power comes out of the barrel of a gun again becomes a real possibility for the global society of the Age of Aquarius.

DEFENDER OF FAITH

You know the world has changed when the British royal family changes. Earlier monarchs of the House of Windsor were far from angels. But Charles is the first modern royal and heir to the throne to admit, without remorse and on prime time telly, that he is an adulterer. The future king justified his sexual pluralism—having more than one woman—because, like most of his Western contemporaries, he has bought the new "truth" of religious pluralism (having more than one truth).

For His Royal Highness, there are many ways to God—and possibly many gods. Since 1521 the British monarch has borne the title "Defender of the Faith." When Charles becomes king, he intends to drop the definite article and be known as "Defender of Faith" since, as he explains, with an exquisite sense of modern-day tolerance, all religions "contain common elements of truth."[10]

Charles will be the first deconstructed king (if by then that title is not politically incorrect) on the British throne. Charles may be in for a surpise, for a deconstructed king may discover that there is no longer a throne awaiting him.

THE DETHRONING OF GOD

The new view of truth as power tries to saw the legs off the throne of the universe. Employing their principle for Bible study, Fewell and Gunn, Methodist
and Presbyterian Bible scholars, argue that everyone has his own truth and a
right to empowerment. Everything else (especially one-sided revelation) must be
treated with suspicion. They further argue that "gender relations, at least as
constructed in . . . patriarchy, are power relations." This false totalizing discourse of patriarchy produces "the binary world of heterosexuality."[11]

In their technical language these scholars affirm that "the Bible, which
masquerades as 'truth' is really an exercise of male social control." It needs to
be deconstructed, along with its "binary world" (the belief in right and
wrong, good and evil). Our Methodist and Presbyterian scholars have entered
the strange "new" world of pagan monism. The immediate result is the
deconstruction of the Bible as truth and of God the Father Almighty, maker
of heaven and Earth, as distinct from His creation, the only true expression
of divinity.

"Deconstructed" evangelical Virginia Mollenkott speaks of "the one really foolish assumption . . . that anyone could possibly arrive at a situationless,
culture-free, objective interpretation of any text, let alone a text as complex
as the Bible."[12] What happened to the sufficiency and perspicuity of
Scripture?

"PRO-CHOICE" HERMENEUTICS

Deconstructionism and the loss of the sense of absolute truth have clearly
affected the way people read the Scriptures, or for that matter, any piece of
writing. Interpretation has become much more complicated, to the detriment of the Bible and to the advantage of the Bible interpreter. The following three stages trace this slide from confidence in the text to confidence in
the reader.

The Author

Traditional Bible study has always tried to discover what the author of a passage meant to say, otherwise known as authorial intent. If you know Paul was in prison, might that not help in understanding some of his letters written from prison? Using the "worst case scenario" method, some have recently argued that authors may be the worst judge of their writing,[13] and therefore justify eliminating authorial intent in the interpretation of texts.

The Text

Those who minimize the author's intention tend to adopt an approach known as "literary theory."[14] This approach believes that a literary work is self-sufficient and has no need of outside information about the author's meaning and the history in which the text was written. Understanding depends on the underlying structure of the narrative. The text has a life of its own, independent of the author. To discover meaning, the reader must expose the deep structures of the text itself. Recently the emphasis has moved from the text to the reader's decisive contribution to the meaning of a text.

The Reader

Most readers of the Bible go there for a deeper knowledge of the will and mind of God. Not modern literary theorists. Due to their relativistic approach to truth, interpretation is a matter of personal taste.[15] They argue that since the author's intention cannot be known and the structural approach is too mechanical, the meaning of a text is always obscure. If readers are to derive meaning, it is because *they bring their own questions* and, in interaction with the text, *create their own ever-renewed meaning*. This has become known as reader-response theory. As one can imagine, it is enthusiastically taken up by readers with an agenda, e.g., liberation theologies of all stripes, which take experience as divine revelation. This method has become a major force in our experience-saturated world. "Hardly any sphere of the interpretative process has escaped major restructuring and rethinking since the decade of the sixties."[16]

While these new methods contain valuable insights,[17] the extremist employment of reader-response methodology in particular blunts the two-edged sword of God's Word and allows advocates of all kinds of agendas, including the homosexual, to maintain the appearance of knowing Scripture, while actually ignoring it and the power of God.

Reader-response Bible study is part of the sweeping change in Western intellectual history over the past generation. The old rationalistic method has given rise to a new definition of what constitutes responsible scholarship. Here are some of the ingredients of the new method of Bible study.

THE NEW BIBLE STUDY: ALL METHODS ARE FAIR

Today's Bible sits on the family table, trussed-up like a Christmas turkey, from which everyone carves his choice piece of meat: white for some, dark for others, a wing or leg to suit your fancy. Hendrik Hart, a Christian Reformed theologian, defends homosexual marriage to his conservative denomination. While admitting that no biblical texts favor homosexual behavior, he urges the Church to step out: "Most churches can now make use of legitimate and accepted hermeneutical approaches to the Bible that would enable them to consider that these texts do not directly apply to our modern situation."[18]

With these new liberating methods, Scripture cannot touch us even if it wanted to. Some, not ready to ditch the Bible, content themselves with "radical transformation."[19] "New rules," says a feminist theorist, "will require feminist interpreters to assume that Scripture is *not* 'the word of God'. . . is *not* a container of revelation" and to "correct as we read . . . in the way one might say to a friend, 'I know that is what you said, but I know that's not what you meant.'"[20] Notice how radical this judgment is. Scripture is not even a container of revelation. You cannot find jewels within the rubble. Everything must be reinterpreted by feminist interpreters who know what the Bible really wants to say but is incapable of articulating. The Bible needs lots of help, and lots of help now exists.

Eclecticism—Pick and Choose

Often known as the cut-and-paste method, this has been a classic liberal method of Bible study. What fits liberal theory stays, what doesn't goes. Old-style liberals tried to remain within Scripture as long as they could, but today's reconstructed liberals make no such pretense. Ruether states without embarrassment:

Religious feminists . . . seek to reclaim aspects of the biblical tradition . . . but . . . recognize the need both to go back behind biblical religion and to transcend it. . . . looking backward to options in biblical
and prebiblical faith.[21]

She recommends the use of any text, whether pagan Greek or heretical
Gnostic.[22] The scriptural texts that do not fit, she deletes. Ephesians 6 stays,
for it supports her interpretation of patriarchy as an expression of the evil
principalities and powers against which liberationists must wrestle,[23] whereas
Ephesians 5:21-23 must go. (This text and other "satanic verses," as mentioned in chapter 6, are publicly "exorcised.") Clearly, this is a new way of reading the Bible. It has been called by feminists a hermeneutic of suspicion.

Suspicion

Elizabeth Schlüssler Fiorenza, a leading theorist of feminist interpretation,
proposes a hermeneutic of suspicion capable of unraveling the patriarchal
politics inscribed in the biblical text. Since the Bible is written in androcentric, grammatically masculine language, feminist interpretation must develop a "hermeneutic of critical evaluation for proclamation" that is able to
assess theologically whether scriptural texts function to inculcate patriarchal
values (the reader is left to imagine what she would do with those), or
whether they must be read against their linguistic androcentric grain in
order to set free their liberating vision for today and for the future. Such a
feminist hermeneutics of liberation reconceptualizes the understanding of
Scripture as nourishing bread rather than as unchanging sacred word
engraved in stone.[24]

According to the modern myth of feminism, there exists an oppressive,
pervasive patriarchal conspiracy[25] which demands vigilance, indeed radical
suspicion.[26] Even the most civilizing and noble of all books merits scrutiny.
According to this theory, the men of the Bible were just as scheming and
power-hungry as all the rest and sought to suppress an original goddess worship and the attendant liberation of women that early prebiblical cultures
knew. Rage and anger, empowerment and suspicion are the new "Christian"
values to be turned upon the very source of Christianity, the Holy Scriptures.
Indeed, the Bible is turned upon itself, as the "Exodus myth" is used to exit
from the Bible's authority.

"Exodus" Liberation Interpretation

Such suspicious picking and choosing is motivated by a new understanding of truth and justice, found by the human heart within experience and a personal conviction of what is liberating. By calling this interpretative method "Exodus hermeneutics"[27] an aura of biblical thinking is projected. In fact, one is slowly but surely exiting from the Bible itself. Just as Israel came out of Egyptian bondage, so liberation interpreters believe they are freeing the Bible's essential liberative message from its oppressive patriarchal husk.

Some may not realize how radical this program is. Exodus from patriarchy and suspicion of its oppressive power are proposed by Fewell and Gunn, both mainline Protestant Bible teachers and parents, who love their children enough to ask if they really want them reading such a reactionary book as the Bible.[28] Radical suspicion, convinced that texts are written for social control, asks whose interest the text will serve. For the biblical text, suspicion falls on the ultimate patriarchal Father—God. The biblical God is therefore seen as a construct of the oppressive patriarchy in control when the texts were composed. These radical scholars argue rightly, I believe, that "neither Christianity nor Judaism has yet come to terms with the real challenge of feminist thought." Gender-inclusive translations "only mask the extent of the problem." The real problem, they maintain, is idolatry, worshiping the Bible's "male" construct of God.[29] One can sense the shock that consistent application of the new method produces. "We do not know," they say, "where our own reading takes us. The problems feminist criticism raises for traditional notions of revelation and biblical authority are immense."[30] Their honest reading through the lens of feminist suspicion takes them and their children right out of Christianity into paganism. The void beckons, and imagination is called in to fill the bill.

Imagination

If the Bible is full of androcentric texts, to save it for use in the Church, feminists—male and female—in this theological movement feel compelled to *re-imagine* feminine presence in the Bible, thereby placing women as well as men into the center of early Christian history.

Such a feminist critical method could be likened to the work of a detective insofar as it does not rely solely on historical "facts" nor invents its evidence, but is engaged in an imaginative reconstruction of historical reality.[31]

Fiorenza, who holds the position of professor of New Testament studies and theology at the University of Notre Dame, suggests female authorship for early Christian writings. She does this not because of solid evidence or new facts, but to challenge the androcentric dogmatism that ascribes apostolic authorship only to men. "The issue has become now, not whether or not such suggestions are *true*, but which of the various possibilities is most useful to the feminist case."[32]

Much of this imagining is born within the warming structures of community spirituality as well as the white-hot cauldron of group rage.

Community

Deconstruction leaves the intellectual landscape as barren as a desert after a nuclear explosion. No truth means no significance, and no significant action. If there is no truth, then what is left? There is the individual and his personal truth, but from the point of view of power, the individual is insignificant. Truth must arise from communities.

Stanley Fish explains the importance of communities. "The self does not exist apart from the communal or conventional categories of thought that enable its operations (of thinking, seeing, reading)."[33] But we may wonder how communities survive the skepticism of the deconstructionist worldview. As someone has said: "Those who attack the objectivity of meaning go about their lives assuming that this [meaning] is in fact possible."[34] A glorious example is the statement by Marjorie Suchocki, vice president for academic affairs of the School of Theology at Claremont, in defense of multiculturalism in academia:

> Notions of absolutes and universals have given way to recognition that what we call knowledge is conditioned by its social/cultural location . . . education that implicitly or explicitly promotes the hegemony of one mode of thought and being as if it were universally valid is flawed.[35]

Our arbiter of the intellect denies absolutes, but in so doing makes an absolute statement about the way things should be. Her statement, in making an implicit claim to universality, shows its own hopeless flaws. Living with such absurdity may be easier in communities because they give a semblance of "objectivity," if that is anybody's concern anymore.

There is enormous arbitrariness here. You join a community and accept its story as true and empowering for you, if it fits your life style and sense of justice. The Bible is used, not to establish the Christian community but to give various communities a claim on the Christian faith and family whenever it happens to fit. "A new critical hermeneutics," says feminist Fiorenza, "does not center on the text but on the people whose story with God is remembered in the texts of the Bible."[36]

Such reasoning denies the Bible any objective power. There is no general truth, only subjective truth for me and my community. In this postmodern situation debate and intellectual exchange have become a rarity. If academia does not yet quite resemble the L.A. gang scene, intellectual warfare between communities already typifies American campuses.

Advocacy

If truth is a form of naked power, it is little wonder that our time has discovered a new form of Bible interpretation known as "advocacy exegesis."[37] In particular, communities make better advocates than individuals. Though numbers do not mean that something is true, there is strength in numbers.

Rosemary Ruether states the case for advocacy baldly: "Women's studies do not pretend to an ethical neutrality. This stance is actually a ruling-class ideology. Neutrality hides a commitment to the status quo. All liberation scholarship is advocacy scholarship."[38] Name-calling and disruptive demonstrations characterize even the Church's business. This academic belligerence leaves the old-style liberals breathless. Walter Brueggemann, professor of Old Testament, Columbia Theological Seminary, Decatur, Georgia, recognizes a "new definition of what constitutes responsible scholarship." His article title, "On Writing a Commentary. . . An Emergency," betrays his disarray. He notes that "advocacy exegesis" gives primacy to the situation of the interpreter over what the text once meant. Realizing the excesses of rationalism, Brueggemann feels the pull of spiritual involvement offered in advocacy exegesis, yet he sighs with regret at the loss of objectivity.[39] Brueggemann should not worry. A new constructive vision will rebuild the world.

A New Unity

Behind the wide diversity of readings, and in spite of the rejection of totalizing discourses (especially the Christian one), there is a new, unifying—totalizing!—ideology. It is so diverse it can live within a deconstructed world, but so totalitarian that it leaves room for no one but monists. The "hegemony of one mode of thought and being as if it were universally valid," so feared by modern intellectuals, has not disappeared. It has merely changed form. The original Christian theistic claim to truth is now made by pagan monism. Pagan totalitarianism is coming, if one is to believe Harvey Cox: "We must shape and reconceive our rites and myths in order that they unite and enlarge us [humanity]. . . . We must now take the initiative, not just to predict the future . . . but to shape it." This is the last phrase in his book, appropriately entitled *Many Mansions*.[40] In this new vision of human unity the new Babel becomes heaven on Earth.

Behind the "communities of interpretation," a monistic unity appears that gives direction to exegesis in a deconstructed world that has lost its way. Reader response is to monism what authorial intent is to theism. Let me explain. If truth is to be found within, then the reader holds the keys. If truth is revealed from the God without, then it is the inspired author and his inspired text which hold the keys of the kingdom of heaven. Right now, reader response, like monism in all its forms, is on the cutting edge. Its cutting edge is playing havoc with the text of Scripture. Take a look at what radical reader-response exegesis has done to Genesis 1—3, the foundation pillar of the Christian world and life view—and for that reason was, incidentally, the object of constant reinterpretation by the Gnostics.

Genesis 1—3: A Feminist View of the Garden

Eve was framed. —Mary Daly[41]

The response of the contemporary feminist reader to Genesis 1—3 is one of anger, unbelief and suspicion, a reading against the grain, an imaginative reading that puts woman in the center and drives man and the male biblical God out of the garden. Everything is suspect because:

> The myth of the Father God ensured a world of dominance and dependence . . . Patriarchy, embedded in the creation story of Genesis, *is* the universal religion. What explains the persistence of the myth? What explains its selection? There were other myths available at the time. . . . But the Genesis myth marked the establishment of monotheism and the legitimation of patriarchy as the way of nature—as God's will![42]

How can liberal Christians, committed to radical liberation, continue to use Scripture, which is so committed to an ideology opposed to their agenda? By turning the Genesis account on its head.

Many "Christian" scholars go this far.[43] This "new" reader-response exegesis changes the cast of the original drama. God, Adam, Eve and the serpent mysteriously change places and a new hierarchy emerges—the serpent, Eve, Adam and God. Here is the new interpretation by radical Bible scholars (largely in their own words). Seeing is believing.

God
The procedure is announced.

> The notion that the figure God in the biblical text is actually God . . . [is] a form of idolatry. . . . Unless the character of God is subjected to the same kind of critical scrutiny as all the other characters, we are not really reading the text.[44]

"God as male is part and parcel of this story" and the story is about male oppression that produces "anger and irreverence." Thus, in the Decalogue, God is depicted as "a jealous god who forbids any relationship with any other god . . . [the] perspective [of this metaphor] is the husband's. The deity is the model of the jealous husband."[45]

In Genesis 1—3 God is "a curious figure. . . . [who] has a strong penchant for order . . . and a strong bias for the binary."[46] "This creator God is plainly not . . . omniscient" because he discovers that things are good.[47]

God is the source of evil, because the evil desire for dominance and totalitarian power is first and foremost His. In this, He is not the sophisticated God of the monists.

Where JHWH, the judge of all the earth, might fit on the grid of innocence and evil is no less problematic a question than it is in respect to
Abraham, the family sacrificer. Put another way, theology built on
binary terms is found wanting.[48]

In placing the tree, God is a tempter who tantalizes the first couple: "Trust
me! . . . Stay ignorant—or seek [knowledge] at your own risk."[49] God's control of
the Garden is less than complete. His placing the tree might suggest that God
is "anxious, even insecure" and "jealous of his power. . . .[50] we . . . need . . . to recognize God's vulnerability and culpability. . . . God is not capable of simply fix-
ing up the mess."[51]

This picture of God is reminiscent of a leading feminist's description of
God in Numbers 11–12. Having overcome old religious feelings that caused her
to "overrate the character of Yahweh," in the freedom of the new exegesis, she
can call God "desperate" and "distressed." The people's questioning of His judgment is taken by Yahweh "as personal affront. All he can do is take out his frus-
tration on their bodies, the all-too-common response of a distressed parent."[52]
In the curses following the Fall, Yahweh "does not inspire our gratitude" since
He functions as an "ideological agent" for the creation of the male/female iden-
tities which are the source of oppression.[53] God is duplicitous, for He is immortal and knows good and evil but denies this knowledge to man.[54]

One of the above scholars argues that from a structural analysis, Yahweh
should be seen in the role of the villain who steals the man from the earth to till
His garden.[55] The villain allows one flaw in His plan—the tree that will give man
knowledge. The serpent and the woman succeed in thwarting the villain's plan
by getting the man to eat the fruit, which restores the tiller to the real earth.
God is careless, only remembering the Tree of Life at the last moment as an
afterthought.[56]

The above scholars certainly do not "overrate" the God of the Bible. Clearly,
like the Gnostics, they are in touch with a higher god than the God revealed in
Scripture.

Adam

In the new tradition, Adam gets short shrift. He is a pale reflection of God—
like God, a blame shifter, who, in the fine tradition of Ahab, simply sulks
when he cannot get Naboth's vineyard.[57] The Earth creature, Adam, is the

original "clod."[58] Adam is a profoundly passive character throughout the story.[59] "If the woman be intelligent, sensitive and ingenious, the man is passive, brutish and inept."[60] "The Woman gives him the fruit and he eats it as if he were a baby."[61]

Eve

Elizabeth Cady Stanton, the first modern feminist interpreter of the Bible, stated in 1895: "The reader must be impressed with the courage, the dignity and the lofty ambition of the woman" in whom was aroused "that intense thirst for knowledge."[62] "Eve is unable to know the difference between good and evil. How then can she be blamed for her actions?"[63] She only does what comes naturally. She reaches for sustenance, beauty and wisdom, and in doing so, is blamed forever by the male text and the male commentators.[64] Eve, indeed, was framed! "Though Eve's behavior is condemned by God and berated by centuries of readers, she emerges as a character with initiative and courage. . . . she is a child testing her boundaries, weighing her options, making her choices. She makes her decision independent of those who claim authority over her."[65]

Like God, the woman is an explorer. "She seeks, reasonably, to be in a position to make a choice."[66] "Eve's decision is . . . the first act of human independence."[67] She shares God's image of free will.[68] "Eve does not 'sin'; she chooses reality over her naive paradisiacal existence. Her choice marks the emergence of human character."[69] In this, Eve anticipates Lot's wife (whose looking back is "a choice to be human,"[70]) as well as Jezebel who is seen as "a woman of strength . . . acting independently. . . . As the quintessential foreign woman of power she is for the patriarchal Subject the quintessential Other, to be feared and blamed."[71]

The woman is associated with knowledge. "At the deepest level of the text . . . the human transformation in which the woman took powerful initiative was positive rather than negative [and] that complex human world is to be preferred over any male ideal."[72] What has been called sheer disobedience is, from another perspective, emancipation from blind command.[73] Eve gains wisdom, i.e., "the acceptance of the human condition, including death, and the continuity of history it allows," showing that "Eve is open to reality and ready to adopt it."[74]

The woman and the serpent "heroically oppose Yahweh the villain."[75] The woman "is no easy prey for a seducing demon, as later tradition represents her, but a conscious actor choosing knowledge. Together with the snake, she is a bringer of culture."[76]

Paul's arguments in 1 Timothy 2:11-14 are most obviously wrong—in particular, man and woman were created at the same time, a son and a daughter of the androgynous Earth creature, *Ha Adam*, and in this sense Eve was created first.[77]

The Serpent

The serpent is not evil, but is the other face of God, the tempter, who proposes both good and evil. This profound fact the God of Genesis refuses to recognize.[78] With regard to truth, the serpent and Yahweh share the same position. Both are sly, withholding information. Both in collaboration trick the humans. The serpent seems to be God's helper.[79] He asks intelligent questions, and he could have asked others to embarrass God.[80]

The serpent is the spokesman of the tree of the knowledge of good and evil.[81] "The serpent is an agent of regeneration . . . and assists in the delivery of the human race. He contains also the possibility of imaginative integration, for in the garden his is the voice of hope and ambition."[82] The snake does not lie, and has the "capacity to transform situations and overturn the status quo."[83]

This new-style exegesis has popped up everywhere, in more or less radical forms.[84] Take, for example, the scholarly British publication, the *Journal for the Study of the New Testament*, published at the University of Sheffield and known for its conservative, even "evangelical" leanings. Francis Watson, now professor of New Testament at the University of Aberdeen, who was at the time editor of the *Journal*, published an article in which he found the biblical text (new and old) hopelessly patriarchal and hierarchical. Watson considered quite unconvincing (no doubt correctly) all attempts to save these texts by recovering between the lines a sort of pristine egalitarianism. He left the reader with what he judges the "more appropriate strategy . . . resistance." Such resistance, according to Watson, would take the form of a "counter-reading," reading the text "defiantly 'against the grain.'" In practice, this would involve seeing

The serpent as liberator, Eve as heroine in her courageous quest for wisdom and the Lord God as a jealous tyrant concerned only with the preservation of his own prerogatives. *Such a reading was, of course, adopted within Gnosticism.*[85]

This conscious adoption of ancient Gnostic exegesis, in a respected scholarly journal of classic Christian roots at the end of the twentieth century, may make the most skeptical concede that *the Gnostic empire is striking back.*

This theological reversal is the end result of the singular commitment to gender-liberation ideology. Everything else can be jettisoned—traditional family values, biblical canonical authority, the wisdom and goodness of God the creator and the very definition of the source of evil—and especially the plain sense of the text.

BIBLE STUDY FOR THE END OF CHRISTIAN CIVILIZATION

John Richard Neuhaus, Roman Catholic priest and respected commentator on the state of religion in America, has said:

> The teaching of the Bible in theological schools is in the grip of gnosticism, the belief that it is necessary to appeal away from the plain sense of Scripture to a higher knowledge that lies above or behind the text. The aim of biblical studies is to put the students "in the know" so that they will be privy to an esoteric knowledge that even most intelligent and educated folks cannot get from their reading of the Scriptures in Hebrew, Greek or English.[86]

The new version of Genesis is living proof of this statement, as well as a chilling example of how the new Bible study has quite simply shaken itself free of the Bible.

The "higher knowledge" behind this reversal of Genesis is not another interesting hypothesis to enliven our tired traditionalism. In its destruction of Genesis 1–3, which makes the devil God and God the devil, this "knowledge" is the most radical expression of Christian apostasy. It lays the axe to the roots of Western Christian civilization, which was built upon the Bible. Orthodox believers, especially those tempted by certain aspects of the new agenda, must take stock of the enormity of the revolution. The God of the Bible is now rejected as a symbol of evil oppression in favor of an unknown god whose wisdom the serpent speaks. The new Bible study seems to lead ineluctably not to readers' "innocent" questions but to the seducer's age-old lies.

There is nothing new in that, as ancient Gnosticism shows.

CHAPTER NINE

GNOSTIC BIBLE STUDY

They try to adapt to their own sayings in a manner worthy of credence, either the Lord's parables, or the prophets' sayings, or the apostles' words . . . They disregard the order and the connection of the Scriptures . . . They transfer passages and rearrange them.[1]

IRENAEUS

THE TEXT: ANYTHING YOU WANT IT TO BE

Readers shocked by the manipulation of Genesis described in the previous chapter may take solace in knowing that this "new" version is as old as the hills. Its wild implausibility may have contributed to its 1,500-year disappearance. No betting man would have given odds for its resurrection by intelligent scholars at the end of the twentieth century. But the new reader-response view of Adam and Eve is only a rehash of the heretical interpretation invented by Gnostics in the second and third centuries A.D.[2]

Ancient Textual Arm-Wrestling with Yahweh

According to the Gnostic *Hypostasis of the Archons*, the struggle of the true spiritual Gnostic is not with flesh and blood but with "the authorities, against the
powers of this dark world and against the spiritual forces of evil in the heavenly realms" (Eph. 6:12). All Christians could agree with this citation from the
apostle Paul. Most would be shocked, however, to learn that the chief of these
evil authorities is the God of the Old Testament, the Creator of heaven and
Earth, who in ignorance and arrogance claims, "It is I who am God; there is
none [apart from me]."[3]

These Rulers, or *Archons* (the biblical Lord God and His angelic host), are
from "Below" whereas the Spirit is from "Above," from the "Entirety." They create a man of "soil from the earth" and place him in their Garden, depriving him
of the fruit of "the tree of recognizing good and evil." Unbeknownst to the
Rulers, however, the "Spirit from Above" enters the man. The Rulers cause a
great sleep to fall upon him. This is the sleep of spiritual ignorance, from which
all mankind suffers until illuminated with knowledge. During the sleep, they
open his side, and out comes "the spirit-endowed Woman." She awakens Adam
to spiritual life again, and Adam praises her: "It is you who have given me life;
you will be called 'Mother of the Living'—for it is she who is my mother. It is she
who is the Physician."[4]

The "Female Spiritual Principle," the heavenly Eve, enters the Snake, called
the "Teacher,"[5] and teaches Adam and Eve the true way of salvation. The Snake
is Teacher, "the one who is wiser than all of them."[6] This is a recurring theme in
Gnostic literature.[7] The serpent is the redeemer. The God of Scripture is the evil
usurper. "But of what kind is this God?" asked the exasperated author of the
Testimony of Truth.[8]

> First [he] begrudged Adam that he should eat from the tree of knowl-
> edge. And, second, he asked, "Where are you, Adam?" And God does
> not possess foreknowledge, that is, at the beginning he did not know
> this? And later he said, "Let us banish him from this place lest he eat of
> the tree of life and live for eternity." He has truly shown that he is a
> jealous envier.

Hippolytus reports that Justinus, one of the Gnostic leaders of the second century, identified the tree of the knowledge of good and evil with Naas (the serpent), "'For so,' says (Justinus), 'one ought to interpret the words of Moses [for

Moses said these things disguisedly, from the fact that all do not attain to the truth.'"[9]

On the Origin of the World, another text of the *Nag Hammadi Library*, has a similar inverted interpretation of Genesis. The author of this text claims to reveal what existed "prior to Chaos."[10] This is perhaps a reference to the "chaos" referred to in Genesis 1:2, "Now the earth was formless and empty." As with all Gnostic systems that speculate about the time before creation, this one spins a complicated tale of divine emanations from the ultimate "Father of the All." At one point in this process, Sophia, whom "the Hebrews call . . . Eve of Life, i.e. the teacher of life" gives birth to an androgynous being whom the authorities called "the beast" but who in reality is the "lord" and "the Teacher" for "he was found to be wiser than all of them."[11]

"Then the one who is wiser than all of them, this one who is called 'the beast' came," and revealed the truth about the tree of knowledge, that it was actually good, and that "god" had prohibited them from eating its fruit out of jealousy. When "Eve was certain concerning the word of the teacher . . . their minds opened. For when they ate, the light of knowledge (gnosis) illuminated them." Having gained this gnosis, Adam and Eve despise "god." "When they saw their makers (God the Creator and His angels), they loathed them since they were beastly forms. They understood very much."[12] In a further statement of loathing the text goes on to describe God as impotent since the only thing he can do is curse the teacher (serpent), as well as curse everything they created. Of the Creator God it is said: "There is no blessing for them. Good is not able to come from evil."[13] Here is *total reversal*. Good has become evil, and evil has become good.

GNOSTIC METHOD

How could the Gnostics get away with this kind of exegesis, present everywhere in their writing?[14] In much the same way that modern Bible scholars turn the obvious meaning to their personal and communal agendas. Without the technical apparatus and sophisticated intellectual jargon of their modern cousins, the Gnostics created a similar justification for their reader-response approach to Holy Scripture. The contemporary explosion in the production of interpretative techniques should not surprise us. Whenever "Christian" theology looks to pagan polytheism for inspiration—as it is doing now and as it did then—it discovers a titillating variety of reading techniques, without which the Scriptures of the one, true God would be strictly unusable.

Imagination

The Christian Gnostic revival, like its contemporary counterpart, laid great store on imagination. Like other monists and pantheists, they believed that God is "the unknown God," totally distinct and untouched by creation, yet confounded with every part of it. The Gnostics concluded that there is no direct, special communication from such a God. So where is truth found? They looked to the spark of the divine within. Imagination, part of the divine spark, helps in the discovery of ever-renewing and expanding truth. In Gnostic texts, others who have looked within share their experience of gnosis. Even authoritative Scripture is useful to the extent that it serves the monistic understanding of life.

If truth is fundamentally personal, depending upon individual experiences of inner divine illumination, it follows that experience is to be preferred over rational discourse. It will be imagination freed from reason. So the *Apocryphon of James* 4:19-20 exhorts Gnostic believers: "be filled with the Spirit but be lacking in reason." The *First Apocalypse of James* 27:1-5 states: "until you fling away from yourself blind understanding, this chain of flesh which surrounds you. And then you will attain The One Who Exists. And no longer will you be James, instead you yourself are The One Who Exists." This antirational bent reappears in New age spirituality: "the conditions necessary for new faith, hope and love . . . [are that] you have to be flexible, open, have high energy and be non-linear or intuitive."[15] The very spiritual feminist witch, Mary Daly, excoriates the contemporary use of (male) reason for trying to snuff out intuitive contact with the spirits:

> This removal from the philosophical enterprise of intuitive/imaginative reasoning about angels (which some identify as "Elemental Spirits") is associated with the bore-ocratization of philosophy. It is connected . . . with the "philosophical" discrediting and erasure of "final causality" . . . (viz.,) spirit-force.[16]

The great comeback story of our age is the return of "the spirits." The ancient world was full of them, as Plutarch, a first-century Greek historian notes. He described the Greco-Roman culture of the Mediterranean as "a gob-

let seething with myths."[17] The "Christian" Gnostic teachers were only following the culture. Gnostic expert Giovanni Filoramo speaks of the Gnostic
"mythological revival."[18] With no particular reflection on the present situation,
he notes that after a period of rationalism and the critique of the old Greek
myths—*muthos*—by Plato and Aristotle using *logos* (reason), myth is rediscovered
and given new meaning. Gnosticism is no longer interested in the stories of the
gods per se, but only as they relate to human experience.[19] A new person-
centered spirituality was born. Parallels with the present time are fascinating. As
we come to the end of the twentieth century after the so-called Enlightenment
or Age of Reason, people are rediscovering gods, goddesses, myths and spirituality, sometimes under the guise of a revitalized Christianity.

So it was in the ancient world. The Gnostics claimed a new understanding
of the myths. Gnostic gospels seem to have been written this way. The "living
Jesus" reveals timeless wisdom not tied to any historical moment, thus giving
prophetic insight and imagination free course. Observes Irenaeus: "They adduce
an untold multitude of apocryphal and spurious writings, which they have
composed."[20] "No limits," says a modern commentator, "were set to free representation and theological speculation."[21]

Here are two of many possible examples recorded by the Church father,
Hippolytus:

· Valentinus believed the "Creator [acted] from fear: [and] that is what
  Scripture affirms: 'The fear of the Lord is the beginning of wisdom.'
  For this is the beginning of the affections of Sophia."[22]
· Marcus, using the mystical number system of Pythagorus, finds "each
  of the particulars of Scripture to accord with the aforesaid numbers."
  They thus attempt, says Hippolytus, to "criminate Moses and the
  Prophets, alleging that these speak allegorically of the measures of
  the Aeons."[23]

Eclecticism: Picking and Choosing at Will

What they did not write themselves they "borrowed" from other sources, thereby
picking and choosing at will. Gnosticism, observes Rudolf, "frequently draws its
material from the most varied existing traditions, attaches itself to it, and at the
same time sets it in a new frame . . . the Gnostic view of the world . . . attaches
itself . . . to old religious imagery, almost as a parasite prospers on the soil of host

religions, it can also be described as parasitic. To this extent Gnosticism strictly speaking has no tradition of its own," continues Rudolf, "but only a borrowed one. Its mythology is a tradition consciously created from alien material."[24]

If truth is to be found within, it can be found anywhere, so long as it agrees with the subjective experience of gnosis. "Christianity," says Rudolf, "tended to drive towards doctrinal unity while Gnostic thinkers apparently preferred their independent ways. They seemed to seek and incorporate into their systems any bit of 'truth' or 'knowledge' they found, regardless of the source."[25]

A case in point is the Gnostic treatment of gospel material, especially as expressed in the Gnostic *Gospel of Thomas*, as discussed above. There is no interest in real history. The Gnostic gospels were only vehicles to express their thoughts, picking what might be superficially appropriate and adding it to their system, leaving the rest as so much husk.

Tertullian rejects the Gnostics' constant illegitimate search for truth:

Away with the person who is seeking where he never finds; for he seeks where nothing can be found. Away with him who is always knocking; because it will never be opened to him, for he knocks where there is no one to open. Away with the one who is always asking, because he will never be heard, for he asks of one who does not hear.[26]

Ancient Reader-Response Hermeneutics
Rudolf calls the Gnostic exegetical method a

masterful practice . . . of extracting as much as possible . . . (via) the interpretative method of allegory and symbolism . . . a statement of the text was given a deeper meaning, or even several, in order to claim it for one's own doctrine or to display its inner richness. This method of exegesis is in Gnosis a chief means of producing one's own ideas under the cloak of the older literature—above all the sacred and canonical.[27]

This same scholar, who in his own theology is not entirely opposed to Gnostic thinking, nevertheless speaks of "contortionist tricks" and "protest exegesis."[28]

Regarding their approach to Genesis, Filoramo, the Italian Gnostic scholar, notes that the "Gnostic editors manipulate the sacred text in order to make it suit their purpose . . . by retouching, adding a phrase or choosing a different translation."[29] The Church father, Clement of Alexandria (A.D. 150-215), gives an example of reader-response exegesis. He mentions Epiphanes, son of Carpocrates, who believed in the common sharing of all things including wives and husbands, and who argued that the Mosaic injunction not to desire the goods or wife of one's neighbor "turned what was [originally] communal into private property."[30] Again, Irenaeus is forthright in his denunciation of their method: "They do violence to the good words [of Scripture] in adapting them to their wicked fabrications." He also decries their clever distortion of texts. In "allegories [which] have been spoken and can be made to mean many things, what is ambiguous they cleverly and deceitfully adapt to their fabrication by an unusual explanation." Finally, Irenaeus notes, to suit their own theological questions and answers, "They divide the prophecies into various classes: one portion they hold was spoken by the Mother, another by the offspring, and still another by Demiurge."[31]

Community Interpretation

The Gnostics developed communities rallying around teachers and agendas. Epiphanius (A.D. 315-403) complains: "The leaders of Gnosis falsely so-called have begun their evil growth upon the world, namely the so-called gnostics. . . . For each of these [leaders] has contrived his own sect to suit his own passions and has devised thousands of ways of evil."[32] Each sect had its own angle on the "truth" and produced endless variations. The modern historian, Elaine Pagels,[33] herself a theological liberal, grants that the Gnostics show something of the liberal spirit of modern-day pluralism; i.e., the tolerance for all kinds of religious expression. Long ago Tertullian observed that the tolerance only went so far: "They do not care how differently they treat topics," so long as they . . . approach "the city of the sole truth"; that is, the Gnostic version of the monistic circle. Orthodoxy was nevertheless rejected as toxic error. Their "truth" was "approaches." Pagels notes that this commitment to truth is not the same as that of the Orthodox. "Gnostics tended to regard all doctrines, speculations, and myths—their own as well as others—as only *approaches* to the truth."[34]

For the Gnostics, truth was found only in community: No one can know truth in any absolute sense, but each community must find its own. As in modern multiculturalism, the ancient Gnostics were *absolutely* sure that there was no absolute truth.

With this notion of private or communal truth goes the idea of initiation and secrecy. Revelation is secret, reserved for the initiated. Irenaeus notes the communal consciousness of Gnostic groups, which functioned as secret societies. As always, everyone had his price.

> They [are] unwilling to teach these things to all in public but only to those who are able to pay a large sum for such mysteries! . . . They are abstruse and portentous and profound mysteries, acquired with much toil by lovers of falsehood.[35]

Hermeneutics of Gnostic Suspicion

A number of modern-day experts agree that Gnostic Bible interpretation is an exercise in subterfuge and self-serving reinterpretation. Says one:

> If the starting point of gnostic myth is the exegesis of the Book of Genesis, it is not an innocent exegesis. On the contrary, this exegesis reverses, constantly and systematically, the received and accepted interpretations of the Bible. "Inverse exegesis" may be singled out as the main hermeneutical principle of the gnostics.[36]

In this inverse exegesis, "the content of the Bible is not taken at face value but in the light of previous information that contributes to the escalation of a 'hermeneutic of suspicion.' . . . of which gnostics seem to be the earliest systematic representatives."[37] Though the text is about original innocence, there is no innocence in the interpretations the Gnostics forced upon it.

One path that this inverse exegesis takes is that "anything that the Bible calls good is taken to be evil, and vice versa." In the *Paraphrase of Shem,* the Sodomites are the righteous members of the immovable race of Seth which is why they incur the wrath of the Demiurge.[38] These Sethians naturally claimed that their accounts of creation are the true Bible and that the biblical accounts are false, deceptive distortions.[39]

On the Origin of the World demonstrates how the story of the rib of Adam is a manifest falsehood:

> But we will not speak of this to Adam, for (s)he is not from among us.
> Let us instead put a deep sleep upon him and let us rehearse to him in

his sleep that she came into being from his rib, so that his wife may submit, and he may be master over her.[40]

Similarly, the *Apocryphon of John* exhibits radical suspicion of the Genesis account:

> And he caused sleep to come upon Adam. And I said to the Savior, "What is sleep?" And he said, "It is not as Moses wrote and you heard." Then the Epinoia of light concealed herself in him (Adam) and the leader of the archons desired to bring her out of his rib. But the Epinoia of light is unreachable. While the darkness pursued her, it was unable to catch her, and he brought forth a portion of his power from himself. And he made another creation in the form of a woman, according to the likeness of Epinoia, which was revealed to him. And he put the portion of the power he had taken from the power of the man into the womanly creation, and not, as according to Moses, "his rib."[41]

Four times in this short text the author exhibits his profound suspicion of the biblical account by repeating the refrain "not as Moses said." At the same time his far-fetched interpretation must be right because it fits with his Gnostic theory.

A. F. J. Klijn, the Dutch scholar and authority on Gnosticism, says, "Finally we have to conclude . . . that the Jewish elements [the use of Genesis] were thoroughly reinterpreted or inverted in Gnosticism. . . . [and that] Gnosticism had a thorough disdain for its sources which it only used for its own aims."[42]

Gnostic Exodus from Yahweh

Modern radical scholars at the end of the twentieth century seek to lead readers in an exodus from patriarchy and from the great Patriarch, the God of Scripture. Ancient Gnostic teachers invited believers to leave their slavery/submission to the great Archon, the biblical God, Creator of heaven and Earth. The *First Apocalypse of James* surveys the mighty works of creation and, with a little help from ancient astrology, enumerates 72 heavens. But the author reassures the Gnostic believer that in spite of this massive display of power, the Creator is inferior to the true God, to Him Who Is. Indeed since all Gnostics become "He Who Is," they too are superior to the Maker of the Heavens and the Earth.[43]

Similarly, in the Gnostic text the *Dialogue of the Savior*, Judas says to Jesus: "Behold, the Archons dwell in heaven; surely, then, it is they who will rule over us." But Jesus replies: "You will rule over them."[44]

So the whole system of creation, impressive though it is, comes tumbling down in the Gnostic megainterpretation of reality and of Scripture. Modern Bible interpreters argue that the worship of the God of the Bible is idolatry since Yahweh is but an intellectual construct of male oppression, and the true God is beyond all human words. Gnostics saw the God of Scripture as a usurper to be spurned and the true God as the unknown God who was only known in the divine spark within the human soul. The former "god" belongs to the realm of darkness which is also creation, matter, the body, the planets, and fate—a prison from which there is no escape. The latter, true God, the "unknown God" beyond all that is visible or sensible, who incorporates a "fullness" (pleroma) of heavenly beings, inhabits the realm of light. Ancient Gnostic Bible teachers were willing to "deconstruct" the Bible's fundamental teaching about God in order to beat a path of freedom to the unknown God beyond the Bible. Theirs certainly was liberation exegesis, but the exodus from the God of Scripture led not to the promised land but to diabolical slavery.

Ultimate Unity: Pagan Monism

Behind the great diversity of ancient Gnosticism lay a coherent ideology, profoundly opposed to Christian theism, but able to embrace most other religious options. Since the true God was unknown, except through the human heart, all interpretative paths that passed through the experience of "spiritual knowledge" led to God. Though it is common to describe Gnosticism as dualistic, rejecting the flesh and embracing the spirit, recognized expert, Kurt Rudolf, describes the movement as a "dualism on a monistic background."[45] Monism, old and new, welcomes all paths that lead to the "ultimate mystery"—all except one, the plain sense of Scripture and the God of the Bible.

CONCLUSION

In the second century, Irenaeus, who devoted his life to reading, evaluating and finally denouncing Gnostic teaching as heretical, saw that an essential element of their pernicious teaching, which aided in the seduction of ordinary

Christians, involved their twisting of Scripture to suit their own ends. He called their Bible study method a "misuse of Scripture" producing "distort[ed] exegesis." The procedure was, for him, patently obvious: "After having entirely fabricated their own system, they gather together sayings and names from scattered places and transfer them, as we have already said, from their natural meaning to an unnatural one."[46]

In Bible interpretation too, history repeats itself. From sexuality and morals to Bible study methods, the "unnatural" once again claims to be "natural." A fabricated system of liberation, backed by new myths and "self-evident" truths, has descended on the biblical text, skewing its obvious and natural sense.

The parchments of Gnosticism lie unrolled before us on our strategy tables. These plans have been used before, and the Church fathers have shown us effective defense tactics. Their vigilance against heresy both warns and arms us in our own defense of the faith. Christians today will remain ignorant of the past to their own and their children's peril. Church history teaches us what the Scriptures have declared: defense includes offense. If we do not denounce and reject Gnostic Bible study techniques, the Church's foundations will crumble.

CHAPTER TEN

A NEW GOD
FOR A
NEW WORLD
ORDER

*[God is] not transcendence—that orgy of self-alienation beloved of the
fathers—but immanence, god working out god's self in everything.*

RITA NAKASHIMA BROCK
JEWISH FEMINIST, 1979

GOD VERSUS GODDESS

Not even a four-letter word, "God" is still the most dynamite of notions. It
stands for ultimate power and supreme truth. The stakes of the present
debate concerning the nature and person of God could not be higher.[1] Whoever
defines God determines the human society of tomorrow. Far from being secular and humanistic, the future will be, according to many expert observers,

"hyperreligious."[2] The new world order is not satisfied with international trade agreements, arms reduction and innovative planetary politics. Such an order must develop a global ethic, a syncretistic religion with a new god on the throne. Every civilization has had its god. The utopian Age of Aquarius will crown an Aquarian god. "The emergence of a new cultural paradigm,"[3] calls for a new worldview.[4] The popular Christian writer, Madeleine L'Engle, judges that the new worldview needs a new god "who's big enough for the atomic age," since the God of Christ's time "has deteriorated."[5]

Carol Christ, a leading feminist theologian, declares:

> We are living in a revolutionary time when new religious symbols are being formed by a process of syncretism and creativity. . . . the work that feminists are doing to transform the image of God has profound . . . consequences for social life.[6]

This deep work has made great progress. In 1995, Roman Catholic theologian Richard Grigg announced what he considers to be the only hope for maintaining our thinking about God in the third millennium. The title of his book says it all: *When God Becomes Goddess: The Transformation of American Religion.*[7] So if you are really looking for a new god with transformative power,[8] you certainly need to meet Sophia.

SOPHIA: THE DIVINE HOMECOMING FOR THE QUEEN OF MINNEAPOLIS

Sophia is the new god for the new world, the new myth for the Age of Aquarius. In a strange and disorienting twist in feminine seductive power, it is "Sophia, . . . the Logos . . . Christ Herself," according to "evangelical" Virginia Mollenkott, who will make all things new and all things possible. She will give birth to the "New Humanity."[9] Without her, the planet will implode and the glorious human story will never make its final rendezvous of destiny with evolution. Sister Madonna Kolbenschlag, the influential ex-nun and militant feminist in the Roman Catholic church, sees in the goddess movement a "stage, necessary for some, in an evolutionary process that is moving humanity—and the 'God-who-is-coming-to-be'—toward transformation in a 'New Faith.'"[10]

Many met Sophia for the first time in Minneapolis when she was the guest of honor at the RE-Imagining Conference organized by mainline Protestant Christian feminists. In the first session participants repeated the litany: "It is time to . . . dream wildly . . . about who we intend to be in the future through the power and guidance of the spirit of wisdom whom we name Sophia." Like a theme chorus at a Youth for Christ rally, the following line was constantly repeated: "Now Sophia, dream the vision, share the wisdom dwelling deep within."[11] Program literature declared: "Sophia's voice has been silenced too long. Let her speak and bless us throughout these days." Though organizers claimed Sophia to be the personified Wisdom (*sophia* in Greek) of Proverbs 8, her teaching in Minneapolis was at best the teaching of Dame Folly, and at worst the rank paganism associated with ancient goddess worship.[12] Various definitions of Sophia sprouted: "Sophia is the divine energy in women being unlocked by the goddess rituals." "Sophia is the wisdom within me." The program definition said it all: "Sophia is the place in you where the entire universe resides."[13]

Conference speakers filled in the blanks. Aruna Gnanadason, an Indian feminist from the Church of South India, and a director of the WCC subunit on Women in the Church and Society in Geneva, explained that her red dot was a protest against those who saw the forehead as a place for the sign of the cross. For her, it was the sign of "the divine in each other." Naturally, all the participants drew a red dot on their foreheads.[14] Rita Nakashima Brock, associate professor at Hamline University in St. Paul, Minnesota, declared, in terms reminiscent of ancient heretical Gnosticism:

> Although . . . he (Jahweh) refers to himself in the plural form . . . [he] remind[s] us inadvertently, of *the goddess and the earth from which he came*.[15]

Elizabeth Bettenhausen, coordinator of the Study/Action Program at the Women's Theological Center in Boston, Massachusetts, and a member of the Evangelical Lutheran church in America, declared: "We have to [re]imagine the doctrine of creation." Rejecting the biblical view of the creation of the earth, she made the astonishing statement: "Women, not God, are the true creators."[16]

This Sophia is the very antithesis of Wisdom in the Bible, for it denies the very legitimacy of God's creative handiwork. On the contrary, Proverbs shows Wisdom "at his side" as God made the heavens and the earth. As the New Testament reveals, the Wisdom at God's side was Christ, the eternal Son and

Wisdom of God, by whom and through whom all things were created.[17] Use of this text is a pretext to import alien notions into the Christian Church and make a mockery of God the Creator. There is no relationship between personified Wisdom in Holy Scripture and the debutante divinity of Minneapolis. Who is Sophia? Why was the massive head of a beast without name paraded four times a day through the conference hall?

The real agenda of the conference answers this question: "Be speculative, there is no 'answer.' We can't imagine what God is like. Being together in our own images is the ultimate." One astute observer noted that imprecision was part of the program:

> Sophia is the answer to the prayers of a multi-cultural, therapeutic world. . . . [She] serves "reformers" of this ilk as an invaluable *tabula rasa*. Their adherents' ignorance of Sophia—far from being an obstacle—is essential to the project of fashioning a new religion while retaining tenuous and self-interested links to the Christian faith.[18]

The link is tenuous indeed. But Christian believers need to meet and recognize Sophia, the god of the brave new Aquarian world our children will inherit.

SOPHIA: GODDESS OF ANCIENT PAGANISM

One of the brilliant theoreticians of the "re-imagining" feminist movement, Rosemary Radford Ruether, stated already in 1983: "A new God is being born in our hearts."[19] This is a strange place for a god to get started, but Ruether seems to know her subject. Such an unusual birth is occurring because of a new power, "our power to name ourselves . . . and God."[20] Her *Women-Church* serves as a model for many of the movers and shakers in Sophia's retinue. This "church's" creed makes no mention of the God of Scripture or of Christ.[21] Ruether sees spiritual awakening as "a new rapprochement" between Christianity and paganism.[22] In a *Rite of Healing from Rape*, the worshipers in *Women-Church* use their power to name the new pagano-Christian deity: "The Mother-Spirit of Original Blessing surrounds you, upholds you on all sides, flows round about you, caresses you, loves you, and wills you to be whole."[23]

SOPHIA: PAGAN DARLING

Caitlín Matthews is an ordained priestess in the ancient Egyptian cult for the worship of the Goddess, Isis, Queen of the Witches. You cannot get much more pagan than that. In 1992 she published a book in praise of her goddess entitled *Sophia, Goddess of Wisdom*.[24] This neo-pagan notes that "Sophia appears in nearly every culture and society," and that "the connections between Isis and Sophia are very significant and show us Sophia's strongest links to the ancient Goddess tradition."[25] In other words, there is much to connect Sophia with Isis, the Egyptian Goddess of magic and witchcraft. Isis, "the Goddess of a Thousand Names in the Completeness of Her Majesty,"[26] has one name in particular— Sophia.

Conference participants in Minneapolis invoked the following blessing over the elements of milk and honey in their blasphemous simulacre of the Lord's Supper: "Our maker, Sophia, we are women in your spirit."[27] Sophia is not an abstract feminist principle. As Creator, she has the attributes of deity. The "innocent" Sophia theme, developed by imaginative and creative "Christian" women in Minneapolis, is pagan goddess religion, as many gladly admit.

SOPHIA: ALL-AMERICAN GIRL

Goddess spirituality in America at the end of the twentieth century? Thirty years ago, the very idea would have been preposterous. Today it is a powerful reality in the lives of many feminist movers and shakers. The new edition of *The Politics of Women's Spirituality* shows how power and goddess spirituality have come together in our day. [28] Forty-five feminist thinkers, including Charlene Spretnak, Gloria Steinem, Mary Daly and Naomi Goldenberg make an impassioned plea for the rediscovery of women's spirituality through the goddess. Some of the articles deserve particular note, especially the following: "The Great Goddess: Who Was She?" "The Origins of Music: Women's Goddess Worship," "Witchcraft as Goddess Religion," "Why Women Need the Goddess: Phenomenological, Psychological, and Political Reflections." These and many others are written by extremely intelligent Western women at the end of our very sophisticated twentieth century. We are acquainted with Christian spirituality and with the nonspirituality of Western intellectuals toying with atheistic humanism and Marxist philosophy. These contemporary thinkers espouse spirituality, but a spirituality that jumps the millennia to find sustenance in the long-lost traditions of pagan goddess worship. Such thinking is no longer the speculation of a lunatic fringe. Many of the women mentioned are leaders in contemporary society and in mainline churches. Moreover, the presence of the word "politics" indicates a movement not content with secret societies and private fantasies. We are already seeing the first signs of this renewed paganism in legislation, gender issues, the media and in education. The *spiritual* power of the goddess threatens to take *political* power as we enter the Age of Aquarius.

The spirit entity, Lazaris, speaking through an ex-insurance salesman from California, confirms the place of the goddess in modern America:

> Though She never left, the Goddess is returning to you . . . and She brings a Light. . . . Yours is the Great Work: Receiving and then bringing Her Light into a seemingly darkening world. She is returning to you and She brings gifts and treasures that are bountiful and without limit. . . . As She returns, you can come to know the Goddess and you can know God. And . . . you can come to know who you are.[29]

The introduction of Sophia into "Christian" worship is actually, as a recent book title suggests, the "restoring [of] the Goddess to Judaism and Christianity."[30] The goddess being restored is that divinity found "at the intersection of Christianity and paganism," the Gnostic female divinity Sophia, revealed in one Gnostic text as "Thunder Perfect Mind."

> Thunder Perfect Mind . . . appears to be everywhere and encompasses everything: . . . She is everything and everybody and its opposite. She is female and within her there is the whole range of female life from birth to death, from the mundane woman in the world to the divine Wisdom of Heaven. She shows for me that there is no disunity between something and its opposite. A totality includes all aspects. Linear and dualistic divisions do not exist. . . . Asherah and Ashteroth were called whore, abomination and death, by those who hated them. Hochma [Hebrew for Sophia], their sister and descendant, was called the tree of life (Proverbs) before she was divested of her female form. I see in the "Thunder" the vision of a goddess human and divine who speaks again. Her words are taken over by the newer male-oriented religions.

"I am the first and the last" is a description of God and of Christ (Rev. 21:6; 22:13); it not only recalls "Thunder" but also Egyptian Isis.[31]

Here Sophia is clearly identified with the form of pagan monism that joins all opposites in the pagan Mother goddess of Egypt, Isis, patron goddess of the witches. "Today women are rediscovering Isis," says radical feminist Alexander-Berghorn. She goes on:

> The re-awakening of Isis as a source of inspiration for contemporary women is exemplified by the healing ministry of Selena Fox, co-founder and High Priestess of Circle Sanctuary near Madison, Wisconsin. Every month at New Moon, Selena holds a spiritual Healing Circle centered around an Isis Healing Altar . . . each of us can personally experience the healing presence of the Goddess within us. All women are Isis and Isis is all women.[32]

SOPHIA: QUEEN OF THE WITCHES

Witchcraft is the wave of the future. In the rethinking of witchcraft "the feminist religion of the future is presently being formed."[33] This programmatic statement comes from Miriam Starhawk, a leading theorist of goddess worship and witchcraft and wiccan priestess/licensed minister of the Covenant of the Goddess. Raised a Jew, she finds in witchcraft a perfect foil to the "divisive absolutism" of the Judeo-Christian heritage and an excellent bridge to the notion of balanced polarities in many Eastern religions. This *yin* and *yang* balance undermines the idea that something could be "wrong." Everything is useful.

Starhawk brings together in witchcraft all the concerns of the New Age movement—a new world religion for a new world order, ecology and science based on goddess/Mother Nature spirituality, consciousness transformation through "magical" techniques—and adds a zest of feminist eschatology—ultimate salvation through the woman.

"Out of the Broom Closet"

The above title appeared on the front page spread of my local paper. The favorable article about the return of witchcraft supports the attempt to find a "church" building where "parents can bring their children to learn about [Wicca's] ancient heritage."[34] Homosexuals are not the only ones coming out of the closet. Our multicultural time tolerates almost anything. Witches were granted official status at the Parliament of the World's Religions; academics are rewriting their history, especially the history of the famous witch hunts as "ethnic cleansing . . . of independent women in Reformation Europe";[35] Virginia Mollenkott includes witchcraft as a valid expression of today's quest for authentic spirituality;[36] a leading Catholic feminist, Sister Madonna Kolbenschlag in her book, *Kiss Sleeping Beauty Goodbye*, approves of witchcraft;[37] as does Madeleine L'Engle;[38] "Christian" feminist theologian Rosemary Radford Ruether promotes rituals in her *Women-Church* such as a Halloween ceremony in remembrance of the persecution of witches.[39]

Christianity with its distinction between God and the creation, right and wrong, man and woman, is joyfully abandoned as the essence of an outmoded worldview that produced "inquisitions, witch-hunts, pogroms, executions, censorship and concentration camps." In the brave new world of this apocalyptic vision, "the Goddess is ourselves *and* the world." All distinctions are eliminated and everything goes as "our culture as a whole . . . evolve(s) toward life."[40]

> Mother Goddess is reawakening and we can begin to recover our primal birthright, the sheer intoxicating joy of being alive. We can open our eyes and see that there is nothing to be saved from . . . no God outside the world to be feared and obeyed.[41]

Anticipating what transpired in Minneapolis in 1993, Starhawk said in 1979: "Today women are creating new myths, singing a new liturgy, painting our own icons, and drawing strength from the new-old symbols of the Goddess, of the 'legitimacy and beneficence of female power.'"[42] Just before the RE-Imagining Conference, Christian theologian Mary Elizabeth Moore of the Claremont School of Theology and Claremont Graduate School stated that many women found Starhawk's work "compatible with, or at least, adaptable to, Christian teaching."[43]

Through feminism and the religion of the goddess, witchcraft is "adapted" to Christianity. We can no longer dismiss witchcraft as the lunatic radical fringe of far-out feminism.[44] Even if it denies connection with Satanism,[45] witchcraft is at the very least a virulent form of occult, monistic paganism, standing at the opposite pole from Christian theism.

What is a Witch?

Zsuzsanna E. Budapest, a "feminist" witch whose mother was a medium and practicing witch in Budapest, Hungary, provides a very simple and clear description of a witch: "A witch is a woman or a man who considers the earth a living, breathing, conscious being—part of the family of the vast universe—to be regarded and respected as God herself. To be a witch you have to see yourself as part of God, who is present in, not separate from us and all living beings."[46] It would certainly appear that there is very little to distinguish between modern-day witches and other spiritually attuned New Age people such as shamans, mediums and channelers. At the very least, they all claim to plug into the spiritual power of the earth, and turn away from the biblical God, distinct from the earth He created. Roman Catholic journalist Donna Steichen documents, with chilling accuracy, how witchcraft has masterminded a progressive takeover of a substantial portion of the Catholic church in the United States. She shows how witchcraft has swept through the convents of America and decimated many orders. Her studied judgment is disturbing: "Most of the old Catholic culture has been devoured by spiritual termites, leaving behind a structure that looks solid to the eye but crumbles at a touch."[47]

Isis, the "great prototype of all goddesses,"[48] called "the Mighty in Magic," the queen of the witches, was one of the chief antagonists of Christianity during the first three centuries of the Christian era. As we shall later show (see chapter 11), Isis already appeared as Sophia in the heretical Christianity of ancient Gnosticism. Modern Christianity, if it is to be true to its forebears in the faith, will have to resist this same occult, nature magic of witchcraft that centers on the Goddess.

SOPHIA: QUICK CHANGE ARTIST

Have you ever met a polytheist—someone who believes in the existence of many (*poly*) gods (*theoi*)? You probably think of exotic places like Polynesia where everyone wears grass skirts and not much else and people dance to the haunting beat of native tom-toms. But David Miller, a bespectacled "suit," the epitome of middle-class urbane America, the Watson-Ledden professor of religion at Syracuse University and once a candidate for the presidency of the American Academy of Religion, is a polytheist.

SOPHIA: BORN FROM THE ASHES OF GOD

Using the titles Goddess and God the Mother is probably the only way
to shatter the hold of [the] idolatrous male God on the psyche.
—Nelle Morton[49]

Before becoming a polytheist, Miller was part of the death-of-God movement of
the '60s. Radical theologians led by William Hamilton and Thomas Altizer
declared God dead. Come of age, man no longer needed an external divinity.
When the movement fizzled, Altizer ended up teaching American literature to
undergraduates at a state university. One more outrageous radical thesis, no
more clever than a newspaper headline, had passed away. Or so it seemed.

Princess Elizabeth of England flew home from Australia hastily when her
father, George VI, passed away in 1952. As she stepped onto the tarmac in
London, an official greeted her with the phrase I heard then as a young boy:
"The king is dead; long live the queen." Just a decade after George VI went to
meet his maker, William Hamilton might have said: "God is dead, long live the
Goddess." He actually said: "The revolution does not look like monotheism,
Christian or post-Christian. What it looks like is polytheism."[50] Hamilton's
analysis has proved accurate, in spite of Nixon, Reagan, Bush and the powerful
Religious Right of the '80s.

In 1974, David Miller recognized

The announcement of the death of God was the obituary of a useless
single-minded and one-dimensional norm of a civilization that has
been predominantly monotheistic, not only in its religion, but also in
its politics, its history, its social order, its ethics, and its psychology.
When released from the tyrannical imperialism of monotheism by the
death of God, man has the opportunity of discovering new dimensions
hidden in the depths of reality's history.[51]

At the funeral of the God of the Bible, Miller announced "the rebirth of the
Gods and Goddesses." Such an experience, the experience of paganism, he
found to be "liberating." He found freedom in the "multiple patterns of polytheism [which] allow room to move meaningfully through a pluralistic universe. They free one to affirm the radical plurality of the self, an affirmation

that one has seldom been able to manage because of the guilt surrounding monotheism's insidious implication that we have to "get it all together."[52]

As he solemnly proclaimed the death of God, Miller proudly declared: "The Gods and Goddesses of Greece are our heritage. Sooner or later it is they who will reappear."[53] Polytheistic paganism does not hinder one's career, especially when it includes a feminist angle. David Miller for many years wielded considerable influence both in the American Academy of Religion and, ironically, as a member of the publications board of the Society of Biblical Literature.

The goddesses have returned. Secular feminism has developed a psychology of women based on Greek goddess archetypes. Our local community college offers an evening course for 8- to 13-year-old girls designed to help them develop identity through the study of six Greek goddesses. Radical "Christian" feminists are not far behind. Their rediscovery of Sophia dates from the death-of-God movement in the '60s. But is it legitimate to associate Sophia with polytheism?

Sophia: Legion

Sophia is the gateway to polytheism for those still imprisoned by biblical monotheism. At the RE-Imagining Conference, Chung Hyun Kyung, assistant professor in theology, Ewha Women's University, Seoul, Korea, spoke of three goddesses—Kali (Hindu), Quani (Buddhist) and Enna (animist) whom she integrates with Christianity to produce a "change of perspective" and the "fusion of different horizons."[54] Virginia Mollenkott agreed.[55] So the fusion of goddesses leads to the fusion of religions, which is to be expected since all pagan religions begin with man, not God. The acceptance of polytheism throws the net wide.

Lois M. Wilson, chancellor at Lakehead University, Thunder Bay, Canada is also an ordained minister in the United Church of Canada and a past president of the World Council of Churches and of the Canadian Council of Churches. Of the passage in the Acts of the Apostles, "I shall pour out my spirit on all humanity," she said, "Did he mean neo pagans, did she mean the wiccans, the Sikhs, the Muslims, the Hindus, the men and the women?"[56] One ritual at the RE-Imagining Conference included a liturgical song, listing names for God, from different religious traditions:

Divine ancestor, Mother God, Father God, Elohim, Adonai, Spirit, Ruach, mystery, lover, eternal goodness, alpha and omega, fire of love, living presence, she who is eternal, she who will be, Sophia, Earth Mother, spirit woman, she who is, ninjan, cosmic maxim, weaver God, transforming laughter, womb of creation, higher power, yin and yang, unknown God, unnameable God, holy one of blessing.[57]

The witches and goddess worshipers echo these names. Starhawk speaks of "the Goddess [who] has infinite aspects and thousands of names."[58] Witches Sjoo and Mor describe "the Great goddess of All Living [who] gave birth to her-self and the entire cosmos—she is the world egg, containing the yin and the yang . . . [she is] Kali [the Hindu goddess of life and death] dancing the universe into being and then to destruction and death."[59] David Miller prophesied it: "A polytheistic theology will be a feminine theology, but in the manner of all the Goddesses—the thousands of daughters of Oceanus and Tethys, to name only a few. By being many, these Goddesses avoid a monotheistically chauvinistic view of the feminine."[60]

Today there exists in many churches a modified polytheism, first suggested by one of the great feminist foremothers, Elizabeth Cady Stanton, mastermind behind *The Women's Bible* of 1895. Cady Stanton saw in the plural of Genesis 1, not a hint of the Christian Trinity, but rather a trinity of Heavenly Father, Mother and Son.[61] She continues: "The first step in the elevation of women . . . is the cultivation . . . by the rising generation . . . of an ideal Heavenly Mother, to whom their prayers should be addressed." Such an understanding of God, she claimed (rightly), is "witnessed to in the holy books of all religions."[62] Today that vision is taken up by "Christian" feminists such as Virginia Mollenkott. "We had better learn," says Mollenkott, to "bring *many* names" by which to address this God who is our strong Mother as well as our tender Father, a "young, growing God" as well as an "old, aching God," a "great, living God" who is "never fully known" even though She is "closer yet than breathing."[63]

This solution seems less drastic than the eradication of God the Father and the adoption of goddess polytheism. It seeks to "balance" our idea of God by such liturgical formulae as "in the name of the Father and the Mother, the Son and the Spirit." But enormous difficulties soon arise. Such formulations force Christians to one of two solutions:

- enlarge the Trinity by the addition of the Mother Goddess. But to remain a Christian we cannot enlarge the Trinity. The apparently innocuous search for many names leads to the inclusion of names of pagan gods and to the elimination of the names (Father, Lord, King) by which the one true God has revealed himself;

- produce a Trinitarian God, one of whose persons becomes an androgynous "parent," "God the Mother/Father,"[64] a being who bears no resemblance to anything we know in created reality. By such a notion the personhood of God is subtly dissolved into nonpersonal symbols, which finally leads to the impersonal All of Eastern monism. This is clear in Cady Stanton. Her deep understanding of God is "our ideal first cause, the 'Spirit of all Good,'" witnessed to in "the holy books of all religions."[65]

SOPHIA: FEMININE SYMBOL OF THE MONISTIC ALL

The RE-Imaging Conference gave Sophia the opportunity to endorse monism. Said Mollenkott, a leading speaker at the conference:

> Everything that lives is holy . . . the one divine presence . . . in everybody. . . . The monism I'm talking about assumes that god is so all-inclusive that she is involved in every cell of those who are thoughts in her mind. . . . Like Jesus, we and the source are one.[66]

To think of God in the specific sense of Scripture as the transcendent God who may never be identified with the substance of the creation He has made is now dismissed as the "mythical-literal" faith of "elementary school."[67] "Christian" believers must move to the "Universalizing stage" of oneness with the divine,[68] and understand the world as "God's body."[69]

These notions about God bring together odd bedfellows. The Theosophical Society of the late nineteenth century, a precursor of the New Age movement, was a minuscule elitist minority dedicated to eradicating Christianity and to promoting both the occult and a Western form of Hindu mysticism. The society's vision has made enormous strides. In 1994, Theosophy was adopted as a recognized section of the annual meeting of the American Academy of Religion. The Theosophical Society pronounced valid the contemporary mystical notions of unification and convergence as well as any other ideas about God found in all the world's religions—all but one, biblical/Christian monotheism. As the Society's brochure states:

> Esoteric Philosophy [read proto-New Age thinking] reconciles all nations, strips every one of its outward human garments, and shows the root of each to be identical with that of every other great religion. It proves the necessity of a Divine Absolute Principle in Nature. It denies Deity no more than it does the sun. Esoteric Philosophy has never rejected God in Nature, nor Deity as the absolute and abstract *End*. It only refuses to accept any of the gods of the so-called monotheistic religions, gods created by man in his own image and likeness, a blasphemous and sorry caricature of the Ever Unknowable.[70]

The "Divine Absolute Principle" of monism is finally so diffuse, and ultimately so indefinable, that "god" loses all specific identity. The highest title monism can give to this god is that of "the Deity, *who is beyond all our knowing.*"[71] That contemporary "Christian" thinkers adopt such a "God," proves how successful is the project to eliminate the revealed monotheistic God of Scripture.[72]

Toward the end of the heyday of the cultural revolution of the '60s, cultural analyst Os Guinness predicted the probability that Hinduism would seek, by a "fraternal embrace" especially directed to mainline liberalism, to "strangle" Christianity. Guinness argued that Eastern tolerance, which has been widely adopted as an unquestioned "democratic" value in our day, is actually the kiss of death. Hinduism embraced Buddhism by declaring that Buddha was a further revelation of Krishna. Some Hindu gurus have similarly spoken of the "Blessed Lord Jesus Christ" as an expression of Hinduism. Guinness predicted: "Probably the same approach will be made openly to Christian theology in the next few years. Liberalism is already showing signs of response before the overtures are made."[73] Guinness was right.

SOPHIA: EVERY WOMAN

"Hey, we are God." Such is one writer's estimation of the result of Shirley MacLaine's TV miniseries "Out on a Limb."[74] Her book states the message clearly.

God lies within, and therefore we are each part of God. Since there is
no separateness, we are each Godlike, and God is in each of us. . . . We
are literally made up of God energy, therefore we can create whatever
we want in life because we are each co-creating with the energy of
God—the energy that makes the universe itself.[75]

Recently MacLaine claimed that the mainstream had gone New Age. How right
she is. Says Virginia Mollenkott: "When Shirley MacLaine teaches people to
chant 'I am God,' she is correct."[76]

There is one final surprise. The RE-Imagining Conference has already
taught us that God is unknowable, and that Humanity is God: "We can't imagine what God is like. *Being together in our own images is the ultimate.*"[77] The perverse
sexuality at the conference underlines the nature of its theology. According to
the apostle Paul, when mankind worships the creature rather than the Creator
and exchanges the truth of God for an (imaginative) lie God gives them over to
sexual impurity.[78]

But the ultimate blasphemy might surprise even some at the conference.
The end point of the reduction of God, as ancient Gnosticism eloquently
shows, is not the identification of God as an impersonal, unknowable force nor
even the elevation of man as God. The ultimate blasphemy is to make Satan
God. For behind the force and divinized humanity is the ultimate personal
source of evil, the devil.

Sophia: Satan

Is this life imitating art or art imitating life? Radical religious feminist theater
interprets in vivid green the true nature of Sophia. In this view, the serpent was
actually Lilith, a female spirit, who, according to the stage directions of this
feminist drama "in green body make-up or leotard, slithers into view round a
tree." With "serpentine" movements "she slithers round the tree again, and
reappears immediately with a red apple in her hand, which she offers to Eve,"
and utters the classic words: "Well, Eve?"[79]

The Jewish feminist, Alix Pirani, whose book attempts to restore the
Goddess to Judaism and Christianity, explains who Lilith is. Though the name
appears but once in the Bible and means "night creature,"[80] modern religious
feminists, following a few speculations by medieval rabbis,[81] have resurrected

the myth. Pirani herself claims that Lilith appears to her in her study,[82] and that she is a manifestation of the goddess.[83] In particular, modern feminism identifies Lilith with the serpent of Genesis.[84]

> Lilith appeared to her [Eve] in the shape of a serpent in the garden of Eden and tempted her to defy God by biting into the apple of the tree of knowledge of good and evil . . . . Saturn is also Satan and the fallen angel Lucifer, who descends to earth in the guise of the immortal lightning serpent Sata. When God denied Adam and Eve the fruit of the tree of knowledge in order to keep them ignorant, it was Lucifer, in the form of the serpent Lilith, who offered them the "light" of consciousness.[85]

Pirani does not miss the relationship with Gnosticism, which she approves.[86] So this "ancient Goddess who appeared in the form of the serpent is now insistently demanding the restoration of her rightful position—that of the Great Mother Goddess who is bestower of life as well as being a powerful Queen of the Otherworld. Otherwise we shall continue to suffer the consequences: the curse of Lilith."[87] Needless to say, the curse of Lilith is the Christian faith.

Who is Sophia? Sophia is Lilith, the feminine expression of Satan. The head of the beast paraded in Minneapolis did have a name. Its name was Sophia.

SOPHIA: FUTURE OF THE PLANET

The many faces of Sophia represent the continuum of pagan thinking within the present society and much of the Christian Church. Not everyone espouses the whole philosophy. Some may not see the ramifications. But Sophia's ratings are improving. She is an attractive alternative to the God of Scripture, for she fits the aspirations of the Age of Aquarius. She is the new star in the pantheon of the gods, the divine Tinkerbell upon whom the hopes and wishes of the modern world ride. In her person she expresses the "manifold wisdom" of the pagan agenda:

> The new spiritual evolution.[88]
> The new popularity of Process Theology and the God who is coming-to-be.[89]

The rejection of patriarchy in all its forms.[90]
The new view of pro-choice democracy.[91]
The new global vision of religious unity.[92]
The new deep ecology, focused on divine Mother Earth.[93]
The new psychology of the self without limits.[94]
The new pro-choice ethics.[95]
The new understanding of Jesus as Sophia's prophet.[96]

These are just some of the reasons why the future of the "new" god on the block looks bright. Can anything stop the thunderous return of Sophia?

CHAPTER ELEVEN

THE GOD OF ANCIENT GNOSTICISM

I am the prostitute and the venerable one.
I am the wife and the virgin . . .
I am the one whose likeness is great in Egypt.

THUNDER, PERFECT MIND

M inneapolis 1993 was not the first sighting of Sophia in Christian circles. She made an early appearance in the heretical Gnostic writings of the early centuries of the Church's history. Mainline women in Minneapolis imagined they were creating new images of the divine *ex nihilo* (out of nothing). But Gnostic musings of 1,500 years ago give their vain imaginations, in the unforgettable phrase of Yogi Berra, a surprising aura of *"déjà vu* all over again!"

Sophia appeared among the Gnostics as a fresh young goddess with fascinating new ideas that got her in trouble but brought redemption.[1] For those tired of the male God of the Bible, she promised liberation and radical freedom.

Her wisdom surpassed the biblical wisdom of Proverbs, for under her mysterious and alluring mantle lay hidden both the pearls of Lady Wisdom and the dark secrets of Dame Folly. This Gnostic prayer to Sophia would have been welcomed in Minneapolis: "May She who is before all things, the incomprehensible and indescribable Grace, fill you within, and increase in you her own knowledge."[2]

SOPHIA IN GNOSTICISM

Sophia is God's First Thought. She becomes "fallen" wisdom because through her inquisitiveness, like that of Eve, the physical world eventually comes into being. Ialdabaoth (Yahweh), her aborted fetus, born from her desire to know, creates the physical world.[3] Because she realizes her mistake, Sophia "misses no occasion to cheat the Rulers, [namely God and his angels] in order to help [humankind]."[4] Her mission of self-redemption is twofold: to expose the truly evil nature of the biblical God, and to point mankind to the true God behind the Creator and the visible oppressive world He foolishly created.

According to Gnostic theory, Sophia's function has both a negative and a positive side. Negatively, her revelation deconstructs the Creator of heaven and earth and all his works, thus clearing the way for her positive function, that of revealing the true, unknown God from whom she emanates. These two functions must be seen in order to appreciate just how extreme is the "Christian" Gnostic attack against orthodoxy. While the feminine Sophia evokes notions of tenderness and creativity, her true work is a violent death blow to the Christian God. This is why we need to know these ancient texts, for they can tell us something about our own future.

Sophia: Overthrowing God

Recognized specialists of Gnosticism have consistently emphasized the truly radical nature of the Gnostic system. Kurt Rudolf notes, for instance, that the *Gospel of Philip* produces a "fundamental re-evaluation of things and names—the names of this world belong to error, introduced by the archons."[5] According to Rudolf, the Gnostic conception of God is "thoroughly revolutionary."[6] Hans Jonas, the great German expert of Gnosticism, argued in the '50s that the syncretistic tendency in Gnostic circles was not "directionless" but had a distinct purpose—to collect and use "any material that can set the scene in a world other than this world," that is, in a world other than the world of the created order made by the Creator of heaven and Earth.[7]

Recent feminist thinkers have discovered the revolutionary character of Gnosticism as it applies to gender and patriarchal civilization. Says one, "Gnosticism is becoming a powerful influence in feminist research into the overthrow of the male in the divine."[8] An egalitarian, nonpatriarchal vision constitutes the agenda of cutting-edge theology, sociology and global politics in the West. Gnosticism and antipatriarchal feminism are a match made in heaven since divine Sophia's mission was [and apparently still is] the overthrow of Yahweh. Sophia's key role in the overthrow of patriarchy has not always been acknowledged in the analysis of this second- and third-century heresy. But present preoccupation with gender liberation makes the nature of her mission jump off the ancient pages.

Sophia: Proving Yahweh a Fool

Like a blustering earthly macho brute who thinks that because he is male he knows everything, the heavenly prototype of all patriarchal oppression, Yahweh, foolishly thinks He is the creator of all things. He is mistaken. Sophia is the Creator.[9] According to Ptolemy, a Gnostic theologian of the second century, she is the true origin of creation:

> They say that the Demiurge [the Creator] believed that he had created all this himself, but in fact he had made them because Achamoth [another name for Sophia] had prompted him.[10]

As the Goddess of Wisdom, Sophia is all wise, brimming with intellectual vigor, whereas the classic Gnostic name for the male God of Scripture is Samael, the "blind one." Sophia is the "Mother of the Universe."[11] Spiritual illumination is to be desired, whereas Yahweh's work of creation, through the process of childbirth, is to be jettisoned as uncouth and animalistic. So the living Jesus of the *Gospel of Thomas* declares: "My mother [gave me falsehood], but [My] true [Mother] gave me life."[12]

While Sophia instructs in wisdom, Ialdabaoth (Yahweh) is in a fog of confusion. Says one Gnostic text: "[Ialdabaoth] appeared out of the waters, in the likeness of a lion and gynandrous [a mixture of female and male], possessing

great authority in himself, but not knowing where he had come into being."
The only authority He has is the "authority of matter,"[13] which, of course, for
Gnostics, was the one authority which did not matter! Even human beings
know more than this divine fool. Adam tells Seth, "And we are like the great
eternal angels, for we were greater than the god who made us and the powers
who were with him."[14] The *Apocryphon of John* speaks of man's wisdom as making him "greater than those who had made him" and "stronger than that of
the first archon [Yahweh]."[15] So Paul's statement in 1 Corinthians 2:9 is
turned against Paul's God: To the Gnostic believer is promised what no
"angel-eye" has seen and what no "archon-ear" has heard.[16] (Archon, "ruler,"
is a derogatory title for the God of the Bible). The Gnostic believer sees and
hears more than the God of Scripture. "Sola Scriptura" were not Gnostic
watchwords.

As souls at death return to their divine origin, met by the Archons (Yahweh
and his angels) who seek to bring them under their power, the Gnostic Jesus
reminds them that the power they must evoke is the power of Sophia, "mistress
of [souls]." By this power Gnostic believers will put Yahweh and His hosts to
flight.[17]

To summarize, the God of Scripture, most often known as Ialdabaoth, an
apparent play on Yahweh and Sabaoth, which perhaps means "Son of Shame,"[18]
is presented variously as "ignorant, arrogant,[19] conceited, disdainful, stupid,
mad,[20] assassin . . . a lionlike freak who will exert his ludicrous talents at the
expense of humankind . . . a perfect object for gnostic hatred and contempt."[21]
With such a despicable male god as this, who could not be charmed by the alluring wisdom of sophisticated Sophia?

Yahweh Confused about His Gender

The Gnostic critique implies the foolishness of imagining God in purely masculine terms. We hear the same critique today, even among "progressive" conservatives, who change hymns, liturgies and even the biblical text in order to
conform to a "gender-inclusive" divine image. The Gnostic attempted to dislodge the God of Scripture by positing gender confusion in God.

The *Apocryphon of John* proposes a new revelation of divinity that is as inclusive as any modern jewel of political correctness. The divine reality reveals itself
to John through Barbelo [Sophia] as alternately a youth, an old man and a ser-
vant, and then as the Father, the Mother and the Son.[22] Similarly, in the *Gospel*

of the Egyptians, we read: "There are three powers that come from the ultimate, unknowable God; the Father, the Mother and the Son."[23] Sophia shows in her multiple nature the transformation of gender, exposing the binary, limited character of the male Yahweh. Such a reduction of God to exclusively male metaphors deserves derision, and here it is.

Yahweh the Joke

Both the God of the Bible, who uses male language to describe himself, and biblical patriarchal history deserve mockery and scornful laughter. Everything in the Old Testament is a "laughingstock" from Adam to the Chief Archon. Creation and biblical theology are rejected en bloc. The whole thing is a big joke.

For Greek speakers, the name "Demiurge" for Yahweh was a form of mockery. In Plato and Aristotle a demiurge is an artisan/craftsman who merely follows the ideas of others (the artist) but is incapable himself of true creativity. Thus when the Demiurge presented Himself as Lord of Creation, His folly and pride were obvious to all who knew Greek.[24]

The mockery becomes much less subtle. According to the *Second Treatise of the Great Seth,* the Creator of the world is mocked because He makes the statement: "I am God and there is no other beside me."[25] Seth, the Christ-figure in this version of Gnosticism, with laughter, calls this "empty glory." When God asks, "Who is man?"[26] all the angels cannot conceal their mirth at the smallness of the knowledge of such a God.

Laughter and mockery are back. At the RE-Imagining Conference, the audience erupted in laughter and applause when a speaker pointed out that neither God the Father nor Jesus Christ had been mentioned in their worship.

Behind the laughter Sophia stands, smiling.

YAHWEH IS A DEMON

But it is no laughing matter. When the laughing stops, the hissing begins. There is no neutral ground. God the Creator, the crucified Jesus and all those who foolishly follow them must be denounced as diabolical.

The ancient Gnostic texts explain that Sophia, in order to undo the evil activity of her aborted fetus, Ialdabaoth (Yahweh), sends the good serpent to "seduce Adam and Eve into breaking Ialdabaoth's command."[27] In this reversal exegesis, the serpent has become not just wise but good. God has become both a fool and the personification of the devil. In a number of ways, God is shown as the devil.

God's Work of Creation Is Diabolical
The *Apocryphon of John* paints a very different picture of Eden than the one found on the first pages of the Bible:

> And they, namely, the archons, took him,
> and put him in paradise, and bade him,
> "Eat, for this is delight," for their delight is bitter
> and their beauty is perverted.
> But their delight is a lie and their trees are ungodliness
> and their fruit is a fatal toxin and their oath is death.
> And they put the tree of their life in the middle of Paradise.
> But I will teach you all which is the secret of their life,
> which is the counsel which they took together,
> that is the image of their spirit.
> Its root is bitter and its branches are death,
> hatred is its shadow and deception is in its leaves,
> and its flower is the unguent of evil
> and its fruit is death and lust is its seed.
> And it yields its fruit in the darkness.
> The ones who taste of it, their dwelling place is in Hades
> and their place of rest is darkness.[28]

God's Associates Include the Devil
Ialdabaoth, the "first archon," begat authorities for himself. Some of these authorities bear the various biblical names of God, such as Adonaiou and Sabaoth, but one is Belias "who is over the abyss of Hades."[29]

Another ancient Gnostic text, the *Gospel of the Egyptians*, makes the same association: Sakla (a derogatory name for Yahweh, which in Hebrew means "mad") joins with the demon Nebruel and produces assisting spirits, two of which are named Adonaios and Sabaoth.[30]

God Looks Like the Devil

The God of the Bible, Ialdabaoth, is portrayed as a lion-headed creature born from confusion who is called Ariel (from the Hebrew term *ari* meaning "lion"). This arrogant wild animal form, called Saklas, "the mad one," appears as "a lionfaced serpent with glittering eyes of fire."[31]

God Is the Devil

Finally in bald, unimaginable blasphemy, God is the devil. The Gnostic "reversal exegesis" practiced on the "satanic verses" of Genesis is now turned on Paul's Epistle to the Ephesians. The God of Old Testament Scripture, whom Paul identifies as the God of Israel and the Father of our Lord Jesus Christ,[32] is identified with the principalities and powers and with the devil who throws the flaming darts. In *Trimorphic Protennoia* God the Creator appears without nuance as the great Demon who rules over the lowest part of the underworld, that is, hell. The text calls Him Ialdabaoth, (Yahweh and Sabaoth), and lest there be any doubt as to whom is meant, He is called the "Archigenitor" (the Chief Creator), the one who falsely boasted, saying "I am God and . . . there is no other beside me."[33]

In similar blasphemous manner, the *Apocalypse of Peter* includes the crucified Jesus, Elohim and the cross with the demons:

> And he [the Savior] said to me [Peter], "Strengthen yourself, for it is you to whom these mysteries have been given, to perceive them through revelation, that this one whom they crucified is the firstborn, and the abode of demons, and the stony vessel in which they live, of Elohim, of the cross which exists under the Law.[34]

SOPHIA CASTS YAHWEH INTO HELL

Yahweh gets what any devil deserves—hell. The laughter has long since ceased. Things are deathly serious. Pushing reversal interpretation to its incredible but logical conclusion, in about as audacious a show of against-the-grain exegesis as one can find, Sophia casts the God of Scripture into the destructive fires of hell.

The Italian specialist G. Filoramo recognizes that Gnosticism presses its system to a logical conclusion: The Archons and the Demiurgos are defeated and destroyed in a universal conflagration.[35] There is hardly need of scholarly support. The texts are crystal clear. The *Hypostasis of the Archons* affirms the sad end of Yahweh in no uncertain terms. Ialdabaoth, for His blind arrogance in thinking that He is the one true God is reprimanded by the feminine goddess, Zoe, daughter of Pistis Sophia. "She breathed upon his face, and her breath became an angel of fire and that very angel shackled Ialdabaoth and threw Him down into Tartaros [Hell], under the abyss."[36]

According to *On the Origin of the World*, at the end of the world, Sophia will chase the chaotic divine beings whom she had made, together with the First Father, into the pit where they will devour one another. Finally the First Father (Yahweh), when He has destroyed them, will destroy Himself.[37]

Such is the radical destructive work of Sophia—to bring an end to God. This should be seriously noted. This is the underbelly of an ancient apostasy now being promoted, often by means of its less shocking elements as a valid, alternative expression of early Christianity and as the new form of Christianity for the third millennium.

SOPHIA REVEALS THE TRUE UNKNOWABLE GOD OF PAGAN MONISM

What is left when Yahweh is banished to hell? Having deconstructed the tired old God of orthodoxy, Sophia takes up her "positive" role as revealer of the "true" God standing behind her. As in the dream of the empty Bible that needs rewriting, we now have eerily empty heavens that need an occupant. Swept clean, the cosmos awaits new inhabitants. The God whom Sophia reveals is the unknown and unknowable god of pagan monism that bears a striking resemblance to the new god of contemporary Aquarian spirituality.

GETTING TO KNOW THE UNKNOWN GOD

In the Gnostic system, God is the "unknown God" beyond all that is visible or sensible, who incorporates a "fullness" (pleroma) of heavenly beings.[38] According to the Church fathers, Gnostic theologians delighted in describing the indescribable. The proto-Gnostic Marcion (A.D. 150) called his preaching the "gospel of the alien God." Basilides (second century) spoke of "the primal nonexistent God." Valentinus (second century), perhaps the greatest Gnostic theologian, states with eloquence this pillar of Gnostic thinking:

> There is in invisible and ineffable heights a pre-existent perfect aeon whom they call Pre-beginning, forefather and Primal Ground, that is inconceivable and invisible, eternal and uncreated and that existed in great peace and stillness in unending spaces (aeons).[39]

The recently found texts bear out the Church fathers' witness to Gnostic teaching—God is everything and nothing:

> He is not corporeal [nor] is he incorporeal.
> He is neither large [nor] is he small.
> [There is no] way to say,
> "What is his quantity?" or "What [is his quality?"],
> for no one is able [to know him].[40]

The *Gospel of the Egyptians* describes him as:

> the great unseen [spirit the] Father, the name of whom cannot be spoken . . . the light [of the] [uncorrupted] the limitless light, [the] brilliance, from the aeons of light of the unrepealable, indistinguishable, ageless, unproclaimable, the aeon of aeons, self-producing, the stranger, the truly authentic aeon.[41]

The Gnostics argued that the true God is beyond all representation, biblical or otherwise. The Gnostics, to judge from the following quote from *Allogenes*, would doubtless have said that worship of the God of the Old Testament was idolatry:

> He is neither god-like, nor is he a blessed one nor is he a perfected one . . . Nor is he anything that is which one is able to know. But he is another thing of himself that is superior which one does not have the ability to know. . . . Since he is limitless and impotent and nonexistent.[42]

For the Gnostic, to describe God is proof of inferior spiritual perception. Thus, Yahweh is already shown to be inferior because He is known. The gracious condescension of the scriptural Lord of glory in revealing Himself to His creation and to His people is mocked and thrown back into God's face. In the *Teaching of Silvanus* the comparison is drawn between the inferior God, the Creator, who is easy to know, and the "true" God who is impossible to comprehend.[43]

The Gnostic's ultimate spiritual principle is not a trinity of divine persons but a lone, impersonal cause referred to as "The Father of the Totalities"[44] or the "All."[45] We have come full circle. At the end of the twentieth century, the new spirituality now refers to God in inclusive, politically correct fashion as "the God/Goddess/All That Is." In this grab-bag terminology, everything is included—except a divinity of individual personhood.

GNOSTICISM: DUALIST OR MONIST?

It is often said that Gnosticism is dualist.[46] If Gnosticism rejects matter and embraces spirit, which it does, how can it have an overarching system that includes everything in a monistic embrace? But there are reasons for thinking that Gnosticism is ultimately monist. Like other forms of pantheism, it sees God everywhere, even in matter. While theism separates God from His creation, Gnosticism denies to God any specific identity. God is so diffuse that He is everywhere, and thus nowhere.[47]

While there is an anticosmic emphasis, the essential Gnostic opposition to the world is opposition to God the Creator and His created order. The Christian view of God and creation cedes to a pagan monistic God who is everywhere but unknowable. The so-called *Gospel of Mary* hints of this pagan pantheism when it predicts that all things "exist in and with one another" and "will be resolved again into their own roots."[48] This is not anticosmic. It is anticreational, rejecting things the way they are now. The living Jesus in the *Gospel of Thomas* expresses a similar monistic sentiment:

> Jesus said, "I, myself, am the light above all. I, myself, am the all. The all came forth from me and the all extended to me. Cleave a piece of wood, I am there. Lift up the stone and there I will be found."[49]

These texts whisk matter from the God of Scripture and give it to the monistic God behind all things. Indeed in one text (and many others imply it) matter comes not from Yahweh but from his mother Sophia: "He made the heavens without knowing the heaven; he formed man without knowing him; he brought the earth to light without knowing it. And in every case, they say, He was ignorant of the ideas of the things He made, and even of His own mother, and imagined that He alone was all things."[50]

Even Yahweh's one claim to infamy, the creation of the world, is not His to claim, and is brought into the domain of the divine emanations as the work of Sophia. Even the physical world does not finally belong to Ialdabaoth but is employed by the true and ultimate god as a vehicle whereby he might be known.

THE GNOSTIC SOPHIA: EPITOME OF A MONISTIC PAGAN DEITY

Ultimate divine power is often described in the male imagery of the unknowable Father. Gnostics claim that the knowable, revealing, teaching divine power is female.[51] (The equivalent on Earth is Eve teaching Adam as a wise Instructor). God is so unknown and removed that one must speak of nonbeing existence. The dynamic force that brings one face-to-face with the unknown is female. Sophia is the divine element that spans both the physical and the spiritual worlds and joins the opposites of earthly existence into a mystical unity. *Trimorphic Protennoia* describes "three descents of the Gnostic heavenly redeemer Protennoia, who is actually Sophia. She is the First Thought of the Father. . . . She dwells at all levels of the universe."[52] Notice how Sophia takes the place of the Eternal Son in the divine Trinity. Sophia's revelation is pantheistic monism. She is everywhere, declaring:

I am revealed out of the immeasurable and the unspeakable. I am beyond comprehension, I live in the incomprehensible. I stir in all creation. I myself am the life of my Conception that exists in every power and stirs in every eternal movement and in Lights unseen and in the Archons and Angels and Demons and in every soul which exists in [Tatatros] and in every soul made of matter. I exist in those who came to be in existence.[53]

A Mystical Weather Forecast: Thunder Everywhere

Thunder, Perfect Mind, a mysterious name for Sophia, reveals that while we can never know the source of all unity (God), all is united in Sophia's cosmic embrace. Sophia is the perfect expression of pagan spirituality. She decon-structs rational categories in a monistic joining of the opposites:

> For the first and the last am I.
> I am the adored and the despised one.
> I am the prostitute and the venerable one.
> I am the wife and the virgin.
> I am the mother and the daughter. . . .
> I myself am the stillness that is beyond understanding
> and the conception whose thoughts are numerous.
> I am the voice, the sound of which is myriad
> and the word (logos), whose appearance is manifold. . . .
> I am shame and fearlessness.
> I am without shame; I am ashamed. . . .
> I am without mind and I am wise. . . .
> For I myself am the Greek's wisdom and the barbarian's knowledge.
> I myself am the judgment of the Greeks and the barbarians.
> I am the one whose likeness is great in Egypt. . . .
> I am the one who is called life and whom you call death.
> I am the one who is called law and whom you have called lawless. . . .
> I, I myself am godless, and
> it is I whose God is manifold. . . .
> I am the immutable essence and the one who has no immutable
> essence. . . .
> I am the joining and the dissolution. . . .
> I, I myself am without sin and
> the root of sin originates from me. . . .
> It is I who is called truth and lawlessness. . . .[54]

This text, according to the original editor of the document, has no distinctive-ly Gnostic themes. But contemporary feminists know better. The text bears some resemblance to the personification of Wisdom in Proverbs 8, but the dif-ference in content is radical. In Proverbs Dames Wisdom and Folly are set in opposition. Here wisdom and folly belong to the same divine principle. This female revealer resembles not biblical wisdom but the Egyptian goddess Isis or the Hindu Kali.[55] Little wonder Thunder/Sophia is gratefully welcomed into modern religious feminists' pantheon:

Another female divinity who calls to women and assures us of our divinity and our power is the otherwise un-named Thunder Perfect Mind. She appears to be everywhere and encompasses everything . . . She is everything and everybody and its opposite. She is female and within her there is the whole range of female life from birth to death, from the mundane woman in the world to the divine Wisdom of Heaven. . . . I see in the "Thunder" the vision of a goddess human and divine who speaks again. . . . [in the manner of] Egyptian Isis. [56]

Sophia: Hailing from Egypt

This feminist author puts her finger on the pagan origin of Sophia as an expression of the Egyptian Goddess, Isis. Of course, the text itself clearly makes this connection when Thunder/Sophia declares: "[I] am the one whose image is great in Egypt." The connection is appropriate, since Isis was the Egyptian Goddess of Wisdom.[57] It is said of Isis that she is "the still point of the turning world"[58] who proclaims: "I am Nature, the Universal Mother . . . single manifestation of all gods and goddesses am I."[59] Like Thunder/Sophia, Isis joins everything within her all-inclusive embrace. I cite again the description of her wisdom by an Isis scholar:

> Curiously, . . . the Egyptians [when characterizing Isis by her wisdom] called her "great in magical power." [For them] real wisdom consisted of insight into the mystery of life and death. . . . Thus wisdom was to the Egyptians equivalent to the capacity of exerting magical power.[60]

This is also affirmed in more technical language by Caitlín Matthews, the modern priestess of Isis and specialist of the history of Sophia. "The Greek-Egyptian experience (after Alexander the Great's conquest of Egypt) is truly a catalyst in this study of Wisdom, for the strong character of Isis the Goddess became the Sophianic touchstone of . . . Gnosticism."[61] Here you have it stated unambiguously by a pagan priestess that Gnosticism serves most admirably as a bridge for paganism to infiltrate Christianity.

Initiation into the mysteries of Isis and the ecstatic secret experiences in her temples gave adherents a foretaste of transformation into immortality.[62] Isis was thus the giver of magical, occult knowledge and wisdom through which, like Sophia, she revealed the distant, unknown Egyptian God behind all things, Re.[63] Isis "RE-Imagined" God for her adepts!

That "Christian" Gnostics borrow from paganism is here patently obvious—as therefore should be the pagan nature of present-day speculation about Sophia. The Sophia who made a brief appearance in Minneapolis did not fly in from Jerusalem, nor can traces of her identity be found in the Bible. She came from pagan Egypt via "Christian" Gnosticism and her passport bore her real name—Isis.

Protennoia, which means "first thought," another manifestation of Sophia in the ancient Gnostic texts, reveals in the starkest terminology the joining of the opposites in a nonrational unity so essential to pagan thinking both ancient and modern:

> I am gynandrous [I am Mother, I am] Father since [I] [have coitus] with myself. I [have coitus] with myself [and the ones who love] me [and] I am the one through whom the All [endures]. I am the womb [that gives form] to the All by birthing the Light that [shines in] glory.[64]

The text goes on to explain that the above revelation and the androgynous or gynandrous joining of all duality is the ultimate mystery, a mystery called "the Sound of the Mother," hidden from the "Aeons and the Archigenitor, granted to the Sons of the Thought."[65] In other words, Sophia brings a new revelation of divinity that goes beyond anything the ignorant God of Scripture could imagine. It is the "sound" of the monistic mystical experience of connection with all things in the hearts of those who know.

Through the gender confusion Sophia brings, she deconstructs the God of the Bible. But her ultimate role is to point beyond the feminine gender to the androgynous state of true monism. For, as one Gnostic specialist rightly notes, in Gnosticism "the ultimate image of salvation is neither male nor female but the restored unity of an androgynous Mother-Father, who has passed through diversity."[66] This historical fact is all the more interesting in the light of the contemporary promotion of inclusive versions of the Lord's Prayer which address God as "Our Father/Mother in heaven,"[67] as well as radical egalitarian interpretations of Galatians 3:28.

THE HEART OF GNOSTICISM IS THE HEART OF PAGANISM: MAN IS GOD

Sophia brings to light the essence of this diabolical revelation—there is no God other than man. As Gnostic expert Filoramo notes, "God is, in fact, Anthropos, Man/Human, or rather the archetypal Androgyne." In Gnosticism, he adds, "the human has now become the predicate of the divine. The manifestation of God to himself: this is the heart of Gnostic myth."[68] It is also the heart of the original lie of the devil: "You will be as God."[69]

The second-century Church father Irenaeus saw the dreadful consequence of Gnostic teaching. He reports that the Sethian Gnostics called God man:

> Ialdabaoth, becoming arrogant in spirit, boasted himself over all those who were below him, and explained, "I am father, and God, and above me there is no one." His mother, hearing him speak thus, cried out against him: "Do not lie, Ialdabaoth; for the father of all, the primal anthropos, is above you; and so is Anthropos, the son of Anthropos."[70]

This version of primal history declares man to be God. On Earth, Seth's antitype, Jesus, reveals that when James reaches Him Who Is "you will no longer be James; rather *you are the One Who Exists*."[71] Such is surely the most pernicious form of humanism, divinized humanism. Today atheistic humanism is on the run. The new enemy is a spiritualized view of man. He is no longer simply the measure of all things, as rationalism maintained: Man is now also the measure of God, for man is God. This new spirituality is the final expression of idolatry because it is not just disobedience of God's laws: It replaces the divine with the human.

SUCH A GOD/MAN IS THE MOUTHPIECE OF SATAN

Many naively rid themselves of a patriarchal construct and reimagine the divine in more user-friendly ways. It is simple to exchange one set of mythological ideas for another. Replace God with man, and bring heaven to Earth in the establishment of a new utopia. But there is a forgotten element in the equation, a third player in the cosmic contest for the soul—the self-effacing, slithering

Satan. The human heart is not an autonomous place of spiritual goodness. It is a tablet on which either God or Satan writes.

Sophia did not replace the bumbling Yahweh with a third, optimistic option. Sophia, the goddess of occult wisdom is in every way opposed to the wisdom of God. The new spirituality she offers has been offered before. Its Earth-centered wisdom and light-illumination bring unsuspecting and spiritually hungry contemporaries into the foyer of Satan's kingdom. Her voice is his. Our world wobbles on the brink of a great delusion. If it ignores the warning the ancient Gnostic apostasy provides, our brave new world will stagger, inebriated, into the euphoria produced by the dazzling false promise of a liberated humanity and androgynous, uninhibited sexuality.

CHAPTER TWELVE

THE NEW
SEXUALITY

Times and trends do change and unisex is
unquestionably in fashion.

JUSTICE ANTONIN SCALIA[1]

Psst . . . Do you want to invade France? The best time is in August around 2:00 P.M. Those not on vacation are taking a nap. Do you want to capture a civilization? Change perceptions of sexuality. Though few may practice New Age Eastern spirituality with chakras, crystals, astral travel and channeling, everyone is a male or a female. Sexuality keeps a civilization functioning. Insidiously, a new definition of sexuality in tune with New Age liberal monism beckons our world, promising liberation for the oppressed, justice for the deprived and peace on Earth.

Sex and religion make a formidable twosome. Sexuality can never be disassociated from the religious quest. By a new sexuality, liberalism will transform religion and the planet. "We are doomed as a species and a planet," prophesies a religious feminist, "unless we have a radical change of consciousness."[2] The liberation of sexuality accompanies a change of planetary consciousness and the revival of pagan spirituality on the eve of the "Aquarian" millennium.

GOD AND SEX IN THE THIRD MILLENNIUM

The agenda for sexual revolution follows the same logical progression mentioned in earlier chapters: crisis, deconstruction and reconstruction. Take the program for unity of the world's religions. First comes a description of ecological crisis; then a call to dismantle the Christian view of creation. Finally theological syncretism beckons. In the case of sexuality, the crisis is due to the evils of patriarchy; the deconstruction destroys the Christian view of sex and gender roles; and from the ashes rises a monistic phoenix: the new androgynous ideal.[3]

Ruether's Ruthless Rage-Raising Rhetoric

In "Christian" theologian Rosemary Radford Ruether's universe, patriarchy has replaced sin.[4] Since this affirmation cannot be established from Genesis 3, these founding texts become the adopted myths of patriarchal religion. According to Ruether, patriarchy is the work of the devil, the Mark of the Beast, the Great Babylon, the evil land of Egyptian slavery from which the Church should organize a modern-day exodus, the inward reality of which prostitution is the outward expression. "Rapists are the shock troops of patriarchy, while wife-batterers are the army of occupation." The essence of the contemporary Church is liberation from patriarchy[5]—the new culprit to be eliminated in the class struggle for social justice, identified as the enemy in the struggle with the principalities and powers; the idol of masculinity, of father rule—the mechanical idol with flashing eyes and smoking nostrils who spews out blasphemies in the temples of patriarchy and who is about to consume the earth; the great Leviathan of violence and misery whose "evil powers have entered into the deep layers of our unconscious" from which we need to be baptized.[6] As in postmodernism generally, the louder the shouts, the higher the feminist consciousness is raised.[7]

The Great Evil

Pagans might well reject the patriarchal structure of creation (though many do not), but Christians? Extending the evangelical denunciation of patriarchy,

Virginia Mollenkott blames "*hetero*patriarchy" for most social ills, including racism and classism. "It is vital for us to understand the ways in which distorted concepts of human sexuality, gender distortions, and misconstructions of our God-language have blocked human freedom and healthy relationships and therefore have stunted any possibility of feeling fully alive. Only after accurate diagnosis of what is ailing us can we hope for an adequate cure." She defines "heteropatriarchy" as:

> the hierarchial ways of organizing by which everything and everyone is ranked and whatever is male and white tends to get the upper hand. People and things cannot simply be *different* from one another: one way of being, doing, and thinking must always be the norm, everything else being *ab*normal. . . . Patriarchy is a profoundly mistaken social system that has caused misery to millions and could yet cause the destruction of humankind and the planet we share together.[8]

A practicing lesbian, Mollenkott adds: "Compulsory heterosexuality is the very backbone that holds patriarchy together."[9] Homosexuality will break that "backbone." "If society is to turn from patriarchy to partnership," we must learn that lesbian, bisexual and gay issues are not just private bedroom matters of "doing whatever turns you on." They are "wedges driven into the superstructure of the heteropatriarchal system." Mollenkott echoes Kate Millet's pagan vision: "A woman is called lesbian when she functions autonomously. Women's autonomy is what women's liberation is all about."[10]

The revolution is about the personal power to be autonomous of all structures and relationships. It is the power of radical freedom to do what you please. This is a pagan agenda, but in good faith many Christians try to extract good from the revolution by Christianizing it as today's goal for the Christian faith. The glorious liberty and high calling of homosexuality lead some liberal Christians to denounce the "sin of heterosexism." Two Christian scholars, one a Roman Catholic laywoman, the other a Lutheran minister, challenge the Church not only to "accept" homosexuality with Christian tolerance, but to see it as a normative "given." Not only is the Judeo-Christian heterosexual ethic no longer useful; insistence upon it is sin.[11]

On a less radical level, evangelical egalitarian feminism makes a similar move. A systematic theology published by InterVarsity Press (the publishing arm of a historically orthodox parachurch student organization), expresses a blanket rejection of patriarchy typical of radical feminism: "Feminist theology has done a great service to the Christian community by pointing out the evils of andro-centrism, patriarchy and misogyny."[12] Misogyny certainly, and perhaps also androcentrism in some forms could be described as evil—but patriarchy, which is at the very basis of Scripture and of Western civilization? Gretchen Gabelein Hull, a board member of the Council for Biblical Equality, speaks of the "sin of patriarchy. . . . To Christianize patriarchy is to end it."[13] According to Hull, one cannot reform patriarchy in the light of the Christian revelation of God as Father of our Lord Jesus Christ.[14] One can only eliminate it! Egalitarianism is the first step to autonomous individualism just as the relativization of sexual differences is the first step to gender confusion. The new liberalism is feminist to the marrow, as was the Parliament of the World's Religions. Do evangelicals embrace egalitarian feminism as a theological/exegetical discovery of the glorious liberty of the gospel? Or are they encouraged by enormous societal, ideological and economic pressures, and a naive faith in the democratic process?[15]

The Jewish feminist, Naomi Goldenberg, is not so naive. She fingers God the Father of the Judeo-Christian Scripture as the architect of the patriarchal society. Like patriarchy, this God will have to go, as the title of her book, *Changing of the Gods*, affirms:

> The new wave of feminism desperately needs to be not only many-faced but cosmic and ultimately religious in its vision. This means reaching outward and inward toward the God beyond and beneath the gods who have stolen our identity.[16]

Goldenberg's words ring with uncanny certainty: "We women are going to bring an end to God."[17] How are they doing?

DECONSTRUCTION—
THE GOAL: THE DESTRUCTION OF
THE CHRISTIAN VIEW OF SEX
AND GENDER ROLES

Is it fortuitous that liberalism's conversion to monistic spirituality coincides with major changes in sexual practice, gender roles and family structures? The sexuality of Western civilization has been deconstructed in just one generation. The role of women has changed drastically, representing a megashift in the perceptions of human sexuality. Feminism has opened doors to many other changes. Oddly, not many are willing to consider feminism as a driving force of the neo-pagan ideal,[18] even though radicals do at every occasion.

Revolution and Nothing Less

The women's movement, according to its leading theorists, "is not a reformist movement but a revolutionary one."[19] Dissident Roman Catholic priest and professor of sociology, Andrew Greeley prophesied major changes in the Church in the near future: "Women will remake religion."[20]

Some find this revolution exhilarating, the best thing to happen to women, and especially to housewives, since sliced bread. *Time* magazine, like Greeley, is full of optimism, wondering if this movement constitutes a "New Reformation." The radicals chuckle at such naivete, disdaining the very idea of "reformation" which implies a return to purity in some lost form. They prefer to see the women's movement as a "paradigm shift" of "far-reaching ramifications,"[21] a "new dispensation" or a "new revelation." The arrival of "being," which makes everything before it "nothingness," is a radical "conversion to a new consciousness." [22]

Some are appalled. A Roman Catholic journalist, Donna Steichen, in *Ungodly Rage*, her documentation of the progress of feminism in the American Catholic church, entitled, says in the introduction:

> This book is about darkness. Its pages document one of the most devastating religious epidemics of our, or any other, time.[23]

These authors, both for and against, agree on one thing: Feminism is a force of revolutionary power. Its staggering progress in just one generation cannot be dismissed as the normal ticking of the democratic process, the next step in the civilization of the planet. Something else is happening.

A Social Tidal Wave a Mile off the Coast

While sociologists in 1993 did not see any major cultural changes on the religious horizon to alter the face of the mainline churches,[24] in the '70s Naomi Goldenberg, a Jewish feminist, predicted a tsunami of revolutionary change: "When feminists succeed in changing the position of women in Christianity and Judaism, they will shake these religions at their roots."[25] In 1971, when she first met feminists she remembers thinking: "Such women will change the world."[26] Goldenberg's prophecies are unusually perceptive as many feminists now turn to goddess worship and witchcraft. Indeed, Goldenberg herself has since become a witch.[27] Through the use of powerful female images such as the goddess, the gorgon or the amazon, radical feminists intend to bring about "a major change of consciousness, a new symbolic transformation."[28] Transformation into marketable social engineering is rapid. Advertisements in my local supermarket invite 8- to 11-year-old girls to learn empowerment through the study of six pagan goddesses. In schools and day-care centers, apparently innocuous programs of "gender-equality education," which have cost millions of tax dollars, ensure that the biblical teaching on sexual and role distinctions are erased from the future generation's collective consciousness—with most people's silent approval.

The effects are mixed. The reconsideration of the place of the woman in society and the Church, and the creative search to employ women's gifts are salutary and beneficial. However, "true spirituality" without a blush now casts aside the biblical revelation of God as Father; creational sexuality and biblical sexual morality become the ultimate expression of evil oppression. Madeleine L'Engle feels morally entitled to call the God and Father of our Lord Jesus Christ "the paternalistic male chauvinist pig Old Testament God."[29] The new hymnal of the United Church of Christ goes beyond calling God names. It simply removes them. Its general synod has "cleansed" its hymns of unacceptable patriarchal notions like "Father" and "King."[30] The Father-Son relationship at the very heart of the gospel is thereby deconstructed and the blood of what Goldenberg calls the "slow execution of Jahweh and Christ" is on the hands of a mainline "Christian" denomination. At certain evangelical colleges it is appropriate to call God "Parent" in order to avoid the sexist and oppressive term "Father."

Biblical Bull

It was standing room only. Between 500 and 600 Bible scholars, theologians and teachers of religion packed a lecture hall and part of the hallway in a downtown hotel in San Francisco in November 1992 to hear the latest revelations from post-Christian lesbian feminist witch and professor with tenure in the theology department at Boston College, Mary Daly (she has since retired). In the middle of the joint annual meeting of the American Academy of Religion and the Society of Biblical Literature, in the middle of her account of the great inter-galactic reunion of feminist heroines past and present taking place "on the other side of the moon," Daly suddenly stopped. With deliberation, she looked her attentive audience up and down. Then, raising her arms in the form of prophetic utterance, and in a voice halfway between a cackle and a screech, she blurted out: "What's all this biblical bulls--t?" At the end of her lecture, the "biblical" scholars gave her a thunderous ovation. "Theology" has come a long way, baby—all the way back to the Gnostic rejection of Scripture and the God of Scripture.

If publications, reviews and public endorsements are anything to go by, there are thousands of teachers in university departments of religion and in theological seminaries who have adopted some form of this humanist program of ethical, spiritual and sexual liberation.[31] Liberal theology can run the gamut from the white, straight, male Harvard professor of theology to the lesbian ecofeminist witch who has severed all ties with biblical Christianity. But the twain do meet. Mary Daly, who screams blasphemies on virtually every page of her recent books promoting witchcraft and erotic "spiritual" lesbianism, receives accolades from Harvey Cox, respected liberal theologian, Victor S. Thomas professor of divinity at the Harvard Divinity School. Mary Daly dismisses the incarnation of the eternal Son as the "symbolic legitimation of the rape of all women and all matter," and describes as "bull . . . the apostles creed."[32] Cox considers her "a woman who makes a Big Difference" of whom he is a self-styled "fan."

Cox, one of 300 scholars who signed a petition from the American Academy of Religion which helped force Jesuit Boston College to promote Daly to a tenured professorship, even though she had rejected Christianity for paganism, said, "It is hard to imagine where the whole field of religious and theological studies would be today were it not for the contributions she has made."[33]

At one of the leading theological institutions in the country, the Claremont Graduate School, two witches, Naomi Goldenberg and Mary Daly, were featured guest speakers in the Women's Studies in Religion Program. This program also cosponsored a four-day conference on "Women and Goddess Traditions," which included lectures on "The Goddess and Women's Power: A Hindu Case Study" and "Goddess, Matriarch and Pregnancy: A Long Tradition." Participants included Professor Emily Culpepper of the University of Redlands, an ex-Baptist fundamentalist and now a witch and collaborator with Mary Daly, who finds spiritual strength and solace in the Hindu goddess, Kali.

At the Harvard Divinity School studies are dominated by the feminist perspective. In a semihumorous but well-documented article entitled "What's up at Harvard Divinity School," Jewish social commentator, Don Feder, recounts that Buddhist chanting and meditation are more popular than hymn-singing, and the Christian calendar is passed over in favor of pagan holidays. According to Feder, feminist goddess worship is the interpretative grid through which religion, Christian theology and the Bible are interpreted.[34]

Gays R Us

The proof of this megashift and of its radical implications is the growing acceptance and power of the homosexual community. "We are no longer seeking just a right to privacy and a protection from wrong," says a leading spokesman for the movement. "We have a right . . . to see government and society affirm our lives."[35]

The project is clearly succeeding in modern-day America, in spite of the scores of millions of Americans who doubtless oppose it. In 1975 the venerable institution of *Time* magazine opposed this agenda: "It is one thing to remove legal discrimination against homosexuals. It is another to mandate approval."[36] By 1992, *Time* was inviting its readers to accept homosexuality the way they accepted black Americans, women voters or automated-teller machines.[37] The boundaries move every day. In 1994, one of the major debates was the place of gay groups on *high school* campuses.[38] Already the Los Angeles Unified School District was planning an end-of-year prom for gay students. The cutesy reporting of the *Los Angeles Times* asked readers to believe that there is nothing more natural for the progress of American democracy than a teenage boy making himself a lace dress to wear at the end-of-year dance. By now, gay high school groups are commonplace.

Is this a foretaste of the liberated future to which we are headed with unbounded enthusiasm? It sounds more like a Fellini movie about the last orgiastic days of a decadent Roman empire. Indeed, like Fellini, Hollywood is ever obliging and produced in 1993 the first major motion picture, *Philadelphia*, whose leading character/hero is a gay man. But gays are still not satisfied. They want Hollywood to give the general public full-nudity gay love scenes, for equal time in steamy sex.[39] If the L.A. school district can give us gay proms, it will sure-ly only be a matter of time for Hollywood to give us gay sex in full color in a the-ater near you.

In academia, feminism and homosexuality have urged each other to more and more radical positions, as the well-researched and finely titled article, "Coming Out Ahead: The Homosexual Moment in the Academy" demon-strates.[40] The author reports that "at many colleges, gay/lesbian/bisexual stu-dent associations are among the most active . . . on campus, funded by student fees and by institutional funds from the university's Office of Multi-culturalism." At Harvard each dorm has a designated gay tutor; at Columbia University, the chairman of the English department is committed to "hiring, tenuring and working with" gay and lesbian scholars; many universities, including Stanford, Chicago, Iowa and Pitzer College, offer spousal benefits to homosexual partners of faculty members.[41] The Bi-College News of Haverford and Bryn Mawr Colleges describes the workshop on lesbian dominatrix tech-niques. The expert, Kali Morgan, was sponsored by the Bryn Mawr Women's Center.[42]

The homosexual agenda progresses by suggesting that democracy is the source of morality, and many "straights" are buying the line.

Until recently, Western society has borne the name Christendom, implying a Judeo-Christian understanding of male and female. Radical deconstruction favors neo-pagan gender confusion in an androgynous ideal. To succeed, the program must eradicate the last vestiges of Christendom from Western society. Patriarchy and normative heterosexuality must go. The broad liberal agenda behind these societal changes points to an all-inclusive monistic religion. People are profoundly religious.

RECONSTRUCTION—
THE IDEAL: NEITHER MALE NOR FEMALE

Homo Noeticus—The New Spiritual Human

Somewhere over the rainbow, just around the corner, in the third millennium, the earth should tilt on its axis, and a convergence of like-minded believers will bring the final jump in evolutionary progress. A star will be born. A new humanity will sprout wings, and mankind will fly to its ultimate destiny of unity with the All. This kind of evolution is religion, not science, as many now recognize. "Religion," says New Ager and United Nations undersecretary, Robert Muller, and key figure in the Parliament of the World's Religions, "[will] cooperate to bring to unprecedented heights a better understanding of the mysteries of life and of our place in the universe."[43] This rosy religious future on Earth will come about because, according to Muller, "a new and higher form of humanity [is taking] control of the planet. . . . homo noeticus is the name I give to the emerging form of humanity."[44] *Homo noeticus*—the new rational/spiritual human being. This is the New Age savior. Cloned by the thousands, as people reach altered states of consciousness through meditation, this spiritually empowered New Man will save humanity and the planet.

The skeptical listener smiles in disbelief. Thousands of years of human history have not produced rebirth. But tomorrow is always a new day, and the Aquarian revolution *will* be different because mankind will be different.

The Androgynous Ideal—Anything You Want to Be

The New Man (male and female) of pagan monism is an attractive chap. As a hybrid of Eastern and Western monism, he is not the emaciated guru on the streets of Calcutta. That would hardly sell on Madison Avenue. He is an optimist who can realize all his dreams and be whatever he wants to be. He can do "all things"; that is, all things within the monistic circle. He is no longer limited by the hard and fast separation of reality into right and wrong, true and false, male and female. His ultimate goal is union with the all, and on the sexual plane, androgyny.

For Mary Daly, the way forward in God's dealings with the human race is through feminist liberation and the creation of a "mysticism of sorority." Her eschatological vision for the future of humanity is summed up in the following passage:

> What is at stake is *a real leap in human evolution*, initiated by women . . . to an intuition of being which . . . is an intuition of human integrity or of androgynous being.[45]

For most people, androgyny is a mental not a physical state.[46] Very few human beings are born with both male and female organs. The closest most come to androgyny is homosexuality and bisexuality, for in homosexuality and bisexuality, as we have noted, gay males and lesbian females play both the male and the female role. Support of this idea comes from the noted psychologist Carl Jung who suggested that "homosexuality preserve[d] an archetype of the androgynous original person."[47] Homosexuals are thus the true pagan monists, who have succeeded in translating spiritual theory into physical reality. They are the prototype of the Aquarian New Man of the twenty-first century.

HOMOSEXUAL SHAMANS FOR SPIRITUALITY IN THE NEW AGE

The story of the occult in world history is also a story of homosexuality. . . . In pagan cultures, homosexuals often hold an elevated position in religion and society. When pagan civilizations ruled the world, homosexuality and pederasty were widely practiced and accepted.[48]

The move from radical feminism to homosexuality is as rapid as it is logical. Feminism has deconstructed the creational sexuality of Christian theism. Homosexuality reconstructs it according to the norms of pagan monism. A long-time "evangelical" feminist, Virginia Mollenkott, recently announced her homosexuality. Discovering and practicing her homosexuality was for her a moment of deep self-understanding. "To live in the gender I preferred: this striking phrase causes me to think about the native American shamans who were permitted to live and dress like the other sex without stigma and with a great deal of respect for their spiritual power."[49] Such a discovery has led Mollenkott to spiritual monism. Her new "sensuous spirituality" includes comparing her own experience with that of pagan homosexual shamans as well as her adoption of New Age thinking and practice.[50] This is spiritual monism because it is founded upon the joining of the opposites of classic pagan ideology.

It is well documented that pagan religion has always held a special place for androgyny/homosexuality. Mircea Eliade saw androgyny in many traditional religions as:

an archaic and universal formula for the expression of wholeness, the co-existence of the contraries, or *coincidentia oppositorum* . . . symboliz-[ing]. . . perfection. . . [and] ultimate being.[51]

Sex and religion are clearly an inseparable dynamic duo, but not just any sex for any religion. Androgyny is expressive of the monistic vision just as heterosexuality expresses the mystery of theism. The autonomous androgynous individual symbolizes the faceless divine Spirit who inhabits the undifferentiated All just as heterosexuality reflects both the unity and personal distinctiveness of the triune Christian God and the relationship between Christ and His Church. In our day confusion reigns. A new sexuality, alien to everything the Church has known, is forcing itself onto the Christian religion. Dominican "Christian" theologian Matthew Fox actually says: "In some ways, homosexuality is superior to heterosexuality. There's no better birth control . . . and there is cosmological merit in the fact that it is not productive; there's a lot of merit in rediscovering sexuality as play."[52] Radical Episcopalian Bishop Spong affirms: "Feminism and homosexuality lie at the heart and soul of what the Gospel is all about."[53] This new "gospel" is not the announcement of deliverance from sin but an incitation to sin even more.

In the monistic tradition, the same religious claim is made for homosexuality as it is for androgyny. "Lesbian/gay peoples have always held . . . [a] shamanistic function and ceremonial office . . . in every society."[54] Homosexuals see themselves as high priests of the coming new religion.

This is clearly illustrated in Native American religion where homosexual transvestite males functioned as shamans.[55] Examples abound, even closer to home. Emily Culpepper, the ecofeminist lesbian witch with an M.Div. and Th.D. from Harvard Divinity School, was once a "deep South," "highly involved" evangelical Christian. Even now, while calling herself an "amazon, pagan, oddwoman, [and] 'Nag-gnostic,'" Culpepper honestly admits that "Sunday night hymn singing echoes still in my inner ear." In spite of this interference, she sees gays and lesbians as "shamans for a future age."[56] What is a shaman? A shaman is "a charged, potent, awe-inspiring, and even fear-inspiring person who takes true risks by crossing over into other worlds."[57] A fuller definition leaves little to the imagination: "The power and effectiveness of shamans—witches, sibyls, Druids—emerges from their ability to communicate with the *non-human*: extra-terrestrial and subterranean forces, and the spirit-world of the dead."[58] *The Encyclopedia of New Age Beliefs*[59] documents the deeply spiritual relationship between shamanism and homosexuality. Shamans are guided by "guardian spirits" which often take the form of "power animals" or "familiars." This certainly happened in the case of ex-evangelical Emily Culpepper, whose black cat became for her the incarnation of the bloodthirsty Hindu Goddess Kali.

> This incarnation of Kali became my wise companion for eighteen years, teaching me much (as witches' familiars do), about the mysteries of living and dying. . . . My cat taught me that the fearful symmetries of nature . . . included her flashing beauty, her sweet friendliness and playfulness, and her appetite for hunting and killing.[60]

Culpepper's cat taught her how to live "beyond dualism";[61] that is, to join the opposites in both mind and body. The deep spiritual communion between this woman and her cat proves the affirmations of the experts concerning the shaman. From the "power animal" the shaman "derives his psychic abilities, spiritual assistance. . . . Basically, the power animal becomes the shaman's alter ego." By the same token, the shaman "permanently incarnates these spirits into his own body."[62] In an attempt to join the opposites, not only are sexual differences eliminated but the distinction between human and animal has been virtually lost.

Part of the shaman's initiation is sexual perversion. "Many shamans become androgynous, homosexual or lesbian at the insistence of their spirit guides.[63] Homosexuality appears to be not just a physical condition but a spiritual commitment. A recent book traces the history of gay male spirituality, and argues that "gender-variant men have fulfilled a sacred role throughout the millennia." Contemporary examples given include the homosexual priests of the Yoruba religion in Cuba and "young gay witches in Manhattan."[64] In more familiar but strangely comparable terms, Virginia Mollenkott, calling herself "an evangelical lesbian feminist," speaks for gays and lesbians, when she says, "We are God's Ambassadors."[65] Indeed, Mollenkott claims she "was told" by her "guardian angel, a Spirit Guide, the Holy Spirit or Jesus [she is not sure]: 'A great shift is occurring in the world, and you are a part of that shift.'"[66] Similarly, Judy Westerdorf, a United Methodist clergywoman, triumphantly declared to the delegates at the pagano-"Christian" feminist RE-Imagining Conference that "the Church has always been blessed by gays and lesbians, . . . witches . . . [and] shamans."[67] Some see a brave new world of sexual pluralism where all are free to do their own thing. The androgyne will be the spiritual leader and heterosexuality will be tolerated, as in ancient Greece.

Homophobia

Christians are exhorted to love sinners but flee sin. Though sexual revolutionaries throw the charge of homophobia at anyone who opposes homosexuality, theistic Christians have reason to resist acceptance of homosexuality in Western society. While not all homosexuals are overtly anti-Christian—indeed some claim to be Christian—one may not underestimate the role of homosexual theory in the normalization of paganism in the Christian West.

Friedrich Nietzsche was the nineteenth-century philosopher who called for the total overthrow of Christianity, the transvaluation of values (that is, calling good evil and evil good) and the rediscovery of polytheism. Some believe he was a homosexual.[68] The contemporary pagan revival reveres Nietzsche as one of the movement's great patron saints, whose time has now come.[69] If homosexuality is to monism what heterosexuality is to theism, then the transvaluation of sexual values will lead to paganism. Sexuality and spirituality are profoundly related. Harry Britt, gay activist, San Francisco supervisor and ex-Methodist minister, recently admitted as much when he described the struggle for gay liberation as "spiritual warfare."[70]

It is little wonder that a leading voice in the contemporary deconstruction of Western Christendom was the French homosexual, Michel Foucault. Foucault sought to deconstruct the value system of heterosexuality by arguing that truth is only power and that heterosexual values are a power play of the majority imposed upon the homosexual minority. Reducing truth and morals to power has created a place in the culture wars for homosexuals. Gay-bashing is a heinous crime, but so are homosexual bully tactics. Naked power describes the constant, violent persecution of a Protestant pastor, Charles McIlhenny, and his family, who for a number of years have opposed the gay power that controls San Francisco's city government (police department, school board, fire department, health department and much of the religious community).[71] The McIlhenny's simple, disturbing testimony, hauntingly entitled, *When the Wicked Seize a City: A Grim Look at the Future and a Warning to the Church*, should alert all to the kind of "ethics" gays in power will eventually use. Any methods are fair to rid modern Western Sodom of this meddlesome priest. "Straight society," says McIlhenny, "is now out of power (in San Francisco) and without influence—living on the fringes of society."[72] He fears that San Francisco is a foretaste of what America will become.

The rejection of traditional values finds a certain expression in "evangelical" authoress Virginia Mollenkott, who, as an openly practicing lesbian with a new moral code, is now righteously committed to lying and deceiving to bring down the heteropatriarchal culture.[73] In spite of her Christian phrases, she has become a pagan monist, and in the monist circle, where evil is merely the dark side of the force, such "dark" power can be used to promote the new morality. After all, "good" and "evil" are only relatively fixed points on the ever-revolving monistic circle where all is one and one is all.

FEMINISM: A FOOTHOLD FOR PAGANISM IN THE CHURCH OF THE THIRD MILLENNIUM?

In the Gnostic texts found at Nag Hammadi, the dominant theme is asceticism, the refusal of all sexuality (see chapter 13). This has the appearance of Christian holiness and appealed to Christians living in the dissolute Greco-Roman pagan world. Kurt Rudolf posits that it was through asceticism that Gnosticism gained a foothold in the unsuspecting Church.[74] One may well wonder if in our day, through the Christian-sounding notions of gender liberation and egalitarian rights for all, neo-Gnostic New Age liberalism is succeeding in doing the same in an equally unsuspecting twentieth-century Church.

Strangely, much of the Christian literature seeking to appraise the New Age and the new paganism avoids one of their most fundamental themes, namely, the transformation of sexuality and the promotion of a woman as the autonomous savior figure of the race. Because the Church has bowed to societal pressures and bought into a certain kind of feminism, it seems blind to the stakes of this social revolution.

NO AGENDA

A member of the task force on sexuality for the Evangelical Lutheran Church of America, defending the statement's acceptance of masturbation and same-sex "marriage," said, and no doubt quite sincerely: "We are not coming in with an agenda."[75] That most people do not see any agenda is as disturbing as the agenda itself. Many Christian egalitarians believe in good faith that they can avoid contamination by this new religion while using the feminist critique to rid the faith of androcentric abuse and oppressive patriarchy. They want to eliminate the patriarchal husk of Christianity and retain the egalitarian kernel. The radical Jewish feminist Naomi Goldenberg is not convinced.

> The feminist movement in Western culture is engaged in the slow execution of Christ and Jahweh. Yet very few of the women and men now working for sexual equality within Christianity and Judaism realize the extent of their heresy.[76]

Christian feminists are rightly concerned to ask what is the timeless teaching of Scripture on male/female relationships and how the Christian gospel transforms male and female sinners. No doubt the traditional Church has many questions to ask itself. I trust Goldenberg is wrong and my feminist brothers and sisters are right. But the danger of throwing the baby out with the bath water is enormous, especially for following generations.[77] This issue must not be decided on the basis of "inner certainty" or "a sense of call" or "the tide of history" or "societal, democratic progress." The Gnostics could claim all that, and history has shown them to be profoundly wrong. The issue can only be decided on solid exegesis of Holy Scripture, and, alas, of that there is a great dearth. Thus, the danger is great that instead of a recovery of biblical sexuality, the result will be sexual and theological confusion and a failure to see the compromises with paganism in large sectors of the Church. Christians must realize that the religious feminist movement carries with it a frontal assault on the normativeness of creational heterosexuality and, beyond that, on God Himself as the Creator.[78] Its "liberating" fruit can only be destructive for both men and women.

There is an agenda: the theoretical ideal of the androgynous, sexually unfettered New Man of Aquarian liberalism. In its pristine purity, only the radical fringe followed by the intellectual and cultural elite actually believe and promote it as such. It is rather promoted via the emotive democratic notions of freedom and civil rights and pro-choice liberty. But behind popular debates about the place of women in military academies, about coed bathrooms and prisons, and about the determination of the Clinton Administration (through its Justice Department) to eliminate any state-recognized distinctions between men and women, hides a new definition of sexuality that slaps the face of the Creator God of Scripture. As doctrinaire radical feminists scream, "New Women, New Earth,"[79] we witness the stirrings of a revolution that will remake the world.

Perhaps this ideology is a fashionable fad of the effete elite. However, the Early Church's exposure to the Gnostic heresy is hardly encouraging. As one scholar said of Gnosticism, "This kind of gnosis (knowledge) was in the air they breathed and some of it entered their lungs."[80] Anyone from Tokyo will tell you that a few drops of poison can bring a nation to its knees. There is reason to think, as the Evangelical Lutheran situation indicates, that the agenda is already in the mainstream. Perhaps one percent of vocal radicals can infect an entire society and with it large sections of the Christian Church.

CHAPTER THIRTEEN

GNOSTIC SEXUALITY

Feminists . . . engage in dialogue outside [the Judeo-Christian] tradition, and never before allowed by it, [namely] dialogue with heresies . . . dialogue with pre-Christian and pre-biblical religion.

ROSEMARY RADFORD RUETHER[1]

RADICAL FREEDOM FROM THE GOD OF THE BIBLE

The image is unforgettable. As the Gnostic believer exits from the sacramental bridal chamber, having undergone the secret initiation of spiritual wedlock, he shakes his fist at the God of Scripture, the Creator and Law-giver, and declares himself free from His authority.[2] He does this to follow "Christ," the one who leads this ultimate rebellion against "the Almighty of chaos," the "Prime Begetter [or Archprogenitor] who is called Yaldabaoth."[3]

But I [Christ] came to take them [mankind] from their blindness so that I might educate them all about the God who is above all creation [the ultimate unknowable divine spirit]. Therefore trample their [the archons—the creator God and his angels] graves and humiliate their wicked designs, and break their yoke and cause to arise those who are mine. For I have given you the authority of the Sons of Light over everything to crush their power underfoot.[4]

The Masterless—this title, of a recent book on American history, expresses its author's belief that the story of civilization in the New World has been marked, on the one hand, by the eroding of the power of familial and local institutions and, on the other, by the rise of federal power and the autonomous citizen. Americans are *The Masterless*.[5] Oddly, this was the favorite self-designation of the ancient Gnostics.

This ancient liberation movement shook free from existing structures and traditions, especially the God of Scripture. The note of *autonomous* liberty is fundamental to the Gnostic self-understanding. They prided themselves on being a "kingless generation," beholden to no person, institution or tradition.[6]

Enter sex, as it always does when theology is involved. "Sex . . . is the means by which enslavement to the powers is perpetuated," says Douglas M. Parrot, one of the translators of the *Nag Hammadi* texts.[7] A program of sexual liberation is therefore an integral part of the Gnostic system. Liberation from enslavement is either the adoption of religious pagan sexuality, especially that expressed in the Mother goddess cults, or in the total rejection of sexuality.

PAGAN SEX FOR A HERESY: HOMOSEXUAL PRIESTS OF THE MOTHER GODDESS

Gnostics carried goddess worship and homosexuality into "Christianity."[8] This eloquent distortion of orthodox belief is instructive in our day when the same incredible phenomena are recurring.

Hippolytus (A.D. 170-236) reports that the serpent-worshiping, Naasene Gnostics (Hebrew *naas* means "snake") attended celebrations of the mysteries of the Great Mother in order to understand the "universal mystery."[9] Like modern syncretists, the Gnostics believed truth was one, to be found everywhere.

Hippolytus denounces as a fundamental error the Naasene attempt to Christianize and spiritualize a pagan perversion of the created order. In his eyes, and he was not alone in the Early Church, the spiritualizing of such humanistic thinking and practice in no way redeemed this borrowing as a possible Christian option.

An independent witness, the first-century Latin poet, Catullus, attended pagan cultic practices of goddess worship like those attended by the Gnostics. He graphically depicts the self-emasculation of Attis, lover of the goddess Cybele, whereby he becomes a "counterfeit woman." The poet portrays the act and its results:

> Attis, . . . exalted by amorous rage, his mind gone, . . .
> cut off his testicles with a sharp flint.
> She (the emasculated Attis) then, aware of her limbs without the man,
> While the ground was still spotted with fresh blood . . .
> (expressing regret for what he/she has done, says):
> There is nothing for me but misery.
> What shape is there that I have not had?
> A woman now, I have been man, youth and boy;
> I was athlete, the wrestler . . .
> Shall I be a waiting maid to the gods, the slave of Cybele?
> I a Maenad, I a part of myself, I impotent? . . .
> I regret now, now, what I have done, I repent of it, now!

Such equivocation stirs the wrath of Cybele:

> Cybele, letting her lions off the leash
> And urging forward the beast on her left hand,
> Said, "Get on, be fierce, see that he is driven mad;
> Make him insane enough to return to the forest;
> He has the impertinence to want to be out of my power. . . ."

The poem ends with the following three-line stanza:

> Great Goddess, Goddess Cybele, Goddess lady of Dindymus,
> May all your fury be far from my house.
> Incite the others, go. Drive other men mad.[10]

Another form of this cultic spirituality is found in Syria, where Cybele is called Rhea. According to this version, Rhea castrates Attis, who from that moment adopted a female lifestyle, put on women's clothes, and traveled through the ancient world singing the praises of Rhea. The *Galli* or effeminate itinerant priests of Rhea imitated precisely the deeds of the mythological Attis.[11]

The rites of initiation into the Cybele cult included baptism in the blood of a slaughtered bull or ram. This took place in a *taurobolium,* or pit. At the end of the ceremony sometimes certain "powers" of the sacrificial bull, no doubt the animal's genitals, were offered to the Mother of the gods, again a powerful symbol of male emasculation before the female divinity.[12] The obvious intentions and results of such cultic mythology and practice was the feminization and emasculation of men under the power of the goddess. One can only imagine what the revival of goddess worship in our time, in the name of Christianity, could do to our civilization.

These grotesque and perverted practices of *non-Christian* paganism are not included for sensationalism but because they constitute a particularly clear example of how paganism was introduced into Christianity. Hippolytus explains the Naasene procedure. Because they claimed that "everything is spiritual," *the Naasenes did not become Galli physically but rather spiritually*: "They only perform the functions of those who are castrated by abstaining from sexual intercourse."[13] The mythological story of the castration of Attis led the Naasenes to conclude that the image of emasculation was a symbol of salvation.[14]

So, concludes Hippolytus, the Naasene Gnostics imitate the Galli, the castrated priests of Cybele. "For they urge most severely and carefully that one should abstain, as those men (the Galli) do, from intercourse with women; their behavior otherwise . . . is like that of the castrated."[15] Hippolytus indicates that Naas was associated with both adultery and homosexuality, since the Serpent was said to have had relations with both Eve and Adam.[16] It is therefore possible that the Naasenes, who worshiped the Serpent, would have practiced some form of deviant sexuality.

GNOSTICISM AND PAGAN HOMOSEXUALITY

In the *Nag Hammadi* texts, one has to read between the lines for suggestions of homosexuality. The *Paraphrase of Shem* speaks of Sodom as the place of the revelation of the Spirit,[17] and the *Gospel of the Egyptians* traces the origin of the seed of Seth the Revealer to Sodom and Gomorrah.[18] The constant praise of "spiritual" homosexuality [androgyny], as the preferred "sexual" state beyond gender differences, certainly makes the likelihood of homosexual practice among some radical Gnostic groups a possibility.

The Church father Epiphanius who seems to have known radical Gnostic groups better than anyone, unambiguously affirms the practice of sodomy in some expressions of Gnosticism.

> These people [the Gnostic Carpocratians] perform everything unspeakable and unlawful, which is not right to mention, and every kind of homosexual act and carnal intercourse with women, with every member of the body.[19]

This accusation he also makes with respect to the Gnostic Nicolaitans[20] and the Borborites.[21]

Hippolytus's account of the Naasene adoption and spiritualization of the sexual perversions of the Cybele/Rhea goddess cult shows to what extent "Christian" Gnosticism was a variant of non-Christian paganism. The leading Gnostic specialists of a generation ago would have agreed.[22] The theological agenda behind this negation of sexuality is the transformation of creation. Through the mysteries of the Great Mother disclosed to the Egyptians and the Phrygians, these so-called Christian Gnostics come to understand "the universal mystery," i.e., what is true in all religions, viz., "The process of change is displayed by the ineffable, unimaginable, inconceivable, formless being transforming creation."[23] Through pagan sexual perversion the Gnostics discover the divine, which is the unknowable, ineffable spiritual Force of monism, not the Creator and Redeemer of Scripture.

Hippolytus's 1800-year-old example illuminates our present situation. Many seek to recuperate pagan goddess spirituality in order to create a new-look Christianity in step with an ecofeminist, post-patriarchal society. The God of Scripture is ditched for the divine spirit in all things.

The Early Church fathers saw the profound logic in the deconstructionist theology of Gnosticism with regard to sexuality. So should we. The logic builds like this:

- the rejection of God the Creator and the establishment of human independence;
- the denunciation of creational sexuality;
- an elaboration of various forms of androgyny.

REJECTION OF GOD THE CREATOR

The Gnostic system achieves human independence by eliminating God the Creator, the so-called world ruler or Archon. The vehemence of this ancient heresy's rejection is comparable to the prevalent feminist rejection of this same Old Testament "patriarchal" God.[24] Indeed, the parallels are eerily striking. The term "patriarchy" is composed of two Greek words—*pater* (father) and *archon* (authority/ruler). For the ancient Gnostic, liberation comes by shaking one's fist at the archon/creator; for the modern feminist, liberation comes from the rejection of the patri-archon. Today the great "evil" of patriarchy is identified as the sinful structure prohibiting humanity's true freedom. Gnosticism identified the archons (God and his angels) as the great obstacle to authentic, unfettered existence of the Gnostic believer, who "stands alone" (*monachos*).[25] This "standing alone" or autonomy (a law to oneself) produces autarchy (rule by the self).

Such autarchy is an early rejection of the creational structures of patriarchy. The elimination of both God the Father and the dismissal of biological fatherhood and reproduction was as much a powerful polemic against patriarchy as any modern feminist diatribe.

As a counterpoint to this theme of autarchy went the theme of superman (hyperanthropos).[26] According to the *Apocryphon of John*, Adam is superior to the God who created him.[27] Superior to the male Archon, this "creature" knows himself to be a "solitary one"; that is, one standing alone, possessing autonomous power, related only to the unknown god within. This fundamental theological autonomy must be understood sexually.

DENUNCIATION OF CREATIONAL SEX

The *Gospel of Thomas* takes the teaching of Jesus that places all family relationships in *subordination* to the eventual demands of the kingdom of God, and makes of it a Gnostic principle for the outright *rejection* of natural family ties.[28]

The Gnostic is *monachos*, "standing alone," with regard to family and sexual ties. Many claim that *Thomas* is not a radical expression of Gnosticism, but on this subject, this apocryphal gospel is notably extreme. In saying 105, Jesus teaches: "The one who is acquainted with father and mother will be called the son of a prostitute." In saying 101, the living Jesus denies any value in physical fathers and mothers, and opts for his "spiritual mother."[29]

The Gnostic *Apocryphon of John* teaches that sexual intercourse is evil: "Up to today sexual intercourse continued due to the First Archon."[30] The *Book of Thomas the Contender* teaches that intercourse produces beasts and that the elect must "abandon bestiality."[31] "Woe to you," the text continues, "who love sexual relations with women and defiled intercourse with them."[32] In the *Dialogue of the Savior*, Matthew recalls one of the commands of Jesus: "Annihilate the works which pertain to the woman (that is, childbearing) . . . so that they (the works) may cease."[33] The *Authoritative Teaching* denigrates the body: "The body came from sexual desire, and sexual desire came from . . . matter."[34] The *Paraphrase of Shem* speaks of Nature and her "unclean femininity," Nature's "dark vagina,"[35] and the "intercourse of Darkness" which will be destroyed at the end of time." *Zostrianos* tells the Gnostic believer: "Flee from the insanity and fetters of femaleness, and embrace instead the salvation of maleness."[36]

These citations, from a variety of Gnostic documents, are not expressions of male chauvinism (though doubtless there was some of that) but are denunciations of the created order of heterosexuality and the bearing of children. Though *apparently* deriving from a quite different agenda, the end result has deep concordance with today's rejection of heteropatriarchy, motherhood, the traditional family and the right to abortion on demand—because they flow from the same spiritual source.

AN ELABORATION OF ANDROGYNY: SPIRITUAL MARRIAGE

Denying creational sexuality, the Gnostics substituted a new kind of sexuality, symbolized by their sacrament of the "Bridal Chamber."[37] In the holy marriage with the new Christ, the Gnostic believer swears to destroy all that God has made. In particular he swears to join together what God had put asunder and thus to destroy the Creator through his works, in particular, the work of created sexuality.

The *Gospel of Philip* identifies sexual distinction as the cause of death.

> When Eve was still in Adam, death did not come into being. When she was divided from him, death came into being. If he goes in again, attaining his former self, death will not exist any more.[38]

Establishing this completeness is the point of the coming of Christ. "For this purpose, Christ came to reverse the division which was from the beginning and again join the two, and give life to those who died as a result of the division and join them. But the woman is joined to her husband in the wedding chamber. Indeed, those who have joined in the wedding chamber will no longer be divided."[39]

Though on the surface less radical, the *Gospel of Thomas* is similarly driven by the androgynous ideal and the refusal of femininity and motherhood. Doubtless representing the goal of the gospel, the last saying, 114, holds out for the believer the attainment of an androgynous or sexless state.

> Simon Peter said to them: "Mary should depart from us, for women are not worthy of life." Jesus said, "I, myself will draw her, to cause her to become male, that she may also become a living spirit that is like you males. For each woman who will make herself male will enter the kingdom of heaven."

Saying 114 should be understood in the light of saying 22: "Jesus said to them, 'When you make the two as one, and when you make the inside like the outside, and the outside like the inside, and the above like the below, and when you make the male and female one and the same, so that the male may not be male nor the female be female; . . . then will you enter [the kingdom].'" Both these sayings suggest the "neutralization" of sexuality so that the ideal for Gnostics is to become sexless.[40] *Thomas* is *not* a macho attack on women, as Pagels rightly sees.[41] It is a rejection of creational sexuality, a radical refusal of sexual differentiation, as presented in the Genesis account.[42]

When *Thomas* says that females will first become males in order then to become "living spirits," he is speaking about a "backwards" creation, which undoes the original order: from the female rib into the male Adam, back into the "living spirit."[43] Thus Gnostic women become "autonomous males,"[44] and together with males, become "living spirits" beyond sexual differentiation. In this implosion of creation, the two become one by destroying differentiation in a return to unity: the monistic ideal.

The Living Jesus of the *Gospel of Thomas* declares that only the "solitary (*monachos*) will enter the bridal chamber."[45] In other words, only autonomous egalitarian beings can find true spirituality. Just what this Jesus of *Thomas* means is clear in his teaching to Salome. To her he declares himself to be he who "exists from the Whole (or the Undivided)." Salome responds with the confession, "I am your disciple," to which Jesus replies with a statement of pure Gnostic principle: "If he [the Gnostic disciple] is [undivided (or destroyed)], he will be filled with light, but if he should become divided, he will be filled with darkness."[46]

Salome has done what *Zostrianos* recommends, as noted above: "Flee from the insanity and the fetters of femaleness, and embrace instead the salvation of maleness."[47] Salome is the ideal disciple, the liberated, autonomous, egalitarian Gnostic, untrammeled by the sexual distinctions of the original creation. Standing alone she has moved beyond the bondage of her sex. She has become spiritually androgynous.

ANDROGYNY: NEITHER MALE NOR FEMALE, QUITE THE CONTRARY

Gnosticism was not simply a movement of sexual freedom. At a deeper level, it was the introduction of monistic, pagan thinking about God into Christian theism. Noted scholar Giovanni Filoramo speaks of the "androgynous god of the Gnostics," who expresses the "concept of *coniunction oppositorum*, or joining of opposites, to embody the conquest of all duality."[48] There are many texts illustrating this Gnostic monism.[49] In the same way, contemporary feminism is not just about sexuality. The new religious feminism seeks to move beyond God the Father to an imagery of bisexual androgynous deity by "reintroducing the image of god as female to complement the image of God as male."[50] Androgyny has deep religious meaning, and the Gnostic texts ring the changes on this mysterious theme. In *On the Origin of the World* Sophia (Wisdom) outfoxes Yahweh and his angels by creating a man who would instruct the wretched creatures to despise the god who created them (Yahweh) and thus escape from his clutches. After 12 months she produced an "androgynous man . . . whom the Greeks call Hermaphrodite." He was to be "the Teacher." This "son" of Sophia is called "the beast" by Yahweh and his hordes but he is "wiser than all of them."[51] In other words, Christ, the androgynous son, first appeared as the serpent-teacher of Genesis 3.

We have already seen in *Thunder, Perfect Mind* that Sophia herself is an androgynous being who joins male and female together—and everything else as well, including truth and iniquity. This is a perfect expression of monism.[52] Note how *Sophia* joins not just the opposites of sexuality but all the aspects of existence. Androgyny is thus the sexual expression of a deeply religious agenda, that of pagan monism.

Sophia makes an even more sexually explicit statement of androgyny in a text already cited, *Trimorphic Protennoia*.[53]

> I am gynandrous (or androgynous) [I am Mother, I am] Father since [I] [have coitus] with myself. I [have coitus] with myself [and the ones who love] me [and] I am the one through whom the All [endures]. I am the womb [that gives form] to the All by birthing the Light that [shines in] glory.[54]

Androgyny is thus the ideal, as in today's new Aquarian humanity. Having mocked the God who created heterosexuality, the Gnostics propose the opposite as an act of defiance. Sexual rebellion in Gnosticism runs the gamut—from the denial of sexuality and femininity, especially child-bearing and motherhood (as part of the Archon's works and pomps),[55] to heterosexual license,[56] and even, perhaps, to homosexuality. The destruction of normative, creational sexuality has as its ultimate goal the joining of the opposites in androgyny, as the *Apocalypse of James* so eloquently puts it: "The perishable has [gone up] to the imperishable and the female element has attained to this male element."[57] This is the return to the supposed original androgynous state of Genesis 1, where God created man, male and female, an androgynous being.[58]

FROM THEORY TO PRACTICE: THE PLACE OF GNOSTIC WOMEN

Whether in mild or extreme form, Gnostic practice is a logical extension of its theory. If every Gnostic, male or female, is autonomous, and if differentiated sexuality is unspiritual, then a radical egalitarianism is the necessary result. If gender hierarchy and subordination are the accursed work of the evil Archon, they must be eliminated. Epiphanes, an early Gnostic teacher, proposes an extreme egalitarian communism.

> The righteousness of God is a communion with equality, for heaven, equally stretched out on all sides like a circle embraces the whole earth ... God makes no distinction between ... male and female ... he declared righteousness to be fellowship with equality ... that he [the Jewish lawgiver] said "thou shalt not covet" [is] laughable ... that he said "your neighbor's wife" is even more laughable, since he compels what was common possession to become private property.[59]

The egalitarian view of the sexes and ethics in general, according to Rudolf, brings the Gnostics to an "inversion of values" and the removal of earthly distinctions.[60] Tertullian denounces a much less extreme form of the rejection of distinctions which had practical implications in Church life:

> They maintain [ecclesiastical] harmony with all, making no distinction. As a matter of fact, it [harmony] exists among them although they hold different doctrines as long as they wage common warfare against one thing, the truth [orthodoxy]. They are all puffed up, all promise "knowledge." Their catechumens are already perfected before they are taught. Even the heretical women ... make bold to teach, to dispute, to perform exorcisms, to promise cures, perhaps also to baptize.[61]

Historians note that women frequently occupied leading positions as teachers and prophetesses or played a leading role in cultic ceremonies as a way of rejecting the creational distinctions.[62] The Gnostic Marcus practiced not only the prophetic ordination of women but had them function also as priests.[63] The authoritative function of teacher is granted to women through the inversion of the Genesis account where Eve is represented as the teacher of Adam.[64] Is this why Saint Paul insists that women should not teach men in the Church?[65] This inverted exegesis is put into practice in the *Nag Hammadi Gospel of Mary*, where Mary instructs Peter and the other apostles with hidden knowledge the Lord revealed only to her.[66] Mary stands up and demands that all praise the Lord's greatness, for he "has prepared us [and] made us into men."[67]

Andrew identifies what Mary says as "strange ideas,"[68] and Peter cannot believe that the Lord would speak privately with a woman.[69] Levi states that "the Savior knows her very well. That is why he loved her more than us." Peter then begs Mary to tell the words of the Savior, and Mary replies that she will reveal to Peter what was hidden.[70] In this strand of Gnosticism, Christ is building his Church not on Peter but on Mary Magdalene.

Kurt Rudolf and Elaine Pagels, both liberal theologians and recognized experts in the field of Ancient Gnosticism, affirm that the Gnostic *practice* was a consistent application of Gnostic *theory*. "Many gnostic Christians," says Pagels, "correlate their description of God in both masculine and feminine terms with a complimentary description of human nature . . . [and] often take the principle of equality between men and women [based on an androgynous notion of creation] into the social and political structures of their communities."[71] Rudolf argues that dominance of female deities in the Gnostic story translates into female religious power in the Gnostic churches.[72] The same Gnostic theory is back in town. Is there any reason to be surprised that the Gnostic practice is back too?

CHAPTER FOURTEEN

THE NEW SPIRITUAL EXPERIENCE

There is no help from within—without the supernatural
the natural is a pit of horror.

JOHN UPDIKE[1]

IN THE BEGINNING WAS THE
EXPERIENCE: EMBRACED BY THE LIGHT

Whatever turns you on" aptly expresses modern tolerance of experience, in terms reminiscent of an LSD high. Drugs turned on people's lights in the '60s, and still do. According to Marilyn Ferguson, researchers can produce mystical experiences, almost at will. After submitting to an "Altered State of Consciousness Inducing Device" (ASCID—apparently the pun is intended), a willing human guinea pig described the trip in glowing terms:

There was a tremendous slow-motion kind of explosion and upsurge and outgo of energy all around and from the point where the light disappeared. It was incredible. Then the circle grew and grew to infinite proportions within me, and all the sound was white. It was a silent Beethoven symphony throbbing all over the place. . . . I grew huge and transparent, filled and permeated with the light and the fire. And I thought: My God is a God of Love and he lives within me.[2]

Betty Eadie, author of *Embraced by the Light*, a best-seller even among Christians, describes her "near-death" experience in a strikingly similar way:

I saw a pin-point of light in the distance, . . . and felt myself traveling . . . at an even greater speed, rushing toward [it]. . . . As I approached it, I noticed the figure of a man [Jesus Christ] standing in it. . . . As I got closer the light became brilliant . . . beyond any description, far more brilliant than the sun. . . . a brilliant, magnificent whiteness that extended out for some distance. I felt his light blending into mine . . . And as our lights merged, . . . I felt an utter explosion of love.[3]

Everybody wants an experience like that. Apparently both New Agers and Christians can have it. Who would opt for *faith* if you could genuinely have *knowledge* like that? The feeling of flying through the clouds in mind-blowing ecstasy, with no hint of fear, in touch with God and one's true self. . . . Sounds like heaven on Earth. If you could bottle the formula, market possibilities would go off the charts. People have, of course. Especially New Age gurus, for $350 a weekend.

In the new religion *everything* exists to create this experience, as the feminist wing concedes with characteristic clarity. "Wild women" speak of the discovery of a "spiritual tradition as women," which they find/create "in new translations, new interpretations, new language . . . new namings of the holy . . . expressed in a vast array of religious forms . . . [and] new images of God."[4] The ideas we have already studied—the new Bible and Bible study method, the new humanity and the new God—have been created from a new experience. All produce a "new theological paradigm" which both creates and perpetuates the experience.[5] The new paradigm leads to a "paradigm shift," a leap into a new perception of reality for the sake of a "new spiritual experience." In describing ancient pagans, David Wells notes that they "proceeded from the basis of their experience to understand the supernatural."[6] So it is with the religious quest of our modern world. The contemporary *experience* of liberation is "revelation" and "truly . . . redemptive."[7] This experience is, in essence, a rediscovery of the spirituality of ancient paganism, as one "gentle, smiling, silver-haired" Roman Catholic sister explained.

> The whole word [pagan] is taking on new meaning, [it is] being redeemed . . . It is not the belief we condemned in the past . . . I believe that was where Jesus was coming from . . . We *are* part of the earth, and we must work out our evolution into the beings we must become, in harmony with the earth.[8]

Personal experience is raised to a formal philosophical principle by theorists of pagan witchcraft: "Subjectivity, we must know, is the only state of experience in the universe. The only state of being is as the subject experiencing itself and the world, from within."[9] All the blocks fit together to undergird this "new" way of encountering the divine, even if Jesus becomes a pagan. For in our day, as in the heyday of paganism, experience is queen.

THE APPEAL OF THE NEW RELIGIOUS EXPERIENCE: VIRTUAL SPIRITUAL REALITY

Sister Madonna, a feminist nun, sees the new spirituality as world-creating:

> The sign of ultimate religious experience will surely be . . . its power to release truly spiritual redemptive energies. . . . In this "truly catholic" New Faith . . . the Church will wither away, made unnecessary by the direct illumination of "a creative Spiritual Presence that comes from *within* them as well as from *beyond*.[10]

Sister Madonna first rejects "the spirituality of this 'false god' [God the Father of the Bible]" who has "created the world we live in. . . . Spirituality of a different kind will create the world we want to live in."[11]

The self-focused religious experience that will save the world, seen in the light of its pagan roots, is appalling. Most moderns, ignorant of this family background, find this spirituality alluring. Those raised on instant coffee, instant mashed potatoes, instant entertainment at the push of a remote control and instant gratification in virtual reality, will find the ecstatic spirituality of the new religion appealing. What's more, it offers immediate success for the problems of our stressful world.

Some health-care experts foresee the coming of "the Age of Anxiety"—created, ironically enough, by the "age of therapy." The National Institute of Mental Health (NIMH) estimates that 24 million people suffer from anxiety disorders and see in newer, more spiritual techniques like massage and yoga, significant ways of avoiding the "stress monster."[12] The reduction of stress is power. Power makes winners out of victims, and is ultimately religious. Instant religious power is a consumer product whose day has hardly begun.

The new spirituality promises apocalypse now, ecstasy now—you can have it all and you can have it now. Deferred pleasure went out of style with Woodstock and Roe versus Wade. In the TV movie *Thorn Birds*, everyone resonates with the justification given to his bishop by the Roman cleric caught with his pants down: "I never felt such ecstasy as I felt with her."

Roof's study of Boomers found that only 4 percent were atheistic or agnostic. These products of the '60s revolution do not want a lifestyle with no "transcendent symbol," no "overarching 'sacred canopy,' " to use the sociologist's terminology.[13] The "me-generation" of the '60s finds regeneration in the new spirituality, which one observer calls "transformed narcissism," by which God and the self become interchangeable. There is "a new emphasis on God—[but] as the accessible self." "Accessibility must involve alternative ways of experiencing the sacred. . . . [for] we all access God differently."[14] The pro-choice envelope for religion expands to include syncretism and polytheism.

The Loss of Traditional Faith

As a schoolboy, I was hopeless in math and science. I still am, as my family will attest. There is one scientific law that I still remember, however: nature abhors a vacuum. It seems that spirit does, too. The loss of traditional faith and religious experience creates a void that makes the "new" religious experience especially appealing. The Eastern worldview that has flooded into the West since the '60s fills the void. It teaches that the created world is an illusion. In its classic expression, Hinduism,

Maya is the power of God, which creates the illusion of a differentiated universe and conceals the divine unity behind appearances, while ignorance creates the seemingly separate self at the individual level.[15]

This is unadulterated monism, to be found equally clearly in modern feminism, witchcraft and in New Age "Christian" and pagan thinking. Its glittering but false promise is to reconnect our fragmented selves to our higher, better selves and to reconnect us all to the fragmented cosmos. This is a heady brew for the spiritually thirsty who have lost connection with traditional faith.

Witches, Nuns, Gurus and Evangelicals

If God is not a reality outside ourselves, the good news is: The only god to know, the only divine will to obey, the only spiritual imperative to heed is found within the human soul. Clear statements of this monistic view abound, from all otherwise disparate sources:

From modern pagan proponents of witchcraft:
The truth is that "God" is not in a book—"holy," golden, or otherwise. God is not in a church, a cathedral, a synagogue, a mosque. . . . God is the universe. We are all now living inside the body of God. There is nowhere to go to get there, we are already here. There is nowhere to go to get outside of God; there is just a forgetting of this truth. It is impossible not to be living, right now and always, within God's body. It is only possible to be aware, or unaware, of this fact.[16]

From two leading feminist Roman Catholic nuns:
We cannot seek God as an object separate from our world, outside our lived experience, . . . God is experienced not so much as a separate being, but God is sensed as the deepest dimension of our own being. What we find is not God but *ourselves*. . . . The process of self-knowledge is the process of knowing God.[17]

God, who has been imprinted in our minds as a transcendent absolute, must somehow be recovered in an epiphany of immanence, of divine self-revelation.[18]

From a liberal "Christian" New Ager:
Since the unconscious is God all along, we may further define the goal of spiritual growth to be the attainment of godhood by the conscious self. It is for the individual to become totally, wholly god.[19]

From an "Evangelical" New Ager:
The Ultimate, the Sacred, God Herself is everywhere at the core of everything and everyone (including me).[20]

The theoretical structure of the new spirituality is the reduction of God to the human self. Theory is never neutral, and this theory has as its aim the salvation of mankind and the planet.

THE AIM OF THE NEW RELIGIOUS EXPERIENCE

The goal of salvation contains various aspects—utopia, power, knowledge and transformation. To understand the appeal and the workings of this spirituality, one needs to grasp how these aspects function in the system.

Utopia:

The new religious experience is driven by a noble goal, the eradication of oppression and the establishment of a just human society. Who has not imagined an idyllic, rosy future, with no fear, no death, no hell, no crying, no oppression, no rules nor limits, no IRS nor speed limits and no comprehensive health insurance (no one will ever be ill?) But be careful—Pinocchio believed, and turned into a donkey.

John Lennon asked us to imagine an earthly paradise with no heaven and no hell; it is the refrain of the new Western gurus who believe the new world order will come about as more people get turned on to spiritual power.

Power: Masters of Our Own Destiny

Gurus of the new religious experience make no bones about the grab for power: "Whether or not we become all that we may be is up to us. We have been given every opportunity and facility. But we have also been given mastery of our own destiny."[21]

Morrison calls it right: *"Mastery of our own destiny"*. Here we have the fountainhead of all Gnostic teaching—the nuts and bolts of the 'Satanic Initiation' which our first parents received in the Garden of Eden."[22] The first sin, which determines all others, is the desire for an independent, autonomous existence beyond the Word of God. The taste of illegitimate power is intoxicating. Says Virginia Mollenkott:

> Spirituality refers to our ways of believing, belonging, and responding to the power and presence of Divinity, Holiness, the Higher Power, the All-Inclusive One who connects us spiritually to one another and the whole ecosystem. The experience of connectedness is too empowering and joyous to relinquish for any reason.[23]

I have on my desk a glossy magazine called *Shaman's Drum: A Journal of Experimental Shamanism*. Its editorial board has 18 members, 14 of whom have doctorates. This ancient occult practice is doing well in the sophisticated academic world of "Christian" America. Shamanism facilitates contact with the spirit world, and the spirituality accruing is power. Once the domain of the witch doctor, shamanistic power is now available to all—at a small fee (major credit cards accepted). New Age guru and channeler, Lazaris, promises a significant return on your investment: "Conjuring Power: Engaging and Enlisting the Elements" is what your dollars buy. As the brochure explains:

> We seek a deeper, more beautiful spirituality. . . . Conjuring power, an ancient tool of the Shamaness and Shaman, an ancient secret of the mystic and the magician, is too frequently a lost art today. It sounds too clandestine, too "occult," or too old for most of us. [But] Lazaris will lift the essence of what it was and show us an incredible new way. A lost art can become a vibrant new tool in our lives and in our modern world where "practice is over."[24]

"Practice is over." The war has begun. Occult power is nothing less than the Serpent's seductive lie. The lie refuses to reveal to people the truth about themselves, and parades, in particular, as knowledge of the goddess, who holds out a glittering promise of personal transformation.

Shamanism, inspiration, mysteries of drunkenness, vision, madness, ecstasy leading to expansions of consciousness—these are the transformative processes of the Goddess.[25]

Transformation: "No Fear"

Evil is difficult to explain, but no one has difficulty understanding the phrase "the power of evil." The *New Age Encyclopedia* states that

> The New Age Movement can be defined by its primal experience of transformation. . . . Having experienced a personal transformation, New Agers project the possibility of the transformation not just of a number of additional individuals, but of the culture and of humanity itself. . . . (it) has (also) become a movement to heal the earth.[26]

"Christian" feminist Rosemary Radford Ruether recalls her "great excitement" when a course on comparative religion gave her a "new orientation" toward religion as a "metaphor for inner transformation" rather than as a body of revealed truth.[27] Christianity offers transformation, but *this* transformation is not Christian. It was "comparative religions"; that is, paganism, that transformed Ruether. "You gotta serve somebody!"

NO FEAR!! scream the decals from T-shirts and pickup trucks. No fear of life, but especially no fear of death. In the union with the Higher Self and the spirit world, death, the ultimate "stress monster," is relativized. As the father in *Lion King* tells the young cub and future king, as well as millions of young Americans, death holds no fear because we are one with the evolutionary, life-giving process.

God lied. "You will not die." Here is the serpent's promise of eternal life. "Eat and your eyes will be opened."[28] Occult knowledge is transformation into immortality. In this version, death is not the "sting" of the "last enemy."[29] There is no hell. Death is not eternal separation from God. It is the "final state of growth . . . the awakening of the True Self to a higher reality." So says Elisabeth Kübler-Ross, with the help of her spirit-guide, Salem.[30] Many books on near-death experiences, including Christian versions,[31] describe death as a wonderful experience of peace, joy and light. We no longer need Lennon helping us imagine no hell. Near-death experiences prove that there is only love and light.

We don't have to wait for death. Immortality is available now, in ecstatic moments of pure spirit. Says Elizabeth Clare Prophet, a "Christian New Age" teacher in Montana,

> You can pray, you can meditate, you can contact God. The God of very gods is within you. You can make contact if you will it so . . . Jesus is the open door to the individual Christ consciousness—the kingdom of God that is, even now, within you.[32]

Because *self*-transformation includes the transformation of humanity and the planet, spiritual narcissism becomes altruism. Meditation on the self is selfless. It not only eliminates stress but saves the earth. Such is the promise and function of the new spirituality, but how is it practiced?

THE PRACTICE OF THE NEW SPIRITUALITY

Like most human experiences (with the exception of the dentist's chair), the new spirituality is both communal and individual. Usually the community initiates individuals into the secret methods which they then use for personal spiritual advancement. Just as true spirituality affirms both the "communion of the saints" in the Church and a personal devotion to the Lord, so false spirituality has its "churches" and "quiet times."

Isis Visits Chicago

I managed to find a seat in the back left corner of the room, a long way from the door, and began to wonder whether my courage had exceeded my wisdom. As an observer at the Parliament of the World's Religions, I judged it important to observe as much as I could, so here I was in a seance/presentation of the Fellowship of Isis, a modern revival of the Egyptian cult to the goddess Isis. A frail but intense priestess from England, with pale skin—perhaps from countless drenchings of dreary British rain—now resplendent in white, began to recount the myth of Isis and her consort Osiris, as recorded in the ancient text *The Golden Ass*. Suddenly she was caught up in an ecstatic trance and spoke, in powerful wailing tones, a revelation in the name of Isis. Everyone then joined hands (I remained transfixed in my corner, trying to look inconspicuous) in the circle of life, inhaling and exhaling deeply. It was then the turn of a young black American immediately in front of me to enter a trancelike state and utter his soul-devotion to the goddess. All eyes turned on him (and many on me!). Fortunately he was followed by a Japanese priest of Isis doing the same on the other side of the room. I pinched myself, remembering that we were in the luxurious Palmer House in downtown Chicago. I managed to slip out before the séance passed from the "first chamber," open to the world, into the "second chamber" for initiated Isis followers only.

An elaborate process, initiation includes the creation of new stories and rituals, and the acceptance of polytheism, and leads to a consciousness-raising experience that can only be called a "conversion."

New Stories

Even the modern pagan experience requires stories or myths to create a context in which spiritual initiation takes place. A number of the examples given below come from radical religious feminism. This is so for a number of reasons: Feminism provides an encounter with the new spirituality; feminism is an especially powerful vehicle for the introduction of paganism into the Church because of its belief in the equality of males and females; New Age prophets declare the Age of Aquarius to be the age of feminist intuition/experience, so it is not surprising that women are leading the crusade to create new images. Indeed the radical feminist claims special knowledge; her "feminist consciousness" is a sort of gnosis, enabling her for the first time to give a true account of the relations of men and women;[33] feminists themselves gladly claim the leadership of the new religion.

Women Spinning New Stories

Like few others, feminists recognize the importance of new myths and devote great energy to create them. Women are "renaming," "re-imagining" the world from the feminist perspective. God, the "male" Father is "exorcised" in favor of the goddess. The language is strong, and so is the program. "Radical transformation" brings Scripture into line with feminist attitudes and gives women a voice. Women are encouraged to write apocryphal Bible stories with women as heroines—that's right, just make them up![34] Genesis is reinterpreted to elevate Eve as the heroine, and the Serpent is celebrated as the true instructor in wisdom (see chapter 8). Creation includes the mysterious Lilith, known in Scripture as a "night hag" but now reinterpreted as Eve's higher self, who comes to her in the Serpent and liberates her from the control of Adam and God.[35] The program notes of a recent "Christian" feminist conference invites conferees to create a new symbolic world:

> TOGETHER—combining ancient text and modern dreams . . . dance, drama and ritual, we shall draw aside a curtain woven by patriarchal consciousness to reveal within each of us the Goddesses and the Wild Woman.
>
> TOGETHER we shall reckon with Her dark side and honor Her bright side. Related to one another, we shall draw Her energy into our souls and celebrate Her return to our lives.[36]

The products of such "Christian" re-imagining are often expressions of radical paganism. The following is a typical example, a prayer in poetic form to the unknown goddess, suggested as material for the renewal of Christian feminist worship:

> Lady, the unknown goddess, we have prayed long enough only to Yahweh the thunder god. Now we should pray to you again, goddess of a thousand names and faces, Ceres, Venus, Demeter, Isis, Dianna Queen of Heaven, or by whatever name you would be known.[37]

This poetic ritual, invoking many goddesses, was not composed "primarily for women who have moved beyond the structures of the Christian Church," says Anglican minister, William Oddie. It is published in a book which aims to create "materials for prayer, meditation and worship drawn from women's experiences of the holy to provide ways to *enrich the Christian tradition*." This material is offered, by women of impeccable (Christian) "establishment" credentials, as "an excellent resource for any congregation wishing to undertake the difficult task of changing the image of God in its liturgy."[38]

Rosemary Radford Ruether gives the now classic feminist line: "These new stories do not necessarily repudiate the old stories, but they may well enable us to reconceptualize them."[39] Presbyterian and Methodist feminists said the same when they worshiped the goddess Sophia in Minneapolis. A book on experimental feminist worship, from the same radical perspective as that of the RE-Imagining Conference, claimed only to be "revitalizing traditional liturgical expressions."[40] But as this poem makes so abundantly clear, such re-imagining was not enriching Christian conceptuality. Like most expressions of this new spirituality, it was an exercise in unadulterated pagan polytheism. When you join monism and theism, monism wins every time, for the God of heaven and Earth will not share His glory with another.

The electronic gaudiness of the Las Vegas Strip and its larger-than-life casinos disorient the mind. In its unbelievably glitzy, fairy-tale atmosphere of constant fun and continuous daylight, people lose their bearings. Squandering hard-earned cash against impossible odds at the betting tables becomes strangely feasible.

Such is the function of the new stories. The new religion seeks to make its constructions perfectly believable and everything before it a bad dream. This is the first phase of consciousness alteration. Step into the shimmering house of the gods, and you will be drawn into occult initiation, happy to let go the hard-earned cash of revealed truth and the rich experience of creational wisdom.[41]

New Rituals

New stories and openness to the spirituality of other religions produces new rituals. Miriam Starhawk, who teaches with the ex-Dominican, now Episcopalian Matthew Fox, is a goddess-worshiping pagan witch. Her book *Spiral Dance* contains an account of *wiccan* ritual, defined as four procedures: 1) relaxation, 2) concentration, 3) visualization and 4) projection or manifestation.[42] These stages are the goals of wiccan rituals, designed for creating altered states of mind and for practicing magic. Witches cast a "sacred circle" to create a "sacred space" or "portable temple" for the proceedings. Then they "go within" or "center the energy," in order to inform the "forces of the universe" that are being called. This is followed by "raising energy," drawing it up from the earth through "guided meditation," dance or shouting. Later, the "energy" is "directed" through a "cone of power" to the object of "magick."[43] Such pagan witchcraft is an important aspect of much of contemporary radical religious feminism.

We shall observe in the next chapter that the ancient Gnostics frequented the mystery cults to share in the pagan rituals and discover the pagan experience of spirituality. We observe the same phenomenon today. A stark example comes from the Presbyterian publishing house Westminster/John Knox. In a book entitled *Women at Worship* two Christian theologians, Marjorie Procter-Smith, associate professor of worship in the Perkins School of Theology at Southern Methodist University, and Janet R. Walton, associate professor of worship at Union Theological Seminary in New York, offer "glimpses of the changing scene of women at worship" who are claiming "ritual authority."[44] They propose to the Church, and to women in particular, selections from radical Jewish and Christian liturgies as well as pagan and African animistic rituals "for the learning of a new ritual language."[45] The old Gnostic "Christians" participating in pagan cults for deeper spiritual lessons is clearly not just a past memory.

The article by Wendy Hunter Roberts, a "Pagan (Unitarian) Universalist," entitled, "In Her Name: Towards a Feminist Theology of Pagan Ritual," catches the reader's attention. The ritual takes place at night at Samhain, the classic wiccan celebration of the winter solstice, and begins with the casting of the sacred circle and the invocation of the god and the goddess via the chant:

Magic, magic everywhere, in the earth and in the air,
How to hold the magic here?
How to raise it up and bring it down?

Then a priest "invokes the Goddess . . . in the priestess," and the priestess "evokes the Lord of the Underworld into a priest"[46] followed by welcoming of the "beloved dead"—Martin Luther King, Jr., Gandhi, Crooked Fox Woman, Elizabeth Cady Stanton, Margaret Sanger (founder of Planned Parenthood) and other worthies. Roberts notes that only the core initiates are permitted to enter "the holy of holies," for the symbol system is "sexually explicit" and "honors darkness and death," "birth and light" and "good and evil."

In the time of prayer, Roberts "call[s] out for protection of the Goddess's people from the wrath of right-wing fundamentalists and their God,"[47] but she recalls that while, in the past, "the patriarchal hordes" destroyed the temples and defamed the Goddess, there is great hope in the present. "Now we are returning."[48]

These pagans are returning within the Church as well, as the appearance of this article from a mainline denominational publisher testifies. For many "Christian" feminists, a Christianized form of witchcraft characterizes their new rituals, as Donna Steichen has demonstrated for the Roman Catholic church. She shows how the nuns are now into crystal reading, dream work, tarot cards and other New Age techniques for their spiritual quest.[49]

These techniques can be read between the lines in the liturgies practiced in Ruether's *Women-Church*. In "The Coming-Out Rite for a Lesbian," which is described as a "new birth," the lesbian praises the goddess, Sophia:

> It was [Dame] Wisdom who gave me true knowledge of all that is, who taught me the structure of the world and the properties of the elements, the beginning, end and middle of the times, the alternation of the solstices and the succession of the seasons, the revolution of the year and the position of the stars, the nature of animals and the instincts of wild beasts, the varieties of plants and the medicinal properties of roots. All that is hidden, all that is plain, I have come to know, Instructed by Wisdom who designed them all.[50]

The themes in this prayer—knowledge of the elements, astrology, animals, herbal medicines and the joining of the opposites—are all found in witchcraft, where the manipulation of elements is known as the "Craft."

Communal Ecstasy

Stories, rituals and witchcraft produce communal ecstasy. In the "first chamber" the Isis group at the Parliament of the World's Religions had already reached levels of spiritual ecstasy that caused me to head for the door. Another group studying new feminist rituals insisted that the doors be closed. I left that one just in time. Ruether describes what happens through the rituals:

> Awakening often occurs through mystical experiences in nature or with other women. . . . Awakening implies the ability to know or see within oneself, once the sleeping draft is refused. . . . For women, awakening is . . . a gaining of power . . . it is a grounding of selfhood in the powers of being.[51]

> Trust in yourself, believe in yourself. Bring that energy up, up, through your roots, into your body. Let it come in through the soles of your feet, rise up your body, all the way to your fingertips. That energy can handle whatever comes to you. All you need to do is call it

up. Feel the power of that energy. Now allow that energy to spiral around your spinal column, rising . . . and then allow the energy to sprout out your head as branches. . . . Feel your connection with the other women in the circle. . . . Be aware that this circle is not complete without your energy.[52]

The spiritual experience of communal power bonds people together and produce conversion or awakening or altered states of consciousness. "Once the individual feminist has been through the process known as 'consciousness-raising,'" says Oddie, "particularly by attending the women's groups whose purpose is to produce and maintain this psychological effect, it is not merely her understanding of social relationships which has changed, but her whole perception of reality. She has undergone a kind of *metanoia,* or conversion."[53] Feminists themselves speak of "a *conversion* to matriarchal imagery."[54] The power of the group is an essential ingredient, but the new spirituality must also be a personal, individual encounter with the cosmic Oneness. It produces formidable energized opponents to traditional Christian faith.

The pagan Roberts describes the very heart of the pagan goddess ritual. When all is ready, the goddess Hekate enters the circle. Her presence produces healing. Roberts describes the experience: "I place my head on her lap. . . . A roar forms in my belly, catches in my throat, then tears its way out through my vocal cords. I feel the tightness leaving me. . . . I am released."[55]

THE HEART OF THE MATTER: NONRATIONAL EXPERIENCE

Phil Jackson, NBA coach of the year ('95-'96) rediscovered his faith by joining Zen Buddhism to the charismatic Christianity of his youth. In his book *Sacred Hoops,* he credits Zen with clearing his mind of all the interference from Christian prayers and Bible verses, lodged in his brain since childhood. With his newfound "intuitive illumination of the mind and spirit through meditation," his heart is open again.[56] He teaches these winning principles to Michael Jordan, Scotty Pippen and Dennis Rodman. The formula works.

Ever heard of a charismatic Roman Catholic Hindu mystic? Here is the testimony of one concerning his disappointment with traditional forms of Christian devotion:

I began to find mental prayer [discursive meditation] completely
unproductive, and so . . . I stopped reflecting on the Scriptures during
prayer . . . [which was] an immense obstacle to experiencing God. . . .
Only total passivity to the kundalini experience brings serenity. Only
then, too, is there a sense of God's presence.[57]

In the newly discovered Easternized form of "Christian" meditation, which
seeks to realize the True Self, the "I Am," "there is a return to the cosmic experience of the Great Mother, as the 'I' now enjoys the energies of the Dynamic
Ground within."[58] "Kundalini dismantles the defense mechanisms. . . . Thus
open to the Dynamic Ground, the Ego stands disorientated and eventually
drops its conceptual ties."[59]

What is particularly Christian in this kind of meditation?[60]

Deepak Chopra, an Indian Hindu medical doctor and immensely successful New Age guru in the U.S.A, describes his suprarational experience in a similar way. In meditation, the higher self is "in contact with the cosmos and pure
being, beyond the boundaries of rational thought and all distinctions which
originate in nothingness and return there."[61]

This nonconceptual spiritual experience brings many into the enslavement
of spirits, for the witches have a very similar spirituality, and it indicates that
one is not alone in the cosmic All. Listen to a wiccan chant:

Know the mystery, that if that which thou seekest thou findest not within thee, thou will never find it without thee. . . . For behold I Have Been
With Thee From The Beginning. And I await thee now. Blessed Be.[62]

Just who is the "I" who has been there since the beginning? New Age channelers indicate that "going within" through the suspension of rational thought is
the perfect means for spirit possession. The spirit entities, speaking through
Ken Carey, make known their preference:

We are unable to commune with humans whose vibrational fields are
distorted by ego factors, emotional fields, excessive conceptualization,
or past-future orientation.[63]

They prefer minds swept clean of rational thought. There, in the hollow
promise of enlightenment, they make their abode. The mind that makes dis-

tinctions between right and wrong, true and false, good and evil has produced the mess; only a new suprarational spirituality will save us.

Meditation

The centerpiece of the new spirituality is meditation, the individual self-discipline that allows access to the occult domain of spiritual power and liberation through the age-old techniques of Hindu practice. Though the fast track of drugs achieves the same result, passive meditation is less harmful to the body. The modern witches Sjoo and Mor tie the moon, sexual ecstasy [kundalini], and soma (a potent Indian drug) together, but the goal is the same—to reach "the still center of all."[64] Meditation silences the mind, allowing the soul to escape the body and to become one with the universe. Deepak Chopra describes the experience as being liberated from a space/time prison (the body) into the knowledge that "you are infinite and boundless."[65]

To get in touch with "unbounded reality" various techniques are used: repeated mantras (religious phrases such as "aum"), visual stimuli such as crystals, or chakra meditation, which identifies seven ascending points of energy within the body, beginning with the base chakra at the bottom of the spine and rising to a point just above the head. At this point, the soul experiences unity with the whole, with the All of the entire circle of cosmic reality, and the sense of endless time, ultimate power and total liberation and glorious immortality has been achieved.

Says Chopra:

> I . . . experience complete stillness where I am an unbounded, unconditioned, omnipresent field of awareness that transcends space and time. . . . A level of being [at which] . . . you are in touch with the cosmic computer. . . . [Meditation] take[s] a person to the level of spirit beyond the mind. . . . You actually have the direct knowledge that you're not in your body and you're not in your mind: you're beyond both.[66]

Mollenkott calls her experience of enlightenment

> one distinct "holy instant" [a notion taken from A Course in Miracles, as she admits]. . . . like my Elder Brother, Jesus, I am a sinless Self travel-

ling through eternity and temporarily having human experiences in a body known as Virginia Ramey Mollenkott. . . . Perhaps my Self has been on earth before in other bodies, perhaps not.[67]

Again, there is the unmistakable notion of humanity's "natural" unity with the divine All, untrammeled by the divisive, dualistic concepts of sin and death.[68]

Does meditation work? You bet it does. It would be a mistake to think that people are merely staring at their navel and deluding themselves into thinking their navel is the very center of the universe. There is occult power out there, and it can give a powerful sense of well-being. Lazaris offers a three-day intensive course entitled "Beyond the Bridge of Belief: Achieving Permanent Change." He boasts of power to break people of their past belief systems and open them to create "a more beautiful present and a more incredible future. . . of limitless possibilities." "In so many ways," he declares, "we have already achieved permanent change. *Metaphysics works*." [69]

SEXUALITY AND THE NEW SPIRITUALITY

Sex and the Spiritual Woman

Why did 2,000 mostly middle-class, middle-aged women from middle of the road, mainline Christian churches end their conference on imaginative spirituality, as they blessed the sacramental milk and honey of a sort of Lady's Supper, with a hymn to the goddess that bordered on homosexual pornography? Read for yourself:

> Our maker Sophia, we are women in your image;
>> with the hot blood of our wombs we give form to new life.
>> With the courage of our convictions,
>> we pour out lifeblood for justice [a reference to abortion?];
> Our Mother Sophia, we are women in your image;
>> with the milk of our breasts we suckle the children;
>> with the knowledge of our hearts we feed humanity;
> Our sweet Sophia, we are women in your image;
>> with nectar between our thighs we invite a lover,
>> we birth a child:

with warm body fluids we remind the world
of its pleasures and sensations;
Our guide, Sophia, we are women in your image:
with our moist mouths we kiss away a tear,
we smile encouragement:
with the honey of wisdom in our mouths,
we prophesy a full humanity to all the peoples;
We celebrate the sensual life you give us:
we celebrate the sweat that pours from us during our labors:
we celebrate the fingertips vibrating the skin of a lover.
We celebrate the tongue that licks a wound or wets our lips:
we celebrate our bodiliness, our physicality,
the sensations of pleasure,
our oneness with earth and water.[70]

While the Bible joyfully celebrates sexuality within marriage, there is absolutely no equivalent of this in the Hebrew or Christian Scriptures as a description of God, so this is "imagination" with a capital *I*. How can people so much in the middle be so far into the extreme? As Donna Steichen has shown, mainline Protestants "discovered" this kind of spirituality only because orthodox groups in the Presbyterian and Methodist churches blew the whistle.[71] But it has been a feature of feminist religious groups since the early '80s.[72] For some time Matthew Fox has defended sexuality, and in particular homosexuality, as playful worship.[73] For Fox, "there can be no renaissance without a mystical sexual awakening." In prose worthy of D. H. Lawrence, this "creation spirituality" theologian adds: "Love beds are altars. People are temples encountering temples. . . . Wings of Cherubim and Seraphim beat to the groans and passions of human lovers."[74] Someone has said that when beds become altars, altars quickly become beds, as ancient pagan orgies easily illustrate. But these notions are making a stunning comeback in contemporary American society and Church. The modern-day witch, Miriam Starhawk, speaking in the name of the goddess, says: "All acts of love and pleasure are my rituals."[75] Virginia Mollenkott's book, *Sensuous Spirituality*, defends the spirituality of illegitimate sexual expression, while various speakers at the Minneapolis RE-Imagining Conference defended sex for children, and playful sex among friends, as normative and healthy. These examples are but the tip of an enormous iceberg, a sort of religious/theological justification for the sexual liberation of the '60s, and the beat goes on. Though the Presbyterian Church U.S.A. in its General Assembly of 1994, denounced RE-Imagining, a similar conference in June 1994, at San Francisco's Episcopalian Grace Cathedral sounded the same note, as conferees were told to "discover and cultivate sacred Eros in all its ecstatic connections."[76]

We have reached a time when the "vain imaginations of the heathen" are masquerading as divine wisdom in the temple of God. Ecstatic perverse sexuality has always been a part of pagan spirituality. In age-old pagan witchcraft, as modern adepts recognize, "sexual magic was practiced, not for the sake of fertility, but for ecstatic self-transcendence, a sexual-spiritual fusion of the human with the cosmic All."[77] "Shamanism, inspiration, mysteries of drunkenness, vision, madness, ecstasy leading to expansions of consciousness—these are the transformative processes of the Goddess."[78] If human beings are divine, then sexual energy especially is divine energy, in whatever form it gets expressed. Sexual ecstasy is one more powerful way of accessing the nonrational experience of occult knowledge, where the mind and the conscience are put on hold. And if orgasm creates a fusion of the human with the cosmic All, is there any reason why perverse sex should not include bestiality? Is this the logical conclusion of Matthew Fox's diatribes against "dualisms," which "oppose not only distinctions between mind and body but also those between creature and Creator. And between man and beast?"[79]

Snakes and Adders

Goddess worship is a continuum. Moderates have just begun to toy with this "new" faith, while radicals have plumbed its depths. At the logical end of the process is a strange but unquestionable relationship between the goddess and the snake. A major expression of ancient Gnosticism that adopted goddess worship took the name Naasenes, "the worshipers of the snake." Also, one Gnostic monistic symbol is a circle made from a snake with its tail in its mouth—the Ouroboros, or world snake.[80] Generally, as Sjoo and Mor point out,

> Great live snakes were everywhere kept in the Goddess' temples during the Neolithic . . . she is represented carrying snakes in her upraised arms or coiled around her. Or, she was imagined as a serpent herself, with a woman's body and a snake's head. . . . The Sumerian goddess was known as the Great Mother Serpent of Heaven. . . . Everywhere. . . . the Goddess-Creatrix was coupled with the sacred serpent. . . . [in]

Australia, Venezuela, the ancient Middle East . . . [the] South Pacific islands. . . . Ancient Celtic and Teutonic goddesses were wrapped with snakes—as well as in China and Egypt.[81]

The snake symbolizes the "rebellious naughty mysteries" of the goddess, viz., "yoga, kundalini and spinal illumination,"[82] as well as eternal life.[83] "To the serpent was attributed power that can move the entire cosmos." And witches Sjoo and Mor add, pointedly: "And [still] does."[84] Everywhere, "the serpent in paradise is pictured with a woman's head and breasts."[85] Is this possibly part of the meaning of the mysterious head of a beast carried throughout the RE-Imagining Conference in Minneapolis?

The energies generated by these techniques became power used to the benefit of all—which is the only way power can be safely used. Ancient legends speak of "the winged radiance of those who have achieved the dynamic equilibrium, the ecstatic union of the currents"—which is the description of those who have raised evolutionary energy, in the form of kundalini, the cosmic serpent, up through the spinal world tree of all manifest being, until it reaches the highest *chakra* of the human mind, becoming winged illumination.[86]

The amalgam of images from Genesis and Hindu meditation techniques might be unfamiliar, but the new spirituality is increasingly interested in "winged illumination." Kundalini meditation derives from Hindu Tantric yoga, which identifies the seven chakra points with sexual energy, known as Serpent energy. A serpent of sexual energy, coiled at the base of the spine, is aroused through meditation, and passes up the spine through sexual ecstasy, bringing the subject into cosmic consciousness.

Kundalini and the Holy Spirit are identified as East meets West at the base of the spine.[87] One writer explains the process: (a) a sense of energy pulsating between the genitals and the base of the spine, and coming into the brain via the cerebrospinal fluid; (b) an uncoiling of energy knots in the ears; (c) an acute, intelligent sensuality; (d) an internal energy body living in harmony with the physical body, i.e., realization of True Self, "I" (self-awareness) "Am" (Christ).[88]

The signs of kundalini at work are a "sensation of electrical energy rippling through the reproductive organs, and the inability to stay focused in logical-conceptual consciousness. . . . [as well as an] inner resistance to conceptualization."[89] In the true spiritual experience, "sexual energy becomes genitally diminished and more diffused throughout the body."[90] Clearly a mind which, through sex, goes beyond all dualisms of sexual distinctions and rational moral considerations, also gets beyond the limiting notion of sin.

A recent article in *Psychology Today* offers advice for the sexually hung up: "Throwing away the rule book and holding onto yourself can be framed as believing in the God within, believing that there is a good part of you inside. The bedroom becomes a place for spirituality to emerge. Spirituality is the application of faith to everyday life, including when you have your underwear down."[91] Of course, with no rule book, there are no limits and there is no sin.

Sin and Spirituality

To consider nothing wrong was the highest form of religious devotion among them.[92] This statement by a repentant member of the cult of Bacchus, preserved by the Roman historian Livy, early in the first century A.D., could be applied with no exaggeration to the movers and shakers of the new spirituality at the end of the twentieth century. Just as in orthodox Christianity, there is a deep connection between spirituality and holiness—the Holy Spirit is the Spirit of holiness—so in a sort of distorted, perverted mirror image the new spirituality is tied to sin.

Sin has been eliminated from Virginia Mollenkott's newly minted "evangelical" faith. After employing various pagan methods of spirituality, she declares:

> Gone are traditional Christianity's emphasis on sin, guilt, and retribution; instead, we are empowered toward co-creatorship, welcomed to continual renewal on a continuous Great Non-Judgment Day.[93]

This sounds like a notable example of the "instant touchdown trick." Having difficulty scoring points? Just redefine the endzone as the place where you stand, and lo and behold, you have won the game. With no sin, there is no guilt for Mollenkott's lesbian activity, which suddenly becomes "sensuous spirituality." She will not condemn those who engage in "promiscuous or easy [casual] sex,"[94] nor women who have abortions.[95] But the new spirituality goes beyond a refusal to judge others and oneself. It actually promotes sin.

In her book *Pure Lust*, Mary Daly, professor of theology at Boston College, and perhaps the leading spokeswoman for lesbian witchcraft, in a section entitled "The Courage to Sin," points out that "sin" derives from a Latin word meaning "to be." For her, in other words, to exist is to sin. Daly is rewriting the English language in order to create her new, sinful world. One entry in her *Wickedary*, "sinarticulate" is defined as the ability to sin. For radical feminists of her stripe, "The tragedy of Christianity is that it has kept untold millions of human beings from sinning, i.e., from knowing their own souls."[96]

This new spirituality eventually demands total commitment by the committing of sinful actions, especially of a sexual nature. Our actions determine who we become, and disobedience imprisons us in sinful structures. While not all feminists are lesbians, radical feminism leads to lesbianism the way monism in general leads to androgyny and homosexuality. Daly herself believes lesbianism is "almost required by radical feminism," and admitted that "everything I write is an invitation to [lesbianism]."[97] Roman Catholic journalist and author E. Michael Jones,[98] reports on a meeting of nuns for the purpose of promoting the ordination of women that ended with the nuns anointing each other's bare breasts with jasmine.[99] Janie Spahr, a Presbyterian lesbian minister, in her speech at the RE-Imagining Conference, claimed that her theology is first and foremost informed by "making love with Coni," her lesbian partner. She went on: "Sexuality and spirituality have come together and, Church, we're going to teach you."[100] This thinking is expressed by a lesbian nun in the early '80s:

> My spirituality has changed over the years. . . . My experience with feminist spirituality and the Goddess has affirmed my intuition that spirit and body are inseparable. . . . Now my intimacy with Marie involves my whole spiritual/sexual self.[101]

This kind of sexual sinfulness can only lead to enslavement, to being "[given] over in the sinful desires of their hearts to sexual impurity for the degrading of their bodies with one another."[102] In the Bible sexual sins are called "sins against [one's] own body,"[103] no doubt because they sin against the image of God in the body God created for monogamous heterosexual sex.

The redefinition of sin does not involve only sexual sins. Abortion, the killing of defenseless children in their mothers' wombs, is redefined as a noble and necessary act of female empowerment, that puts blood on the hands of many, and forces them into a spirituality that can justify this modern, unprecedented "slaughter of the innocents." The following citation from radical feminism gives the ultimate explanation of the real stakes in the abortion issue—that of spiritual power:

> If it is not to be too late for all of us, all women—on a global scale—have got to regain our ancient ontological power—and intuitive skill—for making life-and-death decisions. . . . This is the real challenge presented by feminist issues, including abortion rights. . . . When women begin to define our own lives, including being ontologically responsible for each life we choose to bring—or not bring—into the world, then women will become fully functioning *definers of the world*. And then we will be fully responsible for the kind of world, the spiritual and physical quality of world, into which we bring new life.[104]

The new spiritual woman claims the right to determine future life on this planet. She adopts a monist view of reality in which there are no absolutes and no clearly defined good or evil. For her, life does not begin in the womb but always is and comes from the far recesses of the universe. It has to do with mystical power of life and death.

> Women describe experiences of being pregnant, of knowing and feeling and believing that it was not the right time or circumstance to have a child; they speak of going into meditation, or into their dreams, and speaking to the fetus as one sacred being to another. This is not the right time or space for us to be together. Please leave now. At the right time, we will meet again.[105]

Here it is. The occult knowledge that claims to define good and evil, kills a baby in cold blood in the name of spiritual health.

This is the true face of the new spirituality, whether people realize it or not, which, through mystical gnosis, joins opposites, stands above the moral absolutes of right and wrong, and creates a genocide. The sheep follow, fed lines like "right to choose," "right to privacy" and "the population time-bomb."

If the new spirituality, behind the warm fuzzies, makes your blood run cold, it should.

The Eschatological Re-Eating of the Apple

Inevitably, this spirituality of sin develops its own sacraments which, with hardly any attempts at subtlety, turn the biblical notion of sin on its head. *Women-Church* practices a new baptism where "the initiate descends unclothed" into the waters.[106] The symbolism here, as in Gnosticism, is both to celebrate eroticism and to affirm human innocence. But the sacramental revisionism gets much more explicit. In a vivid playing out of the rejection of the patriarchal "myth of original sin" and Eve's "victimized" place within it, the Women-Church community celebrates the "blessing of the apple," saying:

> This is the apple of consciousness raising. Let the scales of false con-
> sciousness fall from our eyes, so that we can rightly name truth and
> falsehood, good and evil.[107]

Here is Nietzsche's "transvaluation of values," through which evil becomes good and good evil. Incredibly, the very act of original sin in the Garden of Eden is now elevated as the sacrament of gender liberation. Under the guise of Christian freedom, sin and spirituality are ritually wedded. At the RE-Imagining Conference, one of the speakers held up an apple, bit into it, and then with cheers from the audience asked, "What taboo have you broken today?"[108]

A semi-"sophomoric" gesture, as one commentator condescendingly suggested?[109] Not a bit of it. In their rebellion, these women, especially the leaders, are not sophomores. Their experimental sacrament stands as a perfectly accurate symbolic expression of the neo-Gnostic feminist apostasy from biblical Christianity ravaging many of the mainline churches, from which the American Church may never recover. Never have we so needed the lessons of ancient Gnosticism.

CHAPTER FIFTEEN

GNOSTIC SPIRITUALITY

Anyone who "has worn the flesh" will not be saved, but the ones who "know themselves" will enter the kingdom of heaven.

APOCRYPHON OF JAMES[1]

DEATH: THE GNOSTIC'S BEST FRIEND

Death is not the last enemy. It is the Gnostic's best friend. A cosmic Kevorkian, Dr. Death comes as a *spiritual* "health provider" for the termination of an unwanted physical body. In the Gnostic system death *is* victory,[2] the final triumph of the spirit over matter, the ultimate undoing of God the Creator's evil work. Death is the luminous hallway into the radical freedom of disembodied spirits who have broken free from the restraining power of the physical body. Says the Gnostic specialist, Kurt Rudolf,

Redemption . . . is first realized by the gnostic at the time of his death, for at this moment he encounters the everlasting, reawakening fact of release from the fetters of the body, and is able to set out on the way to his true home.[3]

The Mandeans, a particular sect of Gnostics, called death "the day of escape" (or "release").[4] This moment of liberation is not simply a future hope. What the soul experiences at death is the full payment of what the Gnostic has already attained in life through gnosis—knowledge.

GNOSIS

Did you gnotice? In pronouncing the word "gnosis" (the *g* is silent as in "gnat")[5] one is at the center of the Gnostic system. Gnosticism is a movement centered on knowledge (the *k* is also silent). Of course, all systems of thought claim knowledge, but Gnostic knowledge is neither technical, scientific, logical nor philosophical. The *Tripartite Tractate* warns against Greek knowledge of "philosophy . . . types of medicine . . . rhetoric . . . music or . . . logic . . . [which leads to] confusion."[6] This text teaches that people are *incapable of knowing* the truth because they draw the line at the visible—both Jews and pagan philosophers never get beyond faith in the Demiurge (the Creator) because "the powers themselves seem to hinder them (appearing as if they were the Totality)."[7] In other words, the God of creation fools people into thinking that there is nothing beyond His sphere of authority. The result of this subterfuge is that most people never experience true knowledge.

Gnostic gnosis unlocks the heavens. It transforms, redeems and liberates the human being from the humdrum world of the body into cosmic flights of spiritual ecstasy. This knowledge is not dry theory. It is religious experience.[8] As the *Gospel of Truth* states of the true believer:

If he has knowledge (gnosis), he is from above. If he is called, he always hears, answers, and faces the one who calls him, and goes up to him. And he knows in what way he is called. Possessing knowledge, he always does the will of the one who called him, he desires to be pleasing to him. He is given rest. The names of each come to him. The one who will have knowledge in this way will know from whence he is come and where he is going.[9]

This is the knowledge of true spiritual reality—the knowledge of where one is going.

It is also knowledge of oneself. The "Jesus" of the *Apocryphon of James* reveals true knowledge to the disciples. Anyone who has "worn the flesh" will not be saved, but the ones who "know themselves" will enter the kingdom of heaven.[10]

According to the *Gospel of Truth*, self-knowledge and knowledge of God are one and the same. Those who know the Father, the incomprehensible and inconceivable God, have discovered Him in themselves.[11]

Aristotle said about initiation into the pagan mysteries of his day that at the final stage there was no more "learning" but only "experiencing," producing a change in the state of mind.[12] An expert on the ancient pagan mysteries that formed the model for Gnostic spirituality also sees the importance of transformation. "Mysteries were initiation rituals of a voluntary, personal, and secret character that aimed at a change of mind through experience of the sacred."[13] This is what religious pagan Greeks and Romans got from their mystery rituals. A contemporary observer, the Roman historian Dio (c. A.D. 155-229) gives some indication of the spiritual expectations accompanying an initiation: "Something is bound to happen in the soul." Thus the "initial bewilderment of the candidate is changed into wonder, and acceptance of sense."[14] This is clearly gnosis as transformation.

The Bible distinguishes between faith and sin, submission and rebellion. Gnosticism pits gnosis against faith. The *Paraphrase of Shem* speaks of "the impure practice of faith."[15] According to Rudolf "faith plays only a provisional role . . . relative to knowledge."[16] Gnosticism desires (occult) gnosis just as Eve desired the forbidden fruit and the occult knowledge that would make her like God—hence the Gnostic fixation with Genesis 3 and its counterreading. She refused to have faith in the Word of God, and was seduced by the promise of direct knowledge, by which the world would be reconfigured—not according to God's order, but according to the diabolically inspired human pretension to immortal selfhood.

Disavowing biblical revelation and its divinely created handmaid, human reason, this gnosis puts the believer in touch with the hidden mysteries that lie within the soul.

THE GOAL OF GNOSTIC SPIRITUALITY: UNION WITH THE DIVINE

> And it [the end] is the receiving of knowledge concerning he who is hidden, who is the Father. From whom came the beginning, and to whom all shall return who proceeded from him.[17]

Gnosticism uses the classic terms of monism, as it holds out the possibility of full identification and union with the divine. A much-employed expression to evoke the divine reality is "the Totality," and God is referred to as "the Father of the Totalities." The goal of existence, according to the *Testimony of Truth*, is "knowledge of the All."[18] Such knowledge leads from multiplicity to unity[19] and, hence, to union with the unknown Father. "The whole order of the aeons," says the *Tripartite Tractate*, "has a love and a desire for the perfect, total discovery of the Father and this is their unhindered union."[20]

Beyond the Polarities

The very essence of this ancient heresy is the blissful confusion of man and God. Thus, in union with the All, one simultaneously meets oneself; for the self, as we have seen, is God. Hans Jonas speaks of the "identity or consubstantiality of man's innermost self with the supreme and transmundane God, himself often called 'Man'."[21] In other words, the search for God *is* the search for self. However, the *Gospel of Truth* indicates what happens when the self finally meets the Gnostic God. Such a union is ultimate personal, physical and, no doubt, individual *dissolution*:

> Eventually Unity will complete the space. Each one will attain himself inside Unity, he will cleanse himself from numerosity into unity through knowledge, his internal substance being consumed as by fire. . . . But from that time on [death], the outward form no longer appears, but it will fade away in the union of Unity, for now their works lie scattered.[22]

This dissolving of the many into the one, the annihilation of difference and individuality, is a classic theme of mystical monism. Why is it so in the so-called dualistic system of Gnosticism?

The present bishop of the Ecclesia Gnostica of Los Angeles, Steven Hoeller, a twentieth-century Gnostic, affirms the monistic character of his faith, describing the spiritual experience Gnosticism offers as communion in the "dark sea of deep consciousness."[23]

THE ELEMENTS OF GNOSTIC SPIRITUALITY

Destruction of the Created Order

All deviations from God's creational design must deconstruct the natural order and recreate life in terms of their own desires. Thus, in our day, homosexuals have an influence far beyond their actual numbers in intellectual circles, in the media and the arts. In these fields that help define reality, there is the opportunity to recreate the world by bringing down "heteropatriarchy" and making normative the homosexual view of life. A similar program is espoused by radical feminists. This deconstructive and recreative activity finds spiritual resources in the new spirituality in which marginals see themselves as "shamans." Not surprisingly, a similar program characterizes the spirituality of ancient Gnosticism.

Contemporary writer Philip Lee believes that Gnosticism has returned in our day to disfigure Christianity. He notes that

> for the gnostic personality, religious knowledge [knowledge of God] could never be discovered in terms of earthly pilgrimage. Knowledge of God required the exact opposite, *a turning away from this world.*[24]

Rudolf says the negative spiritual agenda of ancient Gnosticism included "the progressive stripping off of everything associated with the earthly body."[25] Lee sees the Church fathers as a scriptural model of true Christianity:

> The Fathers . . . were no less spiritual than those who claimed a higher spirituality; what so radically distinguished them from their opponents was their determination to see the eternal through the God-given temporal gifts of creation.[26]

For Gnostic spirituality to flourish, God-ordained temporal gifts, especially rationality, have to go. Gnosis gave the Gnostic an understanding of the "nonexistent" God beyond the visible world (see chapter 11). The future for the enlightened soul, according to the *Tripartite Tractate*, would be

> an entry into that which is silent, the place which has no need for utterance nor for comprehending nor for forming a concept nor for making light but [where] everything is light while they have no need to be lighted.[27]

If this is true of the post-death existence, it is true of the spiritual life of the Gnostic on Earth, as the Jesus of the *Apocryphon of James* commands his disciples: "Be filled with the Spirit, but be lacking in reason (logos)."[28]

As we have noted, the rejection of reason is part of the general rejection of bodily existence. Rudolf rightly notes: "The Gnostic must prove that he is a Gnostic by the rejection of the body before he can know final redemption."[29] Some Gnostics were vegetarians for that reason.[30] Many were ascetics, as the *Nag Hammadi* texts show. Some engaged in sexual license, as the Church fathers document, as a way of shaking their fist at the Creator of normative sexuality. This, of course, is where sexuality and spirituality overlap.[31] The Gnostics say this very clearly.

Not so in our day. Major changes in sexual norms and practices, pushed by a massive agenda of religious/pagan monism, are surreptitiously justified, not as issues of religion (which would be prohibited by the logic of church/state separation), but as nonreligious issues of civil rights. Many unconsciously slip into a *religious* redefinition of existence by their political acceptance of an egalitarian, antipatriarchal and pansexual vision. The unseen religious agenda of undifferentiated sexuality is actually monistic union of the opposites within the impersonal divine.

Present Spiritual Technology

A foretaste of that union in immortality is experienced in the present, physical existence, as a "call." "Thus, if [the Gnostic believer] has knowledge," says the *Gospel of Truth*, "he is from above. If he is called, he always hears, answers, and faces the one who calls him, and goes up to him."[32] This ascent of union is anticipated even in the aborted fetus of one's body. Philip Lee notes, correctly, that "the gnostics were able, at least to their own satisfaction, to accomplish in Houdini-like fashion a successful exit from the cosmos prior to physical death."[33] Filoramo identifies the "fundamental experience" of Gnosticism as "the visionary moments of ecstasy . . . [of the] divine reality [which] cannot be known through the ordinary faculties of the mind."[34] Ecstatic experiences, both communal and individual, prepare the Gnostic for that final release from the body and ascent to the Father of the Totalities.

COMMUNAL ECSTASY: THE GNOSTIC SACRAMENTS

Like the pagan mystery religions which they studied and frequented, the Gnostics engaged in highly secretive initiation ceremonies, the details of which are only suggested by our texts. The authors of the recent book *Ancient Christian Magic* call these sacraments "rituals of ascent" in which the Gnostics developed their "practices of ritual power."[35] "Initiation in general," says Burkert, speaking broadly of the ancient pagan mystery cults, has been defined as "status drama-tization" or "ritual change of status."[36] The goal of sacramental initiation, in other words, is spiritual and mystical transformation. Irenaeus observes that in Gnosticism "there are as many redemptions [sacraments of initiation] as there are mystery-teachers of this doctrine."[37] The *Gospel of Philip* enumerates five such sacraments: "a baptism and an anointing and a eucharist and a redemption and a wedding chamber."[38] The very existence of five consecutive sacraments sug-gests progressive ascent into the depth of mystery. Nothing is known of the sacrament of redemption, so we shall comment on only four.

Baptism unto Perfection
The baptism in question is not Christian baptism, representing the removal of sins through the death of Christ. Rather, the Gnostics invented another bap-tism, based on the words of Jesus—"I have another baptism to be baptized with."[39] This they claimed to be a secret, mystical baptism of perfection bestowed by Christ on Jesus,[40] and revealed only to his true followers. For this reason, they argued, you could not find it described in the pages of the Bible.

The Anointing
Beyond spiritual baptism "into perfection," the *Gospel of Philip* mentions the sacrament of the chrism (anointing) which is superior to baptism, "for it is from

the word "chrism" that we have been called "Christians."[41] Though we are not told much about it, this anointing with oil served as a special redemption ceremony and functioned as a prerequisite for partaking of the communal meal and entry into the *pleroma*, the highest mystery of all, "The Holy of Holies," the bridal chamber.[42]

The Lord's Supper with a Twist

Not surprisingly, the Gnostics also modified the central sacrament of orthodoxy, the Lord's Supper. How interesting that today we discover a renewed desire to tamper with the Lord's Supper. In the *Gospel of Philip*, the flesh and blood of Christ, a part of the physical creation so detested by Gnostics, were reinterpreted as "the word" and the "Holy Spirit," given to the perfect Gnostics who have realized oneness with the divine.[43] In a Gnostic text not found in the *Nag Hammadi Library*, the *Acts of Thomas*,[44] prayer at the eucharistic table invokes "perfect compassion . . . intercourse with the male . . . and [the] hidden Mother."[45] This is theological tampering. Some Gnostics, using the same theology, went to quite radical extremes.

Epiphanius gives an account of the Ophite/Naasene (the worshipers of the Serpent) version of the Lord's Supper:

They have a snake which they foster in a particular box; at the hour when they perform their mysteries they coax it out of the hole, and whilst they load the table with bread, they summon the snake forth. When the hole is open, it comes out . . . crawling onto the table and wallowing in the bread: this, they claim, is the "perfect offering." And that is also why, so I heard from them, they not only "break the bread" in which the snake has wallowed, and offer it to the recipients, but everyone kisses the snake on the mouth, once the snake has been charmed by sorcery. . . . They prostrate themselves before it and call this the "thanksgiving" (eucharist).[46]

To modern ears, such a ceremony appears grotesque, but one of the great fathers of modern psychology, C. G. Jung, saw in the snake a representation of the "extra-human quality in man. . . . The cold-blooded, staring serpent, express[ing] man's fear of the inhuman and his awe of the sublime, of what is beyond human ken."[47] Modern versions of the Eucharist do not include the snake, but the "re-eating the apple" at the end of the Supper in Rosemary Radford Ruether's *Women-Church,* in its gnosticizing inversion of the Genesis account, reveals a theology that is potentially just as radically "serpentine."

Degenerate Ancients[48]

The testimony of Epiphanius, the fourth-century Church father, concerning the eucharistic celebration of the Borborians, is often dismissed as exaggeration, fantasy and vicious slander.[49] This is possible. In his favor, he expresses a strong sense of Christian piety and personal holiness, and claims to have been compelled to attend such an initiation as a 20-year-old on a visit to Egypt. In sum, he professes to being an eyewitness, and a number of independent witnesses corroborate his testimony.[50] According to Epiphanius, the Borborians began their Lord's Supper with a gastronomical agape, a lavish meal accompanied by plenty of wine. Then followed "the agape with the brother," in which married couples split up and had intercourse with other members of the group. Since conceiving would be imprisonment in the structures of the Creator, *coitus interruptus* was practiced. The male emission was then held heavenward with the prayer: "This is the body of Christ," and then eaten. If a woman were to become pregnant, the fetus was aborted, and eaten, accompanied by the prayer: "We were not mocked by the archon of lust, but have gathered the brother's blunder up." This they called "the perfect Passover."[51]

Again, the modern reader is shocked. But today we worship a god of unlimited human freedom through condom-aided *coitus interruptus*. Fetal murder of holocaust proportions is the greatest ecological disaster the world has ever known. Our neo-Gnostic devotion only lacks Christian eucharistic terminology—and doubtless that will come. We, too, shake our fists and our twisted technology in the face of the God of creation, radically disfiguring, with the gifts He has given us, the world He made.

The Bridal Chamber: Spirituality and Sin

What went on in the bridal chamber was, as in the pagan mystery cults in general, a very well-kept secret. Rudolf believed that the Valentinians prepared a bridal chamber "after the image of the conjunctions" (syzygies—the joining of opposites) which is held in contrast to normal marriage as the "unsullied marriage."[52] In this conjunction the soul returns to "the arms of her partner or ideal prototype . . . [which] is the decisive event at the end of time."[53] Doubtless some form of enactment of this final conjunction took place in the bridal chamber.[54] Filoramo speaks of the individual Gnostics being "reconstructed in androgynous unity" in the bridal chamber.[55]

At one level, this spirituality appears ascetic and world-denying. "Unpolluted marriage," says *Philip*, "[is] a true mystery. It is not of the flesh but pure. It belongs not to desire but rather to the will. It belongs not to the darkness or the night but rather to the day and the light."[56] This claim to purity notwithstanding, what went on in these spiritual bridal chambers is anyone's guess. This, readers will remember, is the *Gospel of Philip* which recounts that Jesus often kissed Mary Magdalene, the converted prostitute, on the lips.[57] The phrase, "One will clothe himself in this light sacramentally in the union," implies spiritual and perhaps physical nakedness.[58] If the only clothes worn were "perfect light," and physical contact with a woman is held up as the model Jesus leaves his disciples, then the allegations of the Church fathers make a lot of sense.

As noted above, *Philip* declares that the bridal chamber is reserved for "free men and virgins." In other words, like the non Christian pagan mysteries, these initiations are secretive and private.[59] Dio, the Roman historian, also notes the secretive element to the pagan mysteries. "At best," he says, "we are in the situation of eaves-droppers, of strangers at the gate"[60]—or, in modern terms, detectives.

So, who were the "virgins"? Epiphanius in his description of the Borborians, called virgins "women who have never gone on to the point of insemination . . . but are always having intercourse and committing fornication."[61] Admittedly the Borborians who joined together the two "sacraments" of the eucharist and the bridal chamber were no doubt the most radical. But some form of sexual compromise does not appear out of the question, given the context of Gnostic theology in general. Should one be tempted to think that this was limited to the radical extreme, Epiphanius also notes that less radical groups like the followers of Basilides also practiced "promiscuous intercourse."[62] Irenaeus and Hippolytus also note this. And of course, such activity began with one of the earliest of the Gnostic heretics, Simon the Magician.[63]

This lurid information is not for shock value. It illustrates the program of deconstruction of normative, marital, child-producing sexuality. Indeed such deconstruction is served by both radical asceticism and libertinism. No doubt some Gnostic sects were ascetic, particularly the group that collected the *Nag Hammadi* texts.[64] Perhaps most of them were. But others, according to the

Church fathers, went to sexual excess.[65] This latter option serves two functions. It flies in the face of God the creator, and it reproduces ecstasy through sexual orgasm, which is well-documented religious pagan practice. Epiphanius says of the Borborians: "They never have their fill of copulation; the more indecent one of their men is, the more praiseworthy they consider him."[66] Some Gnostics who, as Hippolytus asserts, joined in the pagan mystery religions, probably rivalled them in sexual excess. The Roman historian, Livy, recounts comparable sexual orgies in the initiation ceremonies to Bacchus. He cites their justifying principle: "To consider nothing wrong . . . was the highest form of religious devotion."[67] How incredible that a group claiming to be Christians would have had no difficulty saying "amen" to this radical pagan notion. Indeed, the Gnostic group called the Cainites said as much, according to Irenaeus:

> Not otherwise can one be saved than by passing through every action, as also Carpocrates taught . . . At every sinful and infamous deed an angel is present, and he who commits it . . . addresses him by his name and says, "O thou angel, I use thy work! O thou Power of such and such, I perform thy deed!" And this is the perfect knowledge, unafraid to stray into such actions whose very names are unmentionable.[68]

What a powerful example, in an ancient text, of the joining of sin and spirituality that we find so prevalent today.

Irenaeus further observes that

> according to their writings, their souls before departing must have made sure of every mode of life and must have left no remainder of any sort still to be performed: lest they must again be sent into another body because there is still something lacking to their freedom.[69]

Whether ascetic or libertine, such freedom stems from the rejection of God as Creator and Lawgiver, and from a radical commitment to overturn creation's structures. The apostle John, who knew some form of early Gnosticism, issues a damning judgment against all such deluded people: "No one who continues to sin has either seen him [Christ] or *known* him."[70] Gnosticism affirmed the very opposite. Its religious experience is actually *generated* by acts of sin. John names this too. "He who does what is sinful is of the devil, because the devil has been sinning from the beginning."[71]

Whether sexual ecstasy was part of every Gnostic bridal chamber ceremony, ecstasy of a more spiritual nature (union of the opposites) seems to have been produced in the chamber, perhaps by the chanting of strange mantras. According to Irenaeus, the following words are pronounced in the marriage ceremony:

> [I baptize you] into the name of the unknown Father of the universe, into Truth, the Mother of all, into him who descended upon Jesus, into the union and redemption and participation of the powers.

Then follows a repetition of bizarre words: "Basyma cacabasa eanaa irramista diarbada caëota bafabor camelanthi . . . . Messia ufar magno in seenchaldia mosomeda eaacha faronepseha Iesu Nazarene."[72]

Redemption: Stages/Ascent Through Meditation

Mantras are an important element of some individual mystical meditations. Gnosis was also an intensely personal affair. The challenge of spirituality is immense. Gnostics saw themselves as imprisoned in a physical body and then surrounded by at least seven concentric circles stretching out into the cosmos before them,[73] each representing various levels of illegitimate authority of the principalities and powers instituted by the great Archon/Ruler, the God of Creation. According to the theory, the soul is escorted by beings of light, and goes through the seven horrific domains where Christians, monks, apostate Mandeans and other unworthies are held, until it reaches the world of light.[74] "In departing this world," recounts Epiphanius, "the soul makes its way though these archons, but no one can get through them unless he is perfect in this knowledge."[75] The knowledge serves as a password, at the passage of each circle or aeon. Irenaeus describes the soul's journey: "When they come to the Powers, they are to speak as follows: 'I am a son of Father, of Father who is preexisting. I am a son in the Preexisting one. I have come to see all things that belong to me and to others.'"[76] Each soul has its own "helper" or spiritual "counterpart" who reassures the ascending soul: "I shall cause you to ascend and keep you safe in my garment," which is a garment of light.[77] Clearly, spirit guides are not the invention of New Age spirituality.

THE PROCESS:
TASTING MONISTIC UNION NOW

Again we ask, is this final journey through the stars the only journey of the soul? Certainly reincarnation is present in the Gnostic texts, so that imperfect souls have to do it again, and again, and again.[78] However, in the light of contemporary New Age spirituality, which gives ample documentation concerning earthly mystical experience, it would appear that the Gnostic soul *already in this life*, through meditation, made the trip, if only imperfectly. Hindu and New Age meditation, the reader will recall, also proceed via the number seven—*seven* chakra points in the body, whereby the spirit/soul mounts up and out of the limitations of physical existence into the eighth domain of spiritual freedom on a regular basis.

In the *Nag Hammadi* text *Zostrianos*, a document deeply influenced by the Eastern magical mysticism of Zoroastrianism,[79] the teacher, Zostrianos, "presents a series of revelations made by exalted beings regarding the nature of the heavenly realm."[80] Zostrianos advances from one stage to the next through initiatory baptisms, progressing in spiritual insight through *seven* stages and then enters into the eighth and finally the ninth of perfect knowledge. He recounts his experience of the ascent of the soul, but in the past tense. A number of fascinating statements have a modern New Age ring. "He [the power from a holy spirit higher than God the Creator] came upon me alone . . . I saw the perfect child [a "higher self?"]." Every one of the seven baptisms puts one in "the path to the Self-Begotten One." Toward the end of the process Zostrianos states, in terms similar to the claims of those who have successfully penetrated to the spirit world through meditation: "I was [standing] above my spirit, praying fervently to the great Lights." He finally arrives at the "simplicity of the invisible Spirit within the ninth [which is] unity." At the end of this journey, Zostrianos declares: "I saw how all these (the Hidden Aeon, Barbelo/Sophia) and the Unknown Spirit) dwell within one."[81] In a word, the mystical experience is none other than divinization: "I became divine."[82]

To reproduce this process, the master leads the disciple in a prayer/chant of vowels and nonsense words: Zoxathazo a oo ee ooo eee oooo ee ooooooooooo ooooo uuuuu ooooooooooooo ooo Zozazoth. After this there follows an ecstatic state, and a vision of the divine mediated through the master. "The Discourse closes as the master instructs the student to write his experience in a book . . . to guide others who will advance by stages, and enter into the way of immortality . . . into the understanding of the eighth that reveals the ninth."[83]

A similar use of mystical techniques, mantras and seals is found in the *Second Book of Jeu*, a Gnostic text not found at Nag Hammadi. The adept is initiated into a "baptism by fire" by saying the following prayer: "Make Zorokothora Melchizedek come secretly and bring the water of baptism of fire of the virgin of the light, the judge. Yea, hear me, my father, as I invoke your imperishable names." There then follows a list of undecipherable, mystical names for God: "Azarakaza A . . . Amathkratitath, Yo Yo Yo Amen Amen Yaoth Yaoth Yaoath Phaoph Phaoph Phaoph etc."[84] These esoteric names, of which there are many more, seem to represent a disengagement from rational speech, and thus aid in the process of the ascent through meditation. This method of spirituality is not Christian. Indeed, it is specifically repudiated by Jesus in his teaching on prayer.[85]

This journey of the soul through the heavens, similar to the one the Paul of the Gnostic texts makes to the *seventh* heaven and beyond,[86] becomes the basis for the exhortation to all Gnostic believers to follow the same path.[87] "Release yourselves, and that which bound you will be dissolved." It seems quite probable that the journey of the soul at death is therefore the final experience of the soul in life who has sought through initiations and meditations to escape the confinements of the flesh, even if for only limited periods.

This mystical spirituality of present, temporal and final escape from the body is the very antithesis of Christian spirituality. As Philip Lee rightly notes about Christian discipleship: "Absolutely no escape from this tangible world of sensory perception is allowed. Salvation from the world by any other route than through the world will be called a fraud."[88]

MYSTICAL MAGIC

If this spirituality is not Christian, what are its origins? We have noted that "Christian" Gnostics frequented ceremonies of the pagan mystery cults, adopting and/or spiritualizing the sexual perversions of the Goddess cults.[89] Hippolytus states that:

> The entire system of their [the Sethian Gnostics] doctrine . . . is [derived] from the ancient [Greek pagan] theologians Musaeus, Linus

and Orpheus, who elucidate especially the ceremonies of initiation, as well as the mysteries themselves. For their doctrine concerning the womb is also the tenet of Orpheus; and the [idea of the] navel . . . is [to be found] with the same symbolism attached to it in the Bacchanalian orgies of Orpheus.[90]

This is confirmed by Irenaeus:

The most perfect among them shamelessly do all the forbidden things . . . Food sacrificed to idols . . . they are the first to assemble at every heathen festival held in honor of the idols for the sake of pleasure.[91]

Much of "Christian" Gnosticism, through its contact with Graeco-Roman mystery cults, was a self-conscious variant of non-Christian mystical paganism. "Mystical thinking," says the modern polytheist, David Miller, describing its hoary history:

begins with the mystical mathematics of Pythagoras, moves counterculturally through metaphysical theologies and not a few heresies (gnosticisms of several sorts), comes to manifest itself in Pietism after the Reformation, and ends in various forms of Romanticism, from some nineteenth-century literatures in England and Germany to men and women fascinated by sensitivity training, Don Juan, the Yaqi sorcerer, and the *I Ching*.[92]

Hippolytus and Epiphanius accuse a number of the Gnostic systems for having taken their theories and mystical speculations from the Greek mystical mathematician, Pythagorus (581-497 B.C.).[93] Pythagoras is believed to have gone to India where he was initiated into the spiritual ideas of Hinduism, and into the notion that the true self was "an occult self."[94] Through Pythagoras, in particular, and no doubt by many other connections,[95] Gnostic spirituality includes the crucial ingredient of pagan, monistic Hinduism.

The other significant element is Egyptian goddess magic. As we have already noted, Thunder/Sophia, the feminine principle of revelation, declares: "[I] am the one whose image is great in Egypt." The connection is appropriate since Isis was the Egyptian Goddess of Wisdom,[96] that is, the Goddess of magic.[97] A scholar of Isis notes that the magic of Isis is "real wisdom," since it consisted of insight into the mystery of life and death. . . . Thus wisdom was to the Egyptians equivalent to the capacity of exerting magical power."[98] Initiation into her mysteries and the ecstatic secret experiences in her temples gave adherents a foretaste of transformation into immortality.[99]

We possess but one text (already cited) from the ancient world that describes initiation into the pagan cult of Isis. In the satirical novel written by Apuleius, entitled *Metamorphoses, or The Golden Ass* (first century A.D.), the hero recounts:

> I approached the frontier of death, I set foot on the threshold of Persephone [death], I journeyed through all the elements and came back, I saw at midnight the sun, sparkling in white light, I came close to the gods of the upper and the nether world and adored them from near at hand.[100]

This account has all the ingredients of contemporary New Age experiences— light, union with the all, in a near-death experience.[101] Such tangible occult spirituality, which appears to be the very center of Gnostic spirituality, is dabbling in some form of pagan manipulative magic.

The Witness of Contemporaries

Tertullian accused the Gnostics of meddling in magic. "They hold intercourse with magicians, charlatans, astrologers and philosophers and the reason is that they are men who devote themselves to curious questions (curiositati)."[102] Earlier, Irenaeus made the same accusation against the Simonians. The "mystery priests" and every member of the Simonian school "performed sorceries":

> They practice exorcisms and incantations, love potions and erotic magic, familiar spirits and dream-inducers, invoking those demon companions (typical of Greek magic) who send dreams, and whatever other occult things exist, and are zealously cultivated among them.[103]

While it is fashionable nowadays to accuse the "heresy-hunting" Church fathers of exaggeration, support for their allegations comes from an unusual source, the pagan philosopher, Plotinus (A.D. 205-270), who was scandalized that the Gnostics would use "exorcisms," "appropriate utterances," "melodies," "shrieks," "whisperings and hissings with the voice."[104] Many Gnostics, says Rudolf, "fostered a cult of images, even owning statues of gods such as those found among the archeological remains of mystery cults."[105] We must conclude that the fathers were right and that pagan magic was a significant part of Gnostic spirituality. As Gnosticism is rehabilitated as authentic Christianity, we should not be surprised to see a similar spirituality of magic and the occult reenter the Church, in particular through the goddess of pagan wisdom.

CONCLUSION

The Gnostic revolt against the God of Scripture and the resulting search for a "new" spirituality finally led many so-called Christians into a demonically inspired religious occult paganism. Stripping the Old Testament God from New Testament Christianity did not fill the Church with the Spirit of Christ, but opened her doors to the religious pagan agenda of sexual ecstasy, idols and spirit-inspired magic—about which the silenced Old Testament had a lot to say. In a vision recalling what now goes on in living technicolor at the Cathedral of Saint John the Divine in New York City, and in many other places of "Christian" worship, the prophet Ezekiel is taken to the Temple in Jerusalem[106] where he sees:

- in the entrance north of the gate of the altar, the statue of a pagan god to provoke God to jealousy;
- near the gate to the forecourt of the Temple, in a secret room, seventy lay elders, the official representatives of the house of Israel, usurping the function of the priests, engaging in esoteric practices of pagan worship to unclean idols;
- at the north gate, a woman prostrate before the Babylonian nature god Tammuz;
- in the sanctuary, between the holy place and the altar of burnt offerings, (a traditional place of penitence), 25 priests,[107] with their backs to God, facing East, worshiping the pagan sun god.[108]

There is nothing new under the sun. This worship of idols in the very Temple of Yahweh, this searching for light from the East, says the Old Testament commentator, Walter Zimmerli, represents the "unsurpassable height of blasphemy,"[109] against which God's wrath inevitably breaks out with unremitting sever-ity.[110] To these idolaters who know the truth, and deliberately spurn it, God pronounces a woeful judgment: "I will deal with them in anger; I will not look on them with pity or spare them. Although they shout in my ears, I will not lis-ten to them."[111]

Just as in ancient Israel, so in the Early Church, the mystical pagan spiritu-ality of Gnosticism promised believers occult knowledge and human freedom. How many, then as now, were seduced by the glittering half-truths of salvation without sacrifice, redemption without repentance, triumph without crucifix-ion? How many, then as now, fell knowingly or unknowingly into the power of the great seducer, the "one wiser than them all," whose wisdom masked a lie of cosmic proportions hurtling its adepts to death and destruction? How many will rise up now and warn our spiritually upbeat generation of its deadbeat direction and its foolish ways—before it is too late?

CHAPTER SIXTEEN

CONCLUSIONS

Nothing is going to delay the Goddess's second coming.

CAITLÍN MATTHEWS
PAGAN PRIESTESS[1]

The God of the Bible locked in mortal combat for the souls of men with
the goddess of revived paganism—who would have imagined such a scenario in civilized, Christian America at the end of the twentieth century? In the
last 30 years so many leaders in the news media, entertainment, business,
national and international politics, the judiciary, academia and even the
Church, have turned for personal renewal to a spirituality that they think is
compatible with their past but which at every major point is diametrically
opposed to Christianity. Anti-Christian forces have always stalked the Church's
earthly route, but rarely has religious paganism entered into the temple of God
with such bravado and virulence as it has in our day—except, perhaps, at the
time of Gnosticism.

Short-Term Future—The Sophianic Millennium

What can stop the short-term triumph of this pagan religion both in its Christian and non-Christian forms, with its agenda of tolerance for all, and of planetary peace? Few in the Church and the popular culture realize the enormity of the revolution going on around us. The Age of Aquarius, if one is to believe the leading spokeswomen of the movement, is nothing less than the "Second Coming of the Goddess," or the Sophianic Millennium, the era of goddess blessing and worship when all peoples and faiths will be united around the Divine Feminine. "It may be," says Isis priestess Caitlín Matthews, "that Sophia is about to be discerned in much the same way as she was in first century Alexandria: as a beacon to Christians, Jews, Gnostics and Pagans alike."[2] Sophia is the divine Savior who will lead humanity into another, more peaceful and loving civilization because She will lead us out of "the delusion of duality" and into the "marriage of humanity with Nature" and finally into marriage with the Divine.[3]

The time for this program is now. According to Matthews, "Sophia has been inching her way into popular consciousness throughout the latter half of the twentieth century." She goes on: "Those born in this century are now prospective citizens of the New Age, . . . where spiritual orthodoxy will be replaced by spiritual adventure, [and]. . . where the Divine Feminine will lead the way and where women will rediscover and enter their power."[4] This, Matthews argues, is already happening in the changes that affect gender roles and spirituality in present Western society.

Even without the apparent help of goddess spirituality, national, tax-paid programs at all levels of society deconstruct traditional gender "stereotypes" and produce a new and profoundly egalitarian view of sex, by which, one day, women may take power. When that happens, the biblical male God will appear as an archaic anachronism revered only by right-wing marginal Neanderthals. Sophia will take power, unopposed.

Queer Millennium

A minor variation on the coming age of bliss is the sophianic millennium seen through the eyes of a homosexual. The Rev. Nancy Wilson, senior pastor of the homosexual Metropolitan Community Church in Los Angeles, who calls herself a "lesbian ecu-terrorist" (ecu = ecumenical), proclaims a "queer theology" justifying all sexual choices, that can lead all Christians, gay, lesbian and straight, into the next *Queer* millennium.[5] Virginia Mollenkott, the "evangelical" lesbian applauds Wilson's work as "stunningly important, both for our tribe [gays and lesbians] and for any other person, church or organization that seeks to be whole."[6]

One way or another, the star of the Religious Left, with an appealing social agenda in its train, and the support of many international organizations, is in the ascendant in contemporary American society. One of the great secular world historians, Sir Arnold Toynbee, at the height of the Cold War and the expansion of Communism, made a surprising prophecy. He predicted that the twentieth century would be remembered as the time of the first appearance of the great universal religion of the third millennium blending Eastern religions and Christianity.[7] Christians at ease in modern Zion should realize that there is a tide in modern history and that it does not appear to be going their way.

A NEW CREATION OR A NEW FALL?
NEITHER OF THE ABOVE!

Having just entered the new millennium are we moving toward a "new Creation"? Are we headed for a repetition of the Fall? Or will history continue with its ups and downs without any significant change of intensity? The example of ancient Gnosticism suggests that as we enter the Age of Aquarius, the eschatological Eve stands transfixed once more before the tree of forbidden knowledge, seduced by the "wisdom" of the Serpent through whom speaks the goddess. Lilith, the serpentine Sophia, dangles before the modern woman the titillating fruit of autonomous freedom and power as the modern Adam, like the first, looks on in silence, afraid to say a word.[8]

In one of the most politically incorrect statements of all time, the inspired apostle Paul declared: "Adam was not the one deceived; it was the woman."[9] Paul surely does not mean that Eve was intellectually inferior, morally weak and spiritually immature. Rather he sees that in her role, so essential to the project of civilization,[10] and in her function as "helpmate," so crucial for the revelation of the trinitarian God, Eve was exposed with particular force to the bewitching promise of self-liberation.

How clever the Tempter's misuse of Scripture. And Hollywood's too. In her CD *It's a Man's World: Oh, Really?* popular singer Cher kneels in a seductive pose, her jet-black hair intertwined with a green serpent wrapped seductively around her body, clutching in her long fingers a bright-red apple. This modern Eve eats, convinced she is clarifying the true intentions of the gospel for radical libera- tion. But if the original sound of the bite reverberated through the cavernous halls of the universe, signaling the imminent Fall from paradise, what will be the significance of the feminist liturgical sound bite of the eschatological "re- eating of the apple," if not the final catastrophic disobedience and deconstruc- tion of the race?

AMERICAN DREAM OR PLANETARY NIGHTMARE?

Beyond culture wars and gender wars are *spirit wars*. In this ultimate struggle for mastery, the pagan goddess Sophia seeks to usurp the place of God the Creator and Redeemer. This is not colorful hyperbole. The conflict is real, the protago- nists irreconcilable. Sophia is the very opposite of the God of the Bible. She rep- resents monism as God represents theism. Her all-encompassing, encircling womb gives expression to the pagan notion of the divinity of all things, while her name, Sophia, vaunts the human claim to wisdom. With exquisite subtlety she seduces the modern mind by claiming to be tolerant and nondogmatic. In fact she is neither, for behind the velvet glove is an iron fist; behind the neo-pagan rejection of doctrine is a firm commitment to a nonnegotiable dogmatic belief in the unity of all things to which humanity and the planet are ineluctably head- ed; and behind the tolerance is a global system of unimaginable totalitarian pos- sibilities which cannot tolerate the discordant voice of biblical theism.[11]

Utopian thinking, and the pagan spiritual experience on which it is based, obliterates the truth that there *is* a cosmic conflict, that there *is* a deep antithe- sis between the Law of God and the ways of fallen man. The new eschatology sees history moving to its appointed evolutionary rendezvous with human lib- eration and "redemption." Aided by a leap in consciousness, humanity will evolve from its present immaturity into a new world order of peace and love. Of course, people who attain a "leap in consciousness" cease to perceive the need for objective salvation. Virtual salvation through human engineering and pagan spirituality will do just fine. In such a utopia, breaking the spell by the preach- ing of the Cross will not be tolerated.

Pagan monism is, by its very nature, an all-inclusive, totalitarian move- ment whose success depends upon total conformity to its view of peace. Its vision of a tolerant, all-inclusive world cannot tolerate those who believe in absolute truth, in ultimate right and wrong and in differentiated creational structures. In the future "utopia" there will be "no place for truth." Surveying the totalitarian stance of the politically correct orthodoxy on university campuses, where dissent to the official line is just not tolerated, Philip Johnson wonders if we are not being given a chilling preview of an era of "self-righteous bullying."[12] With little ultimate harm, school bullies control the playground; adult bullies, in matching shirts, can turn a democracy into a police state and wreak unimaginable harm on fellow human beings. The "karma patrol" of today could be the Great Inquisition of the Aquarian tomorrow.

While the Clinton White House described the many homosexual members of its administration as "gentle people," there is another, scarier side to this sexual palace revolution. In a widely circulated article called "Gay Revolutionary," the anonymous author "Michael Swift" warns the straight community, in chilling prose:

> We shall be victorious because we are filled with the ferocious bitterness of the oppressed who have been forced to play seemingly bit parts in your dumb, heterosexual shows throughout the ages. . . . We too are capable of firing guns and manning the barricades of the ultimate revolution. . . . Tremble, hetero swine, when we appear before you without our masks.[13]

Psychologist Peg Thompson, author of the book *Finding Your Own Spiritual Path*, after documenting what she calls the contemporary movement of "spiritual individualism," concludes by wishing she could be around in a hundred years "to see how things turn out."[14] Her naive inquisitiveness, like the optimism of many within and without the Church, does not betray the slightest fear that a return to paganism could produce one of the most radical and costly revolutions in human history. For when people make freedom from God and His laws the highest good, they become enslaved to the lie. This becomes obvious in the radical expressions of the movement. Diana Beguine, once a Christian and now a witch, celebrates her freedom from the gospel of the Cross and the law of God, by singing "A-mazing Grace . . . That saved a Witch like me. I once was lost, myself I found, was bound, but now I'm free."[15] This freedom leads to diabolical chains.

There is another side to the picture of gentleness, peace and love. The hubris that tries to save the self, by flaunting the laws of the Creator, leads in fact into slavery to evil. A repentant former member of a Wicca group has described her experiences in terms that strip away any illusion of harmlessness and genuine freedom:

> When I was a witch, I performed rituals. I evoked spirits. I called enti-
> ties. I cast spells, burned candles, concocted brews. . . . But where did it
> lead to? Into darkness, depression and the creation of an aura of gloom
> around me. I was frequently under demon attack. The house where I
> lived was alive with poltergeist activity . . . due to residual "guests" from
> rituals. My friends and family were afraid of me. I knew I had no future;
> all I had was a dark present. I was always wanted. It wasn't Satan's fault.
> He didn't exist—or so I thought. I gave it all up, and came to Jesus on
> my knees . . . .He freed me from the oppression and gave me back my
> soul—the one I had so foolishly given to evil in exchange for
> power. . . . Our salvation was bought at a great price and all we have to
> do is reach out for it. But we cannot serve two masters.[16]

The new spirituality contains power, and for those sufficiently committed to it, it is a power that binds—with great chains. Perhaps the most significant foremother of the new spirituality is Madame Helena Blavatsky, a Russian princess who, at the end of the nineteenth century, sought to unite Western occultism with Eastern spirituality, and claimed she was in touch with "ascended masters." Madame Blavatsky, whose major work, interestingly, was entitled *Isis Unveiled*, left Russia for the United States where she established the Theosophical Society in New York in 1875, and then set up an ashram in India. In 1884, unburdening her soul to an old Russian friend, Vsevolod Soloviev, whom she met in Paris, she said the remarkable following words:

> I would gladly return, I would gladly be Russian, Christian, Orthodox. I
> yearn for it. But there is no returning; I am in chains; I am not my own.[17]

The trouble with this freedom Madame Blavatsky and others espoused is that it is slavery to the powers of evil. Its glittering promise is the same old lie. Its wages lead to personal dissolution and death. But it is a *real lie*, spoken by the Father of Lies. Those who hope to exploit it to serve ideological ends are, in the powerful image of Donna Steichen, like foolish, perverse, vulnerable children, playing with a plastic bomb as though it were Silly Putty.

THE GREAT CONSPIRACY

This book is not a "conspiracy theory." It does not intend to accuse anyone, whether liberal or progressive conservative, of orchestrating a diabolical plot. If there is conspiracy, it is far greater than any individual or group of individuals could imagine. Rather, the above pages intend to set side by side the various "progressive" agendas, whose proponents may not even see the connections, in order to indicate their deep compatibility and then to compare the result with the ancient Gnostic system for independent confirmation. Under the light of scrutiny, a profound coherence appears in the multihued fabric of diversity: pagan monism. This broad pattern will not account for the myriad particularities, qualifications and inconsistencies of any given position. But in a time of moral, spiritual and theological confusion there is a need to see the broad picture and the ultimate stakes.

A NEW AGE POPE?

Vatican expert Malachi Martin saw it, from his perspective within the Roman Catholic church. In a work of fiction, *Windswept House*,[18] Martin describes an "unspoken alliance" between liberal forces in the Vatican (who in number equal the traditionalists in the Curia, but hold the positions of power), and international humanist organizations like the United Nations. Their desire is to change church doctrine on divorce, contraception, women priests, abortion and homosexuality. This powerful alliance is preparing to elect a pope who shares their liberal, globalist agenda. Martin dismisses the notion of conspiracy. It is just a fact that these people inside and outside the church share the same liberal vision for the planet. It is also a fact, admits Martin, that his novel is not fictional at all.[19]

At the deepest level, the issue rending our civilization is not "commitment to change" versus "nostalgia for the past," nor is it even the conflict between proponents of heterosexuality and those who promote pansexuality. Rather it has to do with the age-long antithesis between the woman and her seed and the Serpent. For the "ferocious bitterness" of feminists and gays is ultimately directed not against "straights" but against God, the Creator of heaven and Earth who made Man male and female. We recall the words of Abraham Kuyper regarding the deep antithesis within human history: "Do not forget that the fundamental contrast has always been, is still, and always will be until the end: Christianity and Paganism, the idols or the living God."[20]

As she covers her anemic body with a fake robe of Christ, Sophia begins to look more and more like the harlot of the Apocalypse,[21] that startling image of an apostate Church, fornicating with the kings of the earth, drunk with the blood of the saints and the martyrs of Jesus. On the threshold of the third millennium, the *spirit wars* have begun in dead earnest, though at present we have only seen the initial skirmishes. Sophia is only at the beginning of her reign.

LONG-TERM FUTURE

I have reached the end. This has been a hard book to write. Doubtless I have stood on toes and unnecessarily offended well-meaning people, for which I humbly beg forgiveness. But I could not avoid putting pen to paper. Since moving to the United States, I have felt the oppression of error masquerading as truth in a land that for so long has been a citadel for the gospel. The urge to warn my fellow brothers and sisters has been heavy upon me and kept me at my desk longer than anyone should sit at a desk. I firmly believe, though I pray I am wrong, that we are witnessing the first signs of an assault against the truth of Christ the likes of which the Church has never seen before. Orthodox Christian faith, instead of being celebrated as the backbone of the West, is now dismissed as its lunatic fringe. As Western civilization, with America in the lead, lurches away from its spiritual moorings, what has constituted its center for so long is now, in our generation, being dismissed to the edges as an embarrassing marginal extremism.

The burden of this book is to expose the growing apostasy around us. In that sense it is a wake up call. I have not given many answers, for I am not sure we have heard all the questions yet. This is surely not a time for quick fix-it solutions. I have not set out the Christian alternative.[22] I have rather looked into "the abyss of madness," to use the words of Irenaeus, to describe how so many professing Christians seem to be hell-bent on leading the bride of Christ into the lap of Satan. I have tried to make mine the motivations of the Church father Hippolytus, who sought to expose the heresy of Gnosticism for two reasons:

- *To show Christians what is truth and what is error*. He set out the heretical beliefs in order that believers "will be assisted by our discourse to become more intelligent, when they have learned the fundamental principles of the heresies . . . [and that] they shall be on their guard against those who are allowing themselves to become victims of these delusions."

- *To win those who are themselves teaching heresy.* "By proclaiming the folly of those who are persuaded by [these heterodox tenets], we shall prevail on them to retrace their course to the serene haven of the truth."[23]

Hippolytus understood the heart of the God of the Bible. Calling to apostate Israel to forsake her "adultery with wood and stone," the Lord, with longsuffering love, invites this wayward nation to turn and to repent.[24]

POST TENEBRAS LUX

The motto of our forebears in the faith, "After darkness, light," should encourage Christians to believe that the light will always triumph over the darkness, and that the gates of hell will not prevail against the Church.[25] Christians must remember that God's kingdom will not come by physical violence and the use of the sword. In the war of the spirits, the weapons are also spiritual. And among those weapons is love of our enemies. This is the way Jesus prevailed. This is the way His Church will prevail.

The message of this book is ultimately not discouraging. There is great darkness in the Church today. She disregards the Scriptures, she drags the name of God the Father in the mud, she mocks and spurns the gracious redemptive work of the eternal Son and makes sin the principle of life.

But the seductive lie is not in control of the situation. In its very nature as deception and counterfeit it cannot help but cause the light of the truth to appear in greater splendor. Looking at false teaching makes the gospel even more convincing, and examining the lie causes the truth to sparkle in all its radiance, and with greater intensity. God promises this to his people: "Even in darkness light dawns for the upright."[26]

Such is the challenge to Christians who will live and witness in the Age of Aquarius. This is a program of *action* for God's people at the threshold of the third millennium—to engage in an act of deep understanding as to the nature of truth and falsehood in our day, and to be faithful Eves and courageous, loving Adams who incarnate obedience to the God of Scripture, our Creator and Redeemer, and who by the power of the Spirit celebrate the presence of the coming Kingdom in godly families, holy lives and unflagging evangelism. For, in the words of Hippolytus, those who "have learned the fundamental principles of the heresies," are the ones who will stand firm in the darkness. They will be able to "warn the sinner of his wicked ways."[27] They will stand as watchmen on the walls. They will keep the flame of the gospel burning brightly in an hour of great apostasy,[28] until, at God's appointed time, at the certain rendezvous of the Son with the nations, the truth will blaze forth, across the planet and the cosmos, in the final word of universal confession—in terms paternal, indeed patriarchal—that "Jesus Christ is Lord, to the glory of God the Father."[29]

> Thy kingdom come that earth's despair may cease
> Beneath the shadow of its healing peace:
> Lift high the cross, the love of Christ proclaim,
> Till all the world adore his sacred name.[30]

ENDNOTES

Preface
1. John Lennon, *Skywriting by Word of Mouth* (San Francisco: Harper and Row, 1986), p. 35, as quoted in Alan Morrison, *The Serpent and the Cross: Religious Corruption in an Evil Age* (Birmingham, UK: K and M Books, 1994), p. 67.
2. Genesis 3:15.

Introduction
1. Uwe Siemon-Netto, "Poll shows Protestant collapse," *UPI* (28 June 2001), n.p.
2. Quotation from a speech she gave at the 1998 RE-Imagining Conference, quoted in *The Presbyterian Layman*, 13/3 (May/June 1998), p. 4.
3. Lee Penn, "The Coming World Religion," *SCP Journal*, 23/2-23/3 (1999), p. 51.
4. Marilyn Ferguson, quoted in *Hidden Dangers of the Rainbow* (Shreveport, LA: Huntingdon House, 1983), p. 147.
5. Ken Carey, *Starseed: The Third Millennium: Living in the Posthistoric World* (San Francisco: Harper San Francisco, 1991), p. ix, xi.

Chapter One
1. Marilyn Ferguson, "Aquarius Now . . . Making It Through the Confusion Gap," *Visions* (July 1994), p. 7.
2. Fritjof Capra, quoted in Alan Morrison, *The Serpent and the Cross: Religious Corruption in an Evil Age* (Birmingham, UK: K and M Books, 1994), p. 119.
3. See Gary W. Aldrich, *Unlimited Access: An FBI Agent Inside the Clinton White House* (Washington, DC: Regnery Publishing, 1996), which describes the Clinton staff's history of drug use.
4. Annie Gottlieb, *Do You Believe in Magic? The Second Coming of the '60s Generation* (New York: Times Books, 1987), n.p.
5. Ferguson, "Aquarius Now," p. 7, emphasis added.
6. Humorist Fran Lebowitz, quoted in Suzanne Garment, *Los Angeles Times* (January 24, 1993), n.p.
7. Marianne Williamson, *A Return to Love: Reflections on the Principles of "A Course in Miracles"* (New York: HarperCollins, 1992).
8. *Chicago Tribune* (December 20, 1994), p. 2.
9. *Parliament of the World's Religions: Program Catalogue* (Chicago: 1993), p. 119-120. Jean Houston described regular meetings during her adolescence with Pierre Teilhard de Chardin, a Jesuit priest and a seminal thinker in New Age spirituality.
10. Bob Woodward describes this incident in his book *The Choice*, recommended reading for the White House staff during the Clinton Administration. See Sonya Ross, "White House Defends First Lady's Use of Spiritual Advisers," *San Diego Union-Tribune* (June 23, 1996).

11. Tim Graham, "Happily after Evertz," *World* (April 21, 2001), p. 15.

12. Gillian Russell Gilhool, "More on Beijing," *Wellesley* (Spring 1996), p. 1.

13. Michael Lerner, one of Mrs. Clinton's ideological gurus, was the leader of the Berkeley SDS in the '60s. This Jewish radical reappeared as part of a left-wing evangelical sit-in protest against the Republican project to balance the federal budget by streamlining the welfare system. Pushing the notion of cobelligerency to new levels of compromise, both he and Tony Campolo were arrested by the same police detail!

14. Peter Collier and David Horowitz, *Destructive Generation* (New York: Simon and Schuster, 1990), p. 304.

15. Ken Carey, *The Starseed Transmissions* (New York: Harper, 1982), quoted in Morrison, *The Serpent*, p. 155.

16. Roger Kimball, *Tenured Radicals* (San Francisco: Harper and Row, 1990).

17. Michael Bauman, "The Chronicle of an Undeception," *Culture Wars*, 1/7 (December 1995), p. 17.

18. This should in no sense be taken as defense of the misuse of patriarchal power. But just as the misuse of judicial power does not imply that we are to dismantle the judicial system (our defense against the chaos of lawlessness), so the misuse of patriarchy does not imply that we should abandon a father's tender protection and loving authority in his home. A healthy "patriarchy," or "father-rule" provides an excellent restraint on violence, by training children to the patient and willing exercise of duty within the structure of love, tenderness, joy and peace.

19. *World* (July 2, 1994), p. 19.

20. See two excellent discussions of deconstruction: Gene Edward Veith, *Postmodern Times: A Christian Guide to Contemporary Thought and Culture* (Wheaton, IL: Crossway, 1994), pp. 47-70, and Charlene Spretnak, *States of Grace: The Recovery of Meaning in the Postmodern Age* (San Francisco: Harper, 1991), pp. 233-244.

21. Jerry Rubin, *Do It* (New York: Simon and Schuster, 1970), p. 249.

22. The "Stonewall" riot of 1964 in Greenwich Village, where homosexuals resisted a police sweep of this famous gay bar, is revered as a defining moment for the homosexual movement.

23. In his book, *The Politics of Meaning: Restoring Hope and Possibility in an Age of Cynicism* (New York: Addison-Wesley, 1996), Lerner, a true postmodern, attacks liberalism/modernity from the "high" ground of the new spirituality.

24. NAMBLA (North American Man-Boy Love Association) managed to be included in the Stonewall 25 gay/lesbian parade, sponsored by the City of New York. Meanwhile, a San Diego Superior Court judge ruled that the Boy Scouts could not exclude homosexuals as Scout leaders (*San Diego Union-Tribune*, July 8, 1994).

25. See Genesis 15:16. I am grateful to Rev. Steve Schlissel for this insight.

26. Gary L. Bauer, president of Family Research Council, in a newsletter of February 7, 1994.

27. See the excellent account of this religious search in Os Guinness, *The Dust of Death: A Critique of the Establishment and the Counter-Culture—and a Proposal for a Third Way* (Downers Grove, IL: Intervarsity Press, 1973).

28. Ken Kesey, one of the bards of the movement said: "For a year we've been in the Garden of Eden. Acid opened the door to it. It was the Garden of Eden and Innocence and a ball," quoted in Guinness, *The Dust of Death*, p. 232.

29. David Miller, *The New Polytheism: Rebirth of the Gods and Goddesses* (New York: Harper and Row, 1974), p. 11.

30. Swami Vivekananda, quoted in Morrison, *The Serpent*, p. 228.

31. Gary Bauer, president of the Family Research Council, "American Family Life: Worth Exporting?" *Focus on the Family* (July 1994), p. 2ff. See also William J. Bennett, *The Index of Leading Cultural Indicators: Facts and Figures on the State of the American Society* (New York: Simon and Schuster, 1994), p. 59.

32. The breakdown of the family has enormous impact on a culture—see Bennett, *The Index*, p. 12.

33. Facts from the Census Bureau as reported in the *Escondido (California) Times Advocate* July 20, 1994.

34. No age has expressed the Christian faith in a radical and truly consistent way. Its call to social justice gave the '60s revolution an appearance of moral purity that, in part, explains the longevity of its popularity. There were elements to be criticized in pre-'60s American Christianity, not least its easy acceptance of racial segregation. But the '60s did not call for a return to the sources. It turned away from those sources, finding answers in Eastern paganism.

35. The title of W. C. Roof's sociological study, *A Generation of Seekers: The Spiritual Journeys of the Baby Boom Generation* (San Francisco: Harper, 1993).

36. Ibid., p. 126.

37. Gottlieb, *Do You Believe in Magic?* pp. 249-250.

Chapter Two

1. See Romans 1:25.

2. For parts of this analysis, I am indebted to Professor Jeffrey Haddon of the department of sociology at the University of Virginia, in a public lecture on the major characteristics of the New Age movement. For a more thorough development of the five points of monism, see my *Gospel Truth, Pagan Lies: Can You Tell the Difference?* (Mulkiteo, WA, 2000), a short book, good for schools and study groups. For an opposing view, see Alastair H. B. Logan, *Gnostic Truth and Christian Heresy: A Study in the History of Gnosticism* (Edinburgh, Scotland: T and T Clark, 1996).

3. Asphodel P. Long, *The Absent Mother: Restoring the Goddess to Judaism and Christianity*, edited by Alix Pirani (London: Mandala, 1991).

4. See David F. Wells, *No Place for Truth: Or Whatever Happened to Evangelical Theology?* (Grand Rapids, MI: Eerdmans, 1993).

5. Arthur L. Johnson, *Faith Misguided: Exposing the Dangers of Mysticism* (Chicago: Moody Press, 1988), p. 32. For a good discussion of this issue, see James W. Sire, *The Universe Next Door* (Downers Grove, IL: Intervarsity, 1976), pp. 178-183.

6. Ibid., pp. 35-36.

7. As the great modern Gnostic, C. G. Jung, said: "The self is a circle whose center is everywhere and whose circumference is nowhere." See Miguel Serrano, *C. G. Jung and Hermann Hesse: A Record of Two Friendships*, trans. Frank MacShane (New York: Schoken Books, 1968), pp. 50, 55.

8. Cardinal Bernadin, highly visible in episcopal and sartorial splendor at the opening ceremonies, never once exercised his function as teacher and pastor, and remained silent with regard to historic theistic Christianity.

9. See Matthew 16:2-3.

10. See the Family Research Council newsletter (June 7, 1994).

11. Peter Russell, *The Awakening Earth: The Next Evolutionary Leap,* a standard New Age textbook, quoted in Alan Morrison, *The Serpent and the Cross: Religious Corruption in an Evil Age* (Birmingham, UK: K and M Books, 1994), pp. 135, 138.

12. "The Manson Murders: Twenty Five Years Later," *Los Angeles Times*, August 6, 1994.

13. Ferguson, "Aquarius Now," p. 13, refers to Ilya Progogine's model of dissipative structures.

14. Robert L. Wilken, "No Other Gods," *First Things* (December 1993), p. 13.

15. Ibid., p. 14. See also Stephen Smith, "Worldview, Language, and Radical Feminism: An Evangelical Appraisal," Alvin F. Kimel, Jr., ed., *Speaking the Christian God: The Holy Trinity and the Challenge of Feminism* (Grand Rapids, MI: Eerdmans, 1992), pp. 258-275.

16. See Alan David Bloom, *The Closing of the American Mind: How Higher Education Has Failed Democracy and Impoverished the Souls of Today's Students* (New York: Simon and Schuster, 1987). For a longer view, see George M. Marsden and Bradley J. Longfield, *The Secularization of the Academy* (New York/Oxford: Oxford University Press, 1992).

17. For an excellent documentation see Michael Medved, *Hollywood Versus America: Popular Culture and the War on Traditional Values* (New York: Harper Collins, 1992).

18. See George Grant, *Grand Illusions: The Legacy of Planned Parenthood* (Franklin, TN: Adroit Press, 1992).

19. George Barna, reported in *World* (March 5, 1994).

20. Stephen Smith, "Worldview, Language, and Radical Feminism: An Evangelical Appraisal," Alvin F. Kimel, Jr., ed., *Speaking the Christian God: The Holy Trinity and the Challenge of Feminism* (Grand Rapids, MI: Eerdmans, 1992), p. 275.

21. Os Guinness, *The Dust of Death: A Critique of the Establishment and the Counter-Culture—and a Proposal for a Third Way* (Downers Grove, IL: Intervarsity Press, 1973), p. 209.

Chapter Three

1. Friedrich Nietzsche, "The Greatest Utility of Polytheism," *Joyful Wisdom*, trans. Thomas Common (New York: Ungar Publishing Co., 1960), pp. 178-180.

2. The fatigue sometimes turns to panic. See Walter Brueggemann, "On Writing a Commentary . . . An Emergency?" *ATS Colloquy* (September/October, 1992), pp. 10-11. Brueggemann wonders what will happen as the old scientific, so-called "historical-critical method" is abandoned, and scholars become advocates of whatever turns them on. See chapter 8.

3. Of recent popular liberal theology, Carl A. Raschke, *The Bursting of New Wine Skins: Reflections on Religion and Culture at the End of Affluence* (Pittsburgh, PA: Pickwick Press, 1978), p. 51, says: "Popular liberal theology preached the salvation of the individual, while disregarding the meaning and worth of persons." He sees this same theology as having "so overdone the new that it has sundered its own roots and thereby withered from lack of nourishment" (pp. 24-25).

4. Benton Johnson, Dean R. Hoge and Donald A. Luidens, "Mainline Churches: The Real Reason for Decline," *First Things* (March 1993), p. 13. See also Milton J. Coalter, et al., eds., two volumes: *The Presbyterian Predicament: Six Perspectives and The Mainstream Protestant "Decline": The Presbyterian Pattern* (Louisville, KY: Westminster/John Knox Press, 1990).

5. Edward W. Farley, "The Presbyterian Heritage as Modernism," in *The Presbyterian Predicament*, p. 64.

6. Arthur Matthews, "Emptying the Box," *World* (October 30, 1993), p. 28, gives the details. The central offices of the Presbyterian Church USA and the United Church of Christ, once located·in the "God Box," 475 Riverside Drive, New York, have fled to the heartland: the United Church of Christ to Cleveland, Ohio, and the Presbyterian Church USA to Louisville, Kentucky.

7. Ibid., pp. 14-15.

8. Ibid., p. 18.

9. Ibid., n.p., emphasis added.

10. Stephen Carter, *The Culture of Disbelief: How American Law and Politics Trivialize Religious Devotion* (San Francisco: Harper Collins, 1993).

11. Charlene Spretnak, *States of Grace: The Recovery of Meaning in the Postmodern Age* (San Francisco: Harper, 1991), p. 5.

12. This term is now used by Mary Daly, the radical feminist witch, in *Beyond God the Father: Toward a Philosophy of Women's Liberation* (Boston, MA: Beacon Press, 1985), p. 100, showing again that Nietzsche's ideas are far from dead.

13. Nietzsche, "The Greatest Utility of Polytheism," pp. 178-180.

14. David Miller, *The New Polytheism: Rebirth of the Gods and Goddesses* (New York: Harper and Row, 1974), p. ix.

15. David Cave, *Mircea Eliade's Vision for a New Humanism* (New York: Oxford University Press, 1993), p. 26.

16. Donna Steichen, *Ungodly Rage: The Hidden Face of Catholic Feminism* (San Francisco: Ignatius Press, 1991), p. 286.

17. Spretnak, *States of Grace*, p. 2.

18. See *World* (October 1993), p. 28.

19. Carl A. Raschke, *The Interruption of Eternity: Modern Gnosticism and the Origins of the New Religious Consciousness* (Chicago: Nelson-Hall, 1980). See also James W. Fowler, *Weaving the New Creation: Stages of Faith and the Public Church* (San Francisco: HarperSanFrancisco, 1991), p. 13.

20. Lynn Willeford, "Why I Went Back," *New Age Journal* (August 1993), pp. 35-40.

21. *New Age Journal* (December 1992).

22. W. C. Roof's sociological study, *A Generation of Seekers: The Spiritual Journeys of the Baby Boom Generation* (San Francisco: Harper, 1993), p. 154.

23. Ibid., p. 260ff.

24. A personal letter to Constance Cumbey, quoted in *Hidden Dangers of the Rainbow* (Shreveport, LA: Huntingdon House, 1983), p. 147. One is reminded of the observation by Lee, *Against the Protestant Gnostics* (New York: Oxford University Press, 1987), p. 4: ". . . very few gnostics were to be found outside the main body of the Church. The typical gnostic was a member, often a pillar, of the local and recognized Christian Church."

25. Ken Carey, *Starseed: The Third Millennium: Living in the Posthistoric World* (San Francisco: Harper San Francisco, 1991), p. ix, xi.

26. Duncan Ferguson, ed., *New Age Spirituality: An Assessment* (Louisville, KY: Westminster/John Knox Press, 1993).

27. Only the article by Morton Kelsey, "The Former Age and the New Age," in *New Age Spirituality: An Assessment*, defends a form of reinvigorated traditional Christianity.

28. On page 98 of *New Age Spirituality*, it is true, Spangler disavows this formulation as far too flippant.

29. Ibid., pp. 74-75.

30. Steichen, *Ungodly Rage*, pp. 210, 213 and 232-233, notes this same phenomenon, but argues, as I do, that despite the disclaimer, Fox is as New Age as anyone.

31. Ibid., p. 219.

32. "Matthew Fox: 'Joy Happens,'" *New Age Journal* (December 1992), pp. 26-27.

33. On this term, see Virginia Mollenkott, *Sensuous Spirituality: Out from Fundamentalism* (New York: Crossroads, 1992), p. 73ff.

Chapter Four

1. Mary Daly and Jane Caputi, *Webster's First New Intergalactic Wickedary of the English Language* (Boston, MA: Beacon Press, 1987), p. 88.

2. The title of James Davidson Hunter's best-selling sociological study published in 1991 (Basic Books/Harper).

3. Hunter's subsequent book had a much more ominous title: *Before the Shooting Begins.*

4. Tom Williams, priest of the Church of All Worlds, quoted in Dave Bass, "Drawing Down the Moon," *Christianity Today* (April 1991), p. 17.

5. Japanese proverb quoted in Harold A. Netland, *Dissident Voices: Religious Pluralism and the Question of Truth* (Grand Rapids, MI: Eerdmans, 1991), p. 196.

6. Paul Knitter, *No Other Name? A Critical Survey of Christian Attitudes Toward the World Religions* (Maryknoll, NY: Orbis Books, 1986), p. 225.

7. This is the optimistic read of Leonard Swidler, *The Meaning of Life at the Edge of the Third Millennium* (New York: Paulist Press, 1993), pp. 4, 116.

8. Smart and Konstantine wish to "carry forward" the project proposed by Teilhard and the syncretist theologians Wilfred Cantwell Smith, Raimundo Pannikar, John Hick and John Cobb.

9. Op. cit., pp. 144-145.

10. *Religious Studies, Harper San Francisco Catalog* for 1995, p. 2.

11. Tertullian, *De Praescriptione*, 41, quoted in K. Rudolf, *Gnosis: The Nature and History of an Ancient Religion* (Edinburgh, Scotland: T and T Clark, 1977), p. 216.

12. Matthew Fox, *The Coming of the Cosmic Christ: The Healing of Mother Earth and the Birth of a Global Renaissance* (San Francisco: Harper, 1988), p. 229.

13. Caitlín Matthews, *Sophia, Goddess of Wisdom: The Divine Feminine from Black Goddess to World-Soul* (London: The Aquarian Press/Harper Collins, 1992), p. 368.

14. Katherine Zappone, *The Hope for Wholeness: A Spirituality for Feminists* (Mystic, CT: Twenty-Third Publications, 1991), p. 39.

15. Fox, *Cosmic Christ*, p. 229, says quite plainly: "Deep ecumenical possibilities emerge when we shift from the quest for the historical Jesus to the quest for the Cosmic Christ."

16. See also R. H. Drummond, *A Life of Jesus the Christ* (San Francisco: Harper and Row, 1989).

17. R. H. Drummond, *Towards a New Age in Christian Theology* (Maryknoll, NY: Orbis Books, 1985), p. 183.

18. James W. Fowler, *Weaving the New Creation: Stages of Faith and the Public Church* (San Francisco: HarperSanFrancisco, 1991), p. 21.

19. Sister Madonna Kolbenschlag, quoted in Donna Steichen, *Ungodly Rage: The Hidden Face of Catholic Feminism* (San Francisco: Ignatius Press, 1991), p. 92. Joachim of Fiora (A.D. 1132-1202) first developed the three-age description of history: the age of the Father (Old Testament Faith), the age of the Son (Christian Church), and the age of the Spirit, in which there would be no church.

20. Rosemary Radford Ruether, *Sexism and God-Talk* (Boston, MA: Beacon Press, 1983), p. 11.

21. Marilyn Ferguson, "Aquarius Now . . . Making It Through the Confusion Gap," *Visions* magazine (July 1994), p. 7.

22. Chris Griscom, "Ecstasy Is a New Frequency," *Light Connection* (February 1993), p. 8.

23. Ben Nova, "Future War . . . Future Peace," *Omni* (November 1993), p. 65.

24. Joseph Campbell and Bill Moyers, *The Power of Myth* (New York: AnchorBooks/Doubleday, 1988), p. xix.

25. Alice Bailey, quoted in Alan Morrison, *The Serpent and the Cross: Religious Corruption in an Evil Age* (Birmingham, UK: K and M Books, 1994), pp. 157-158, emphasis added.

26. Ken Carey, *The Starseed Transmissions* (New York: Harper, 1982), pp. 54- 55.
27. James B. Irwin with William A. Emerson, Jr., *To Rule the Night* (Philadelphia and New York: A. J. Holman, 1973), pp. 17-18.

Chapter Five

1. K. C. Johnson and J. H. Coe, *Wildlife in the Kingdom Come* (Grand Rapids, MI: Zondervan, 1993), p. 72.
2. Ecclesiastes 1:9.
3. For a modern, positive expression of Gnosticism, see Harold Bloom, *Omens of Millennium: The Gnosis of Angels, Dreams and Resurrection* (New York: Riverhead Books, 1996).
4. Philip Lee, *Against the Protestant Gnostics* (New York: Oxford University Press, 1987), p. xi.
5. For other works on this general theme, see, in particular Robert N. Bellah, "Civil Religion in America," *American Civil Religion*, ed., Russell E. Richey and Donald G. Jones (New York: Harper and Row, 1974); Carl Raschke, *The Interruption of Eternity;* James Hitchcock, *The New Enthusiasts and What They Are Doing to the Catholic Church* (Chicago: Thomas More Press, 1982); Donna Steichen, *Ungodly Rage: The Hidden Face of Catholic Feminism* (San Francisco: Ignatius Press, 1991); Harold Bloom, *The American Religion: The Emergence of the Post-Christian Nation* (New York: Simon and Schuster, 1992). An important early source is Eric Voegelin, professor of political science, University of Munich, who was a pioneer in developing the category of Gnosticism for the understanding of Western intellectual/religious history. It would be correct to say that his work, begun in the '30s at the University of Vienna, eventually gave rise to a school—see Ellis Sandoz, *The Voegelinian Revolution* (Baton Rouge, LA: Louisiana State University Press, 1981), and Eugene Webb, *Eric Voegelin: Philosopher of History* (Seattle, WA: University of Washington Press, 1981). A profound and sympathetic treatment of Voegelin's contribution is found in David Walsh, *After Ideology: Recovering the Spiritual Foundations of Freedom* (San Francisco: HarperSanFrancisco, 1990), pp. 54-58 and passim. See also Michael Franz, *Eric Voegelin and the Politics of Spiritual Revolt: The Roots of Modern Ideology* (Baton Rouge, LA: Louisiana State University Press, 1992, and Stephen A. McKnight, *Sacralizing the Secular: The Renaissance Origins of Modernity* (Baton Rouge, LA: Louisiana State University Press, 1989). One should also note the important connections between the psychologist C. G. Jung and Gnosticism: see J. F. Satinover, "Jungians and Gnostics," *First Things* (October 1994), pp. 41-48, and Richard Noll, *The Jung Cult: Origins of a Charismatic Movement* (Princeton, NJ: Princeton University Press, 1994).
6. Philip Lee, *Against the Protestant Gnostics*, p. 84.
7. See H. Jonas, *The Gnostic Religion: The Message of the Alien God and the Beginnings of Christianity* (Boston, MA: Beacon Press, 1958), pp. 3-27.
8. G. Filoramo, *A History of Gnosticism* (Cambridge, MA: Basil Blackwell, 1990), p. 34ff.
9. See the works of Gnostic specialists such as U. Bianchi, "Mithraism and Gnosticism," in J. R. Hinnells, ed., *Mithraic Studies: Proceedings of the First International Congress of Mithraic Studies*, I-II (Manchester: 1975), pp. 457-465; S. Giverson, "Der Gnostizismus und Die Mysterienreligionen," in J. P. Asmussen and J. Laessoe, eds., *Handbuch der Religionsgeschichte* (Gittingen: 1975); Mcl. R. Wilson, "Gnosis and the Mysteries," in R. van den Broek and M. J. Vermaseren, eds., *Studies G. Quispel* (Leiden: E. J. Brill, 1975), pp. 451-457.
10. See S. Angus, *The Mystery Religions: A Study in the Religious Background of Early Christianity* (New York: Dover Publications, 1975—originally published in 1925); A. J. Festugière, *Personal*

Religion Among the Greeks, Sather Classical Lectures, 26 (Berkeley, CA: 1954); Walter Burkert, *Ancient Mystery Cults* (Cambridge, MA: Harvard University Press, 1987).

11. Hebrews 13:8.

12. Donna Steichen, *Ungodly Rage: The Hidden Face of Catholic Feminism (San Francisco: Ignatius Press,* 1991), p. 122.

13. Still the standard work on Marcion is Adolf von Harnack, *Marcion: Das Evangelium von fremden Gott,* 2nd ed. TU 45 (1924): see also R. S. Wilson, *Marcion: A Study of a Second-Century Heretic* (London, 1933), and R. Joseph Hoffmann, *Marcion: On the Restitution of Christianity: An Essay on the Development of Radical Paulinist Theology in the Second Century* (Chico, CA: Scholar's Press, 1984).

14. A. von Harnack, Marcion, 235, quoted in P. J. Tomson, *Paul and Jewish Law: Halaka in the Letters of the Apostle to the Gentiles* (Minneapolis, MN: Fortress Press, 1990), p. 10, note 4.

15. Helmut Koester, *Introduction to the New Testament: Volume 2: History and Literature of Early Christianity* (Philadelphia: Fortress Press, 1982), p. 330.

16. Orthodox Roman Catholics might be tempted to breathe a silent "amen" to that comparison, but that would be misplaced. For while it is true that Luther, in his zeal and rhetoric, sometimes went overboard (see his impulsive rejection of James and Revelation—which he later renounced), his love for the gospel and the Scriptures Old and New leaves most of us in the starting blocks.

17. Tertullian, quoted in R. Joseph Hoffmann, *Marcion: On the Restitution of Christianity: An Essay on the Development of Radical Paulinist Theology in the Second Century* (Chico, CA: Scholar's Press, 1984), pp. 110-111.

18. Irenaeus, *Against Heresies* 3:3:4. If Marcion is the prototypical liberal, he may also be the first "modern." E. Michael Jones, in his fascinating study, *Degenerate Moderns: Modernity as Rationalized Sexual Misbehavior* (San Francisco: Ignatius, 1993), claims that the locomotive driving much of modern social science has been the production of "scientific" theory and data to justify the personal deviant sexual behavior of its creators. Jones analyzes the histories of Mead, Kinsey, Keynes, Picasso, Freud and Jung, and argues that their essential methodology consisted in placing desire before truth rather than truth before desire. In this sense, Marcion appears to be the first modern, at least in his methodology. According to early Church tradition, Marcion was originally excommunicated by his own father for having seduced a virgin—see Helmut Koester, *Introduction to the New Testament*, vol. 2, p. 329. Koester dismisses this tradition as a "malicious polemical invention," though he recognizes its important "symbolic meaning." If this tradition were true, all Marcion's later work to demonstrate that the Old Testament law and the Old Testament God were not binding on true, spiritual Christians would be an attempt to justify his own wrongdoing.

19. Duncan Greenlees, *The Gospel of the Gnostics* (Madras, India: The Theosophical Publishing House, 1958), p. vii.

20. J. Gresham Machen, *Christianity and Liberalism* (New York: MacMillan Company, 1923), p. 2. The title states the thesis, though Machen was careful to distinguish between liberalism and liberals.

21. Ibid., pp. 160, 172.

22. Pope Pius X, encyclical on modernism, *Pascendi Gregis* (London: Burns and Oates, 1907). See also *Lamentabile Sane,* and the "Oath Against Modernism," appendices in Michael Davies, *Partisans of Error: St Pius X against the Modernists* (Long Prairie, MN: Neumann Press, 1983), quoted in Steichen, *Ungodly Rage*, p. 257.

23. *Religiousstudies News*, vol. 9, no. 4 (November 1994), p. 15.

24. "The RE-Imagining Conference: A Report," The American Family Association (April 1994), p. 19.

25. James M. Robinson, "Introduction," *The Nag Hammadi Library in English (NHL)*, pp. 1-25, see especially pp. 3, 6-7, 16, 24. In addition, on pp. 5 and 18 he uses the term "heretical" in a similar way.

26. See "RE-Imagining Foments Uproar Among Presbyterians," *The Washington Post* (June 1994).

27. Alan Morrison, *The Serpent and the Cross: Religious Corruption in an Evil Age* (Birmingham, UK: K and M Books, 1994), p. 200.

28. Lee, *Against the Protestant Gnostics*, p. 14. Specifically, Lee is a Barthian, and so technically, from an orthodox point of view, has one foot in the liberal camp.

29. The words of Jesus: Matthew 24:24; Mark 13:22.

Chapter Six

1. David Miller, *The New Polytheism: Rebirth of the Gods and Goddesses* (New York: Harper and Row, 1974), p. 76.

2. Charles Colson, quoted in Cal Thomas, "Manipulating the Bible for Political Ends," *Los Angeles Times* (October 7, 1994).

3. Alicia Suskin Ostriker, *Feminist Revision and the Bible: The Unwritten Volume* (Cambridge, MA: Blackwell, 1995).

4. James Robinson, quoted in K. B. Welton, *Abortion Is Not a Sin: A New Age Look at an Old-Age Problem* (Costa Mesa, CA: Pandit Press, 1987), p. 166.

5. Ibid., p. 67.

6. Rosemary Radford Ruether, *Womanguides: Readings Towards a Feminist Theology* (Boston, MA: Beacon Press, 1985), p. ix.

7. Susan Durber, "The Female Reader of the Parables of the Lost," *Journal for the Study of the New Testament*, 45 (1992), p. 78.

8. Rosemary Radford Ruether, *Women-Church: Theology and Practice* (San Francisco: Harper and Row, 1985), p. 137.

9. Ibid., pp. 47, 142.

10. Danna Nolan Fewell and David M. Gunn, *Gender, Power and Promise* (Nashville, TN: Abingdon, 1993), p. 20.

11. "General Introduction," *The New Testament and Psalms: An Inclusive Version* (New York: Oxford University Press, 1995), p. vii.

12. Ibid., p. ix.

13. Just a generation ago, liberal scholars were hailing Jesus' revelation of God as Father, Abba, as the essence and uniqueness of his message: see E. Loymeyer, *"Our Father": An Introduction to the Lord's Prayer*, translated by John Bowden (New York: Harper and Row, 1966), pp. 41, 42, and Joachim Jeremias, *The Prayers of Jesus, Studies in Biblical Theology: Second Series*, 6 (Naperville, IL: Alec R. Allenson, Inc., 1967), p. 57.

14. For a thorough discussion of the gender-neutral Bible translation issue, see Vern S. Poythress and Wayne Grudem, *The Gender-Neutral Bible Controversy: Muting the Masculinity of God's Words* (Nashville, TN: Broadman and Holman, 2000).

15. James M. Robinson, "How My Mind Has Changed," Society of Biblical Literature: 1985 Seminar Papers (Atlanta, GA: Scholars Press, 1985), p. 495. This might be considered one of the first attempts to apply practical deconstructionism to the Bible.

250   Notes

16. William Farmer, a recognized New Testament critic, professor of New Testament at Perkins School of Theology, "The Church's Stake in the Question of 'Q'," *Perkins Journal*, 39/3 (1986), p. 10, acknowledges that "no one book has been more influential in setting the stage for the present upswing in 'Q' research" than Robinson's and Koester's *Trajectories Through Early Christianity* (Philadelphia: Fortress Press, 1971). Farmer goes on to state that of the essays in that book, "none is more often quoted in the 'Q' literature than Robinson's 'LOGOI SOPHWN.'"

17. Robert Funk, "Three Tributes to James M. Robinson," *Foundations and Facets*, 5:2 (Polebridge Press, June 1989), p. 6.

18. Robinson in Robinson and Koester *Trajectories Through Early Christianity* (Philadelphia: Fortress Press, 1971), pp. 1-19.

19. They build on the work of Walter Bauer, *Orthodoxy and Heresy in Earliest Christianity*, trans. Robert A. Kraft and Gerhard Krodel (Philadelphia: Fortress Press, 1971).

20. In addition to their joint work, *Trajectories*, see Helmut Koester, "GNOMAI DIAPHOROI: The Origin and Nature of Diversification in the History of Early Christianity," *Harvard Theological Review*, 58 (1965), pp. 279-318; also "One Jesus and Four Primitive Gospels," *Harvard Theological Review*, 61 (1968), pp. 203-247; James Robinson, "LOGOI SOPHWN: On the Gattung of Q" *The Future of Our Religious Past: Essays in Honor of Rudolf Bultmann* (London: SCM, 1971), pp. 84-130.

21. Koester, *Trajectories*, p. 270, states in the concluding essay: "The distinctions between canonical and noncanonical, orthodox and heretical are obsolete.... One can only speak of a 'History of Early Christian Literature.'" The gray web of theological confusion is extended to the Early Church.

22. For critiques of the Jesus Seminar from an evangelical point of view, see: Michael J. Wilkins and J. P. Moreland, eds., *Jesus Under Fire: Modern Scholarship Reinvents the Historical Jesus* (Grand Rapids, MI: Zondervan, 1995); Ben Witherington III, *The Jesus Quest: The Third Search for the Jew of Nazareth* (Downers Grove, IL: InterVarsity, 1995); Robert Thomas and F. David Farnell, *The Jesus Crisis: The Inroads of Historical Criticism into Evangelical Scholarship* (Grand Rapids, MI: Kregel, 1998).

23. Robinson, "How My Mind Has Changed," p. 486.

24. Birger A. Pearson, ed., *The Future of Early Christianity: Essays in Honor of Helmut Koester* (Minneapolis, MN: Fortress Press, 1991).

25. Ibid., p. 473.

26. Ibid., p. 472.

27. Ibid., p. 474. The feminist theologian, Elizabeth Schüssler Fiorenza emphasizes the "connections between ... feminist theological questions and those of historical-critical scholarship." See *Bread not Stone: The Challenge of Feminist Biblical Interpretation* (Boston, MA: Beacon, 1984), p. 94.

28. Ibid., pp. 475- 476.

29. The liberal critic Farmer sees this in "The Church's Stake," p. 10. In his own words: "It is Rudolf Bultmann as read through the work of Walter Bauer who lives on in the Trajectories."

30. Pagels, *Gnostic Gospels* (New York: Random House, 1979), pp. 46, 142.

31. Elizabeth Schlusler Fiorenza, *In Memory of Her: A Feminist Theological Reconstruction of Christian Origins* (New York: Crossroads, 1988), p. xv. See also her *Bread not Stone: The Challenge of Feminist Biblical Interpretation* (Boston, MA: Beacon, 1984), pp. 66-67.

32. Robert J. Miller, "The Gospels That Didn't Make the Cut," *Bible Review* (August 1993), p. 21. See also Burton L. Mack, "Q and the Gospel of Mark: Revising Christian Origins," *Semeia*, 55

(1991), p. 31, who says about the struggle of the Q community to survive: "A certain form of Christianity [orthodoxy] finally won over the others." Orthodoxy won not because it was true but because it used social power more effectively.

33. Ruether, *Womanguides*, p. ix.

34. Melanie Morrison, quoted in Susan Cyre, "PCUSA Funds Effort to Re-Create God," *Presbyterian Layman*, 27/1 (January/February 1994), p. 9.

35. James M. Robinson, "Introduction," *The Nag Hammadi Library in English (NHL)*, p. 20.

36. Caitlín Matthews, *Sophia, Goddess of Wisdom: The Divine Feminine from Black Goddess to World-Soul* (London: The Aquarian Press/Harper Collins, 1992), p. 338.

37. Robinson, "Introduction," *NHL*, pp. xiii-xv.

38. Peter Jones, *The Gnostic Empire Strikes Back* (Phillipsburg, NJ: P and R, 1992).

39. Shirley MacLaine, *Going Within: A Guide for Inner Transformation* (New York: Bantam Books, 1989), pp. 29-30.

40. T. Roszak, *Where the Wasteland Ends: Politics and Transcendence in Post-Industrial Society* (New York: Doubleday, 1972), p. 262.

41. Robert J. Miller, ed., *The Complete Gospels* (Sonoma, CA: Polebridge Press, 1992).

42. Robert W. Funk and Roy W. Hoover, *The Five Gospels: The Search for the Authentic Words of Jesus* (New York: Macmillan, 1993).

43. *Polebridge Press Catalog* (Fall/Winter 1991-1992), p. 3.

44. Irenaeus, *Against Heresies* 3:11:8.

45. See Ezekiel 1:4.

46. Stephen Mitchell, *The Gospel According to Jesus* (New York: Harper Collins, 1993), pp. 10-11, has some clearly Gnostic themes—rejection of eschatology, the awakening experience to the kingdom of God within, the Gnostic toying with the sayings of Jesus and censoring what they do not like. On a popular level, this view of Jesus and Christianity is promoted through seminars and lectures throughout the New Age subculture and the diffuse movement of so-called Unity churches. Gary Jones, dean of education at the Unity School of Christianity, lectures on "The Credo of Jesus" that popularizes the "scientific" Jesus of left-wing New Testament scholarship; Wendy Craig Purcell gives a series on "Ancient Wisdom for Modern Times," demonstrating once again that the old Gnosticism has returned.

47. Bentley Layton, *The Gnostic Scriptures* (New York: Doubleday, 1987), p. xxi.

48. *Against Heresies* 3:11:8.

49. Robinson, "Introduction," *NHL*. n.p.

50. See Siegfried Schulz, *Q: Die Spruchquelle der Evangelistisen* (Zürich: Theologischer Verlag, 1972), p. 13.

51. See Farmer, "The Church's Stake," p. 14, who believes Q has staying power because many today are no longer interested in it as a way to explain Matthew and Luke (a thesis that has constantly been challenged), but as a way to reconstruct the history of early Christianity.

52. Bertil Gärtner, *Theology of the Gospel of Thomas*, trans. by Eric J. Sharpe (New York: Harper and Brothers, 1961), p. 30, speaks of its "unique . . . literary form."

53. Even this should be modified. The hymnic material scattered throughout the New Testament is extremely early and includes reflection on the death and resurrection of Christ—see Philippians 2:6-11 and 1 Corinthians 15:3ff.

54. For the proposed relationship between Q and the Gospel of Thomas, see Robinson, "LOGOI SOPHWN," pp. 84-130, and his "On Bridging the Gulf from Q to the Gospel of Thomas (or Vice Versa)," *Nag Hammadi Gnosticism and Early Christianity*, eds. Charles W. Hedrick and Robert Hodgson, Jr., (Peabody, MA: Hendrickson, 1986), pp. 127-176.

55. Stevan Davies, "The Christology and Protology of the Gospel of Thomas," *JBL*, III/4 (1992), p. 663. Stephen J. Patterson, *The Gospel of Thomas and Jesus* (Sonoma, CA: Polebridge Press, 1993), p. 116.

56. See C. M. Tuckett, "Q and Thomas: Evidence of a Primitive Wisdom Gospel: A Response to H. Koester," *Ephemerides Theologicae Lovaniensis*, LXVII/4 (1991), pp. 346-360.

57. John Wenham, *Redating Matthew, Mark and Luke: A Fresh Assault on the Synoptic Problem* (Downers Grove, IL: InterVarsity, 1992), p. xxi. To Wenham's list of scholars we can add James Hardy Ropes, Nigel Turner, Morton Enslin, Wilhelm Wilkens, Robert Morgenthaler, M. D. Goulder and Edward C. Hobbs. Most of these could be called moderate liberals.

58. Ibid. See also the judgment of Hobbs in 1980: "There is no serenity in the field of the sources of the Gospels, there are no longer 'assured results of scholarship.'"

59. A. M. Farrer, "On Dispensing with Q," *Studies in the Gospels*, ed. D. E. Nineham (Oxford: University Press, 1955).

60. M. D. Goulder, a radical critic, nevertheless finds Farrer's arguments still convincing in 1980. See his "Farrer on Q," *Theology*, 83 (1980), pp. 190-195, and also his "On Putting Q to the Test," *New Testament Studies*, 24 (1978), pp. 218-234.

61. Edward C. Hobbs, "A Quarter Century without 'Q'," *Perkins Journal*, 33 (Summer 1980), p. 10.

62. Ibid., p. 19. In the judgment of Hobbs: "Very few are owed so much by so many as Austin Farrer is owed. He is dead these ten years; the posterity of his work lives after him, to declare his wisdom and to summon his successors to honor him, as in fact we do this day." William Farmer, "The Church's Stake," p. 16, still cites Farrer's argument as unanswered in 1986.

63. Marcus Borg, *Jesus: A New Vision: Spirit, Culture and the Life of Discipleship* (San Francisco: Harper, 1987), p. 8.

64. Ibid., pp. 324, 325. This is the same notion that is found in the Gnostic Secret Book of James which is included among the "Complete Gospels." "Heaven's domain is discovered through knowledge . . . [and the major concern of the document] lies in Jesus's teaching and the furnishing of a foundational revelation for a community of Gnostic Christians."

65. Burton Mack, *The Lost Gospel: The Book of Q and Christian Origins* (San Francisco: Harper, 1993), p. 1.

66. Stephen J. Patterson, *The Gospel of Thomas and Jesus* (Sonoma, CA: Polebridge Press, 1993), p. 234.

67. Ibid., p. 235.

68. Fiorenza, *In Memory of Her*, pp. 124, 130ff; see also Louise Schottroff, "Itinerant Prophetesses: A Feminist Analysis of the Sayings Source Q," Institute for Antiquity and Christianity, Occasional Papers, 21 (Claremont, CA: Institute for Antiquity and Christianity, 1991).

69. Ibid., pp. xvi, ivii; though even Fiorenza admits that neutrality is impossible.

70. Kurt Aland, *The Problem of the New Testament Canon* (London: Mowbray, 1962), pp. 25-26; compare E. Hennecke and W. Schneemelcher, *New Testament Apocrypha* (Philadelphia: Westminster Press, 1963), pp. 372, 391.

71. Another approach is to isolate passages and ideas in the Bible and turn them in a New Age direction. See, for instance, Ronald Quillo, *Companions in Consciousness: The Bible and the New Age Movement* (Liguori, MO: Triumph Books, 1994). Quillo admits, nevertheless, that on some points the Bible and the New Age may never agree, so finally the New Age does need a new Bible.

72. Miller, *The New Polytheism*, p. 76.

73. Some well-known Christian liberal scholars are associated with this organization. Ninian Smart, professor of religious studies at the University of California, Santa Barbara, and author of

Christian Systematic Theology in a World Context (Minneapolis, MN: Fortress Press, 1991), is a "presiding council member," and Leonard Swidler, professor of theology, Temple University, Philadelphia, and author of the much quoted and translated article, "Jesus Was a Feminist," *Catholic World* (January 1971), is a member of the "board of advisers." Also, one of the presidents of IRFWP's "Presiding Council" is Paulos Mar Gregorius, Metropolitan of Delhi, of the Syrian Orthodox Church, and one of the leaders in the World Council of Churches. Clearly, by taking a low profile, and no doubt spending lavishly, the "moonies" have begun to live down their bizarre cultic image of a few years ago. The Rev. Moon's name is absent from all the honorary boards and councils of the movement. It does appear, however, in a modest sidebar, where the IRFWP Newsletter does note that the IRFWP "was founded in 1990 by Reverend Sun Myung Moon."

74. See *IRFWP Newsletter*, 12 (Fall 1993), p. 9. See *World Scripture: A Comparative Anthology of Sacred Texts* (New York: Paragon House, 1994).

75. *The Other Bible* (San Francisco: Harper, 1984), p. xvii.

76. Philip Novak, *The World's Wisdom* (San Francisco: HarperSanFrancisco, 1994).

77. Robert O. Batlou, ed., *Portable World Bible* (London: Penguin, 1994).

Chapter Seven

1. According to K. Rudolf, *Gnosis: The Nature and History of an Ancient Religion* (Edinburgh, Scotland: T and T Clark, 1977), p. 53, "there was no Gnostic 'church' or normative theology, no Gnostic rule of faith nor any dogma of exclusive importance. No limits were set to free representation and theological speculation . . . there was no gnostic canon of scripture."

2. Tertullian, *De Praescriptione*, p. 38.

3. Frank Moore Cross, Jr., *The Ancient Library of Qumran* (New York: Doubleday, 1961), p. 40.

4. Rudolf, *Gnosis*, p. 152. See also Bertil Gärtner, *The Theology of the Gospel of Thomas*, p. 271, who dates the Gospel of Thomas about A.D. 140.

5. Ibid., pp. 54-55.

6. Rodolphe Kasser, *L'Evangile Selon Thomas* (Geneva: Delachaux et Niestlé, 1961), p. 58. Kasser lists some 20 allusions to the canonical Gospels in this one saying. See also Gärtner, *Theology of the Gospel of Thomas*, p. 177.

7. Irenaeus, *Against Heresies* 1:8:1. This quotation is taken from a new translation by D. J. Unger, *Ancient Christian Writers* (New York: Paulist Press, 1992), p. 41. If this is a reference to the *Gospel of Thomas*, as it could well be, then Irenaeus is affirming in no uncertain terms that Thomas is dependent on the Synoptics.

8. See Ruether,*Womenguides*, quoted in Mary A. Kassian, *The Feminist Gospel: The Movement to Unite Feminism with the Church* (Wheaton, IL: Crossway Books, 1992), p. 182.

9. G. W. MacRae, "Introduction to the Gospel of Truth," *The Nag Hammadi Library in English*, p. 38.

10. See Romans 3:23.

11. Acts of Peter 20, quoted in Gärtner, *Theology of the Gospel of Thomas*, p. 79.

12. Irenaeus, *Against Heresies* 1:14:1. Compare Hippolytus, *Refutation of All Heresies* 6:42:2.

13. Liddell and Scott, *Greek-English Lexicon* (Oxford: Clarendon, 1968), p. 201.

14. Ibid., p. 204.

15. *Apocryphon of James* 1:1:20-30.

16. *Apocryphon of John* 31:25–32:5, translation taken from Soren Giverson, *Aprocryphon Johannis* (Copenhagen: Prostant Apud Munlsgaard, 1963), plates 70:22—80:5. All the citations from the *Apocryphon of John* in this present book are taken from Giverson.

17. John 20:30-31.
18. John 12:32.
19. *Apocalypse of Paul* 22:24-30, and 23:26-27.
20. William R. Schoedel, *The Nag Hammadi Library in English (NHL),* p. 242.
21. Charles W. Hedrick, *NHL,* p. 249.
22. *Apocalypse of Adam* 85:22-26.
23. *Apocalypse of Peter* 71:21.
24. See Matthew 10:27.
25. *Gospel of Thomas,* prologue.
26. *Gospel of Truth* 22:38–23:15.
27. *Gospel of the Egyptians* 69:6-7,15.
28. *Zostrianos* 132:5-8.
29. *Trimorphic Protennoia* 50:22-24.
30. *Gospel of Truth* 19:34-37.
31. John H. Sieber, "Introduction," *NHL,* p. 368.
32. Ibid.
33. Fritjof Capra, *The Tao of Physics* (Boston, MA: Shambhala Publications, 1975), p. 7.
34. David Miller, *The New Polytheism: Rebirth of the Gods and Goddesses* (New York: Harper and Row, 1974), p. viii.
35. See 1 John 4:1; 1 Corinthians 12:10.

Chapter Eight

1. Burton Throckmorton, Jr., quoted in Virginia Byfield, "The Move to Rewrite the Bible," *Alberta Report* (April 29, 1986), p. 36, quoted in Mary A. Kassian, *The Feminist Gospel: The Movement to Unite Feminism with the Church* (Wheaton, IL: Crossway Books, 1992), p. 169.
2. Sherry Ruth Anderson and Patricia Hopkins, *The Feminine Face of God: The Unfolding of the Sacred in Women* (New York: Bantam Books, 1991), pp. 2-3.
3. Elliot Miller, *A Crash Course on the New Age: Describing and Evaluating a Growing Social Force* (Grand Rapids, MI: Baker, 1989), p. 17.
4. David Wells, *No Place for Truth: Or Whatever Happened to Evangelical Theology?* (Grand Rapids, MI: Eerdmans, 1993).
5. Arthur L. Johnson, *Faith Misguided: Exposing the Dangers of Mysticism* (Chicago: Moody Press, 1988), p. 66.
6. David Jobling, "The Sense of Biblical Narrative: Structural Analysis in the Hebrew Bible," II *JSOTS,* 39 (Sheffield, England: JSOT, 1986), p. 19.
7. For a helpful treatment of this subject, see Gene Edward Veith, *Postmodern Times: A Christian Guide to Contemporary Thought and Culture* (Wheaton, IL: Crossway, 1994), p. 49.
8. Stanley Fish, quoted in Charles Colson, *World* (February 19, 1994), p. 22.
9. Wells, *No Place for Truth,* p. 65. Wells cites David Lehman, *Signs of the Times: Deconstructionism and the Fall of Paul de Man* (London: Andre Deutsch, 1991); Brian McHale, *Post Modernist Fiction* (London: Routledge, Chapman and Hall, 1987); and Linda Hutcheon, *A Poetics of Post-modernism: History, Theory and Fiction* (New York: Routledge, Chapman and Hall, 1988).
10. *Time* (July 11, 1994), p. 47.
11. Danna N. Fewell and David M. Gunn, *Gender, Power and Promise: The Subject of the Bible's First Story* (Nashville, TN: Abingdon, 1993), pp. 14-15.

12. Virginia Mollenkott, *Sensuous Spirituality: Out from Fundamentalism* (New York: Crossroads, 1992), p. 167.

13. E. D. Hirsch, *Validity in Interpretation* (New Haven, CT: Yale University Press, 1967) seeks to defend the importance of the author for establishing some objective meaning. He distinguishes between "meaning," which is the author's intent, and "significance," which depends upon the reader and the various readers' perspectives. "The author's intended meaning is what a text means." This study is quoted in Walter C. Kaiser and Moisès Silva, *An Introduction to Biblical Hermeneutics: The Search for Meaning* (Grand Rapids: Zondervan, 1994), p. 30, which I recommend as an excellent introduction to the details of modern hermeneutical theory and practice. See also V. Poythress, *Science and Hermeneutics: Implications of Scientific Method for Biblical Interpretation* (Grand Rapids, MI: Zondervan, 1988).

14. Of which there are two schools, known as New Criticism of the '40s and '50s, and Structuralism, which came later.

15. Walter C. Kaiser and Moisès Silva, *An Introduction to Biblical Hermeneutics: The Search for Meaning* (Grand Rapids, MI: Zondervan, 1994), p. 29. Kaiser discusses the decisive influence of Gadamer.

16. Ibid., p. 31. See also a programmatic article by D. A. J. Clines, "What Does Eve Do to Help? and Other Readerly Questions to the Old Testament," *JSOTS,* 94 (Sheffield, England: Sheffield Academic Press, 1990), p. 9.

17. Silva, *Biblical Hermeneutics,* with great balance, sees the positive aspects but also the dangers. See pp. 240, 242, 244, 248.

18. D. T. Maurina, *Reformed Believers Press Service* (June 16, 1994), p. 2.

19. Mary Jo Weaver, an associate professor of religious studies at Indiana University and the author of *New Catholic Women: A Contemporary Challenge to Traditional Religious Authority* (San Francisco: Harper and Row, 1985).

20. Donna Steichen, *Ungodly Rage: The Hidden Face of Catholic Feminism* (San Francisco: Ignatius Press, 1991, p. 168, quoting Fiorenza.

21. Rosemary Radford Ruether, *Women-Church: Theology and Practice* (San Francisco: Harper and Row, 1983), p. 3.

22. Ruether, *Womanguides,* quoted in Mary Kassian, *The Feminist Gospel,* p. 182.

23. Ruether, *Women-Church,* p. 63.

24. Elizabeth Schlüssler Fiorenza, "Changing the Paradigms," *How My Mind Has Changed,* ed. James M. Wall and David Heim (Grand Rapids, MI: Eerdmans, 1991), p. 86.

25. For an elaboration of this view of history see Riane Eisler, *The Chalice and the Blade: Our History, Our Future* (San Francisco: Harper and Row, 1987).

26. Oddie, *What Will Happen to God? Feminism and the Reconstruction of Christian Belief* (San Francisco: Ignatius Press, 1988), p. 152.

27. See Ruether, *Women-Church,* p. 41, and Francis Watson, "Strategies of Recovery and Resistance: Hermeneutical Reflections on Genesis 1–3 and its Pauline Reception," *JSNT,* 45 (1992), p. 81ff.

28. Fewell and Gunn, *Gender, Power and Promise* (Nashville, TN: Abingdon, 1993), p. 20.

29. The truly biblical position does not posit God as a male, thus excluding females from the "club." The Bible clearly teaches that both men and women are fully in God's image. Thus one can say that all that is good in the human female is there because of God's good and creative hand and that the female is fully the "image of God" (Gen. 1:27). The same is true of the human male. Thus all that is good about femaleness or maleness is caught up in and sur-

passed by God's infinite "personness." However, God reveals Himself in His creation, and He uses the two-gender nature of the human race to reflect truths about His nature and His relationship with His children. The final revelation Jesus brings concerns the intimacy we can know with God, addressing Him in prayer as "our Father" (Matt. 6:9). This is the true patriarchy, the norm by which human, fallen patriarchy must be redeemed.

30. Fewell and Gunn, *Gender, Power and Promise*, pp. 18-20.

31. Oddie, *What Will Happen to God?* p. 142, discussing Fiorenza.

32. Ibid., p. 143.

33. Stanley Fish, *Is There a Text in This Class? The Authority of Interpretive Communities*, 1980, quoted in Mollenkott, *Sensuous Spirituality*, p. 167.

34. Silva, *Biblical Hermeneutics*, p. 249.

35. Ben Wildavsky, "Agency OKs New Policy on Diversity at Colleges," *San Francisco Chronicle* (February 24, 1994). I am indebted to my colleague, Dennis Johnson, for showing me this article.

36. Elizabeth Schlusler Fiorenza, *Bread not Stone: The Challenge of Feminist Biblical Interpretation* (Boston, MA: Beacon, 1984), p. 147. See also p. 140, where she bases her theory on earlier liberal theory.

37. Thirteen learned societies, including the American Academy of Religion (AAR), sponsored a major multidisciplinary conference on *The Role of Advocacy in the Classroom*, in June 1995, in Pittsburgh.

38. Rosemary Radford Ruether, quoted in Oddie, *What Will Happen to God?* p. 40.

39. Walter Brueggemann, "On Writing a Commentary . . . An Emergency," *ATS/Colloquy* (September/October 1992), pp. 10-11.

40. Harvey Cox, *Many Mansions: A Christian Encounter with Other Faiths* (Boston, MA: Beacon Press, 1988), pp. 210-212.

41. Mary Daly and Jane Caputi, *Webster's First New Intergalactic Wickedary of the English Language* (Boston, MA: Beacon Press, 1987), p. 201.

42. Steichen, *Ungodly Rage*, p. 148, quoting an address by Sister Madonna Kolbenschlag.

43. Elizabeth Cady Stanton, *The Women's Bible* (1895), certainly a significant "foremother" of this modern approach; Phyllis Trible, Baldwin professor of sacred literature, Union Theological Seminary, New York, "Adam and Eve: Genesis 2–3 Reread"; *WomanSpirit Rising: A Feminist Reader in Religion*, ed. Carol Christ and Judith Plaskow (San Francisco: Harper, 1979), pp. 74-83; Carter Heyward, professor of theology at Episcopal Divinity School, Cambridge, MA, *The Redemption of God: A Theology of Mutual Relations* (New York: University Press of America, 1982), pp. 150-152. At the American Academy of Religion's annual meeting in San Francisco in 1992, Heyward boasted, in a public address, of being the only lesbian, pregnant [by artificial insemination] Episcopal priest in the world; Francis Landy, *Paradoxes in Paradise: Identity and Difference in the Song of Songs B and L* (Sheffield, England: Almond, 1983); Dorothee Solle, leading German Protestant theologian and feminist, *The Strength of the Weak: Towards a Christian Feminist Identity*, trans. Robert and Rita Kimber (Philadelphia: Westminster Press, 1984), pp. 126-129; David Jobling, "The Sense of Biblical Narrative: Structural Analysis in the Hebrew Bible," II *JSOTS*, 39 (Sheffield, England: JSOT, 1986); Mieke Bal, *Lethal Love: Feminist Literary Readings of Biblical Love Stories*, ISBL (Bloomington, IN: Indiana University, 1987). pp. 104-132; Anne Primavesi, *From Apocalypse to Genesis* (Minneapolis, MN: Fortress Press, 1991); Frederica Halligan, "Keeping Faith with the Future: Towards Final Conscious Unity," *The Fires of Desire* (New York: Crossroad, 1992), pp. 176-177; Francis Watson, now New Testament professor at the University of

Aberdeen, who was at the time editor of the *Journal for the Study of the New Testament*, "Strategies of Recovery and Resistance: Hermeneutical Reflections on Genesis 1-3 and its Pauline Reception," *JSNT*, 45 (March 1992), pp. 79-103; Susan Niditch, professor of religion at Amherst College, "Genesis," *The Women's Bible Commentary* (Louisville, KY: John Knox/Westminster, 1992); see also the works of certain Jewish scholars: Judith Plaskow, "The Coming of Lilith: Towards a Feminist Theology," *WomanSpirit Rising*; H. Bloom, *The Book of J* (New York: Grove Wiedenfeld, 1990) who argues, from an unbelieving point of view, that the hypothetical source J of the Pentateuch was written by an unbelieving woman of the tenth century B.C. who presents Yahweh as a bungler and favors the serpent. Bruce Waltke's estimation of J as the "most blasphemous writer that ever lived" was written before the appearance of much of this "new" exegesis—see Waltke, "Harold Bloom and 'J': A Review Article," *JETS*, 34/4 (December 1991), p. 509.

44. Fewell and Gunn, *Gender, Power and Promise*, pp. 18, 19.

45. Ibid., p. 95.

46. Ibid., p. 23.

47. Ibid., p. 24.

48. Ibid., pp. 25, 67.

49. Ibid., p. 26.

50. Ibid., p. 24.

51. Ibid., p. 38.

52. Phyllis Trible, "Adam and Eve: Genesis 2—3 Reread," *WomanSpirit Rising: A Feminist Reader in Religion*, ed. Carol Christ and Judith Plaskow (San Francisco: Harper, 1979), quoted in Mieke Bal, *Lethal Love: Feminist Literary Readings of Biblical Love Stories*, ISBL (Bloomington, IN: Indiana University, 1987), p. 113.

53. Ibid., p. 127.

54. Ibid., p. 212.

55. Jobling, "Sense of Biblical Narrative," p. 25.

56. Francis Landy, *Paradoxes in Paradise: Identity and Difference in the Song of Songs B and L* (Sheffield, England: Almond, 1983), p. 219.

57. Fewell and Gunn, *Gender, Power and Promise,* pp. 33, 168.

58. Mieke Bal, *Lethal Love: Feminist Literary Readings of Biblical Love Stories*, ISBL (Bloomington, IN: Indiana University, 1987), p. 113.

59. Jobling, "Sense of Biblical Narrative," p. 26.

60. Phyllis Trible, *God and the Rhetoric of Sexuality* (Philadelphia: Fortress, 1978), p. 113.

61. Niditch, *The Women's Bible Commentary* (Louisville, KY: John Knox/Westminster, 1992), p. 14.

62. Elizabeth Cady Stanton, *The Women's Bible*, republished as *The Original Feminist Attack on the Bible*, intr. Barbara Welton (Arno Press, 1974), pp. 24-25. This surely is a more accurate title since Stanton herself states openly that her "reason had repudiated [the Bible's] divine authority" (ibid., p. 12). Stanton also recognized "general principles of love, charity, liberty, justice and equality . . . in the holy books of all religions," and worshiped the God whom she called "our ideal great first cause, 'the Spirit of all Good'" (ibid., pp. 12-13). Hopefully Christian evangelical "egalitarians," in their rush to embrace this feminist heroine of the past will recognize the pagan character of her thinking.

63. Ibid., p. 31.

64. Fewell and Gunn, *Gender, Power and Promise*, p. 30.

65. Ibid., p. 38.

66. Ibid.

67. Ibid., p. 31, cp., Bal, *Lethal Love*, pp. 124-125.

68. Bal, *Lethal Love*, pp. 124-125.

69. Fewell and Gunn, *Gender, Power and Promise*, p. 31, cp., Bal, *Lethal Love*, p. 125.

70. Fewell and Gunn, *Gender, Power and Promise*, p. 65.

71. Ibid., pp. 166, 167.

72. Ibid., p. 32.

73. Bal, *Lethal Love*, p. 122.

74. Ibid., p. 122.

75. Jobling, "Sense of Biblical Narrative," p. 26.

76. Niditch, *The Women's Bible Commentary*, p. 14.

77. Bal, *Lethal Love*, pp. 109, 116.

78. Fewell and Gunn, *Gender, Power and Promise*, p. 30, cp. Landy, *Paradoxes in Paradise*, p. 189.

79. Bal, *Lethal Love*, p. 124.

80. Fewell and Gunn, *Gender, Power and Promise*, p. 34.

81. Francis Landy, *Paradoxes in Paradise: Identity and Difference in the Song of Songs B and L* (Sheffield, England: Almond, 1983), p. 210.

82. Bal, *Lethal Love*, p. l23.

83. Niditch, *The Women's Bible Commentary*, p. 14.

84. Betty Eadie, *Embraced by the Light* (Goldleaf Press, 1992), p. 109: Halligan, "Keeping Faith with the Future," pp. 176-177. "Eve was seeking truth, and it was the patriarchal church that condemned her."

85. Watson, "Strategies of Recovery and Resistance," pp. 79-103, emphasis added.

86. John Richard Neuhaus, *First Things* (June/July 1994).

Chapter Nine

1. Irenaeus, *Against Heresies*, p. 41.

2. David L. Balas, "The Use and Interpretation of Paul in Irenaeus's Five Books *Adversus Haereses*," *Second Century*, 9 (April 1992), p. 31, notes that "the Gnostic speculations seem to be based primarily on an esoteric exegesis of the Old Testament and the Gospels."

3. *Hypostasis of the Archons* 86:20-30.

4. Ibid., 87:24-26, 88:24-25, 89:3-16.

5. Orval Wintermute, "Gnostic Exegesis of the Old Testament," in J. M. Efird, ed., *The Use of the Old Testament in the New and Other Essays* (Durham, NC: Duke University Press, 1972), p. 252, shows that this was justified by assigning the Aramaic meaning ("teacher") to the Hebrew word HYH—"wild animal" of which the serpent was one (Gen. 3:1).

6. *On the Origin of the World*, 114:3-4. See also the treatment of this theme by Pearson, *Gnosticism, Judaism and Egyptian Christianity*, p. 43ff.

7. Irenaeus, *Against Heresies* 1:27:3 (p. 368 in *Early Church Fathers*) suggests that Marcion believed the serpent possessed him. Marcion certainly believed in the salvation the serpent preached, by which Cain, the men of Sodom and the Egyptians were saved, while Abel, Enoch, Noah, Abraham and the prophets perished. See also the discussions in Hans Jonas, *The Gnostic Religion: The Message of the Alien God and the Beginnings of Christianity* (Boston, MA: Beacon Press, 1958), pp. 92-95, and K. Rudolf, *Gnosis: The Nature and History of an Ancient Religion* (Edinburgh, Scotland: T and T Clark, 1977), p. 84ff.

8. *Testimony of Truth* 47:15-30.

9. Hippolytus, *Refutation of All Heresies* V:xxi.

10. *On the Origin of the World* 97:25.

11. Ibid., 113:21—114:4.

12. Ibid., 118:25—119:19.

13. Ibid., 120:3-6, 9-11.

14. The following texts from the Nag Hammadi collection, in addition to the ones quoted, make direct use of the "reversal exegesis" of Genesis: *Tripartite Tractate* 78:14ff; *Apocryphon of John* 11:15—24:31; *Sophia of Jesus Christ* 106:25—107:15; *Trimorphic Protennoia* 40:23-27; *Second Apocalypse of James* 58:2-6; *Apocalypse of Adam* 64:9—67:14; *Gospel of Philip* 75:3-9; *Letter of Philip to Peter* 136:5-14; *Second Treatise of the Great Seth* 53:19—54:13; *Paraphrase of Shem* 19:26—21:18; *Concept of Our Great Power* 38:1-26; *Interpretation of Knowledge* 6:30-35; *A Valentinian Exposition* 37:32—38:10; *Gospel of Truth* 1:18. On Gnostic hermeneutics in general, see David S. Dockery, *Biblical Interpretation Then and Now: Contemporary Hermeneutics in the Light of the Early Church* (Grand Rapids, MI: Baker, 1992), pp. 45-46, 56-58.

15. Vern Woolf, *Light Connection* (June 1992).

16. Mary Daly, *Pure Lust: Elemental Feminist Philosophy* (Boston, MA: Beacon Press, 1984), p. 155.

17. Plutarch, *Def. or.* 421 A, quoted in G. Filoramo, *A History of Gnosticism* (Cambridge, MA: Basil Blackwell, 1990), p. 47.

18. Ibid., p. 51.

19. Ibid.

20. Irenaeus, *Against Heresies* 1:20:1-3.

21. K. Rudolf, *Gnosis: The Nature and History of an Ancient Religion* (Edinburgh, Scotland: T and T Clark, 1977), p. 53.

22. Hippolytus, *Refutation of All Heresies* 5:27.

23. Ibid., 5:l.

24. Rudolf, *Gnosis*, pp. 54-55.

25. Rudolf, quoted in J. Dart, *The Laughing Savior: The Discovery and the Significance of the Nag Hammadi Gnostic Library* (San Francisco: Harper and Row, 1976), p. 132.

26. Tertullian, *De Praescriptione*, pp. 7, 138.

27. Rudolf, *Gnosis*, pp. 53-54.

28. Ibid.

29. Filoramo, *Gnosticism*, p. 94.

30. Clement of Alexandria, *Stromateis* 3:9:2.

31. Irenaeus, *Against Heresies* 1:3:6 and 1:8:1.

32. *Panarion* 25:2.1.

33. Pagels, *The Gnostic Gospels*, p. 137.

34. Ibid, emphasis added.

35. Irenaeus, *Against Heresies* 1:5:1ff.

36. I. P. Couliano, *The Tree of Gnosis* (San Francisco: Harper, 1992), p. 121.

37. Ibid., p. 124.

38. Ibid., pp. 124-125.

39. Ibid., p. 88.

40. *On the Origin of the World* 116:20-25.

41. *Apocryphon of John* 22:20—23:5.

42. Klijn, in a book review of "G. A. G. Strousma, 'Another Seed: Studies in Gnostic Mythology,'" *Novum Testamentum* XXVII (July 1985:3), p. 278.

43. *First Apocalypse of James* 26:23–27:13.
44. *Dialogue of the Savior* 138:11-15.
45. Rudolf, *Gnosis*, p. 58.
46. Irenaeus, *Against Heresies* 1:9:1-5.

Chapter Ten

1. This will be the great debate of the twenty-first century. See my forthcoming volume on Paul, the apostle to the pagans.
2. Martin Marty, *The Public Church* (New York: Crossroads, 1981), quoted in James W. Fowler, *Weaving the New Creation: Stages of Faith and the Public Church* (San Francisco: HarperSanFrancisco, 1991), p. 14.
3. Fowler, *Weaving*, p. 21.
4. Ibid., p. 20. "Paradigm shifts require more than conversions of the mind and heart: they require the shifting of priorities and resources in institutions; they bring political and economic changes; and, most extensively, they require changes in the worldviews." See also Joseph Campbell and Bill Moyers, *The Power of Myth* (New York: AnchorBooks/Doubleday, 1988), p. 121.
5. Samantha Scott and Barbara Smith, *Trojan Horse: How the New Age Movement Infiltrates the Church* (Lafayette, LA.: Huntingdon House Press, 1993), p. 166: "The God most people are worshiping in churches and temples hasn't grown since Christ's time. He's deteriorated. . . . We need a God who's big enough for the atomic age." See Madeleine L'Engle, *Camilla* (New York: T. Y. Crowell, 1965), pp. 249-250.
6. Carol Christ, "Symbols of Goddess in Feminist Theology," quoted in Carl Olsen, *The Book of the Goddess Past and Present* (New York: Crossroads, 1983), p. 231. On page 250 she speaks of "enormous political and social consequences" of the reemergence of the Goddess.
7. Richard Grigg, *When God Becomes Goddess: The Transformation of American Religion* (New York: Continuum, 1995).
8. Carol Christ, "Symbols of Goddess," p. 249.
9. Virginia Mollenkott, *Sensuous Spirituality: Out from Fundamentalism* (New York: Crossroads, 1992), p. 55.
10. See Donna Steichen, *Ungodly Rage: The Hidden Face of Catholic Feminism* (San Francisco: Ignatius Press, 1991), p. 92.
11. "The RE-Imagining Conference: A Report," The American Family Association (April 1994), p. 2.
12. See also the apocryphal *Wisdom of Solomon* 7:22-27, 29; 8:1; 9:10-12. Here as well, personified Wisdom affirms the creative handiwork of God.
13. "The RE-Imagining Conference: A Report," p. 19.
14. Ibid., p. 3.
15. Ibid., p. 9, emphasis added.
16. Ibid., p. 4.
17. See John 1:1-3, Colossians 1:15-20, and Hebrews 3:1-3.
18. "The RE-Imagining Conference: A Report," p. 18.
19. Rosemary Radford Ruether, *Sexism and God-Talk* (Boston, MA: Beacon Press, 1983), p. 11.
20. Rosemary Radford Ruether, *Women-Church: Theology and Practice* (San Francisco: Harper and Row, 1985), p. 169.
21. Ibid., p. 144.

22. Ibid., p. 104.

23. Ibid., p. 159.

24. Caitlín Matthews, *Sophia, Goddess of Wisdom: The Divine Feminine from Black Goddess to World-Soul* (London: The Aquarian Press/Harper Collins, 1992).

25. Ibid., pp. 11, 65.

26. Carolyn McVickars Edwards, *The Storyteller's Goddess: Tales of the Goddess and Her Wisdom from Around the World* (San Francisco: Harper, 1991), p. 65.

27. "The RE-Imagining Conference: A Report," p. 13.

28. Charlene Spretnak, ed., *The Politics of Women's Spirituality* (New York: Anchor Books Doubleday, 1994).

29. Lazaris, *Concept: Synergy*, P. O. Box 3285, Palm Beach, FL 33480.

30. Alix Pirani, ed., *The Absent Mother: Restoring the Goddess to Judaism and Christianity* (London: Mandala, 1991). See also an earlier book, Merlin Stone, *When God Was a Woman* (San Diego, New York, London: Harvest/HJB, 1976), which attempts a similar reversal.

31. Pirani, *The Absent Mother*, p. 54.

32. Kathleen Alexander-Berghorn, "Isis: The Goddess as Healer," *Women of Power* (Winter 1987), 20, quoted in Ruth Tucker, *Another Gospel: Alternative Religions and the New Age Movement* (Grand Rapids, MI: Zondervan, 1989), pp. 340-341.

33. Pages 187-198 of *The Spiritual Dance* are reproduced in D. W. Ferm, *Contemporary American Theologies II: A Book of Readings* (San Francisco: Harper and Row, 1982), pp. 208-221.

34. *Escondido (California) Times Advocate* (August 28, 1994).

35. Anne Llewelyn Barstow, *Witchcraze: A New History of the European Witch Hunts* (San Francisco: Harper, 1994), n.p.

36. Mollenkott, *Sensuous Spirituality*, p. 97.

37. Referred to in Steichen, *Ungodly Rage*, p. 92.

38. Scott and Smith, *Trojan Horse*, p. 44: "There is a lot of emphasis today, particularly among the more extreme right branches of the church, on the evils of witchcraft. Any book that mentions witches, or magic, or ghosts is automatically to be taken from the shelves." See Madeleine L'Engle, *Trailing Clouds of Glory: Spiritual Values in Children's Books* (Philadelphia: Westminster Press, 1985), pp. 62-63.

39. Ruether, *Women-Church*, p. 223.

40. Ibid.

41. Miriam Starhawk, *Yoga Journal* (May-June 1986), p. 59, quoted in Tucker, *Another Gospel*, p. 340.

42. Miriam Starhawk, *The Spiritual Dance* (San Francisco: Harper and Row, 1979); see also Naomi Goldenberg, *The Changing of the Gods: Feminism and the End of Traditional Religions* (Boston, MA: Beacon Press, 1979), and Carol Christ, ed., *WomanSpirit Rising: A Feminist Reader in Religion* (San Francisco: Harper, 1979) for the same programmatic call for radical overhaul.

43. *Los Angeles Times* (May 22, 1993).

44. As does Tucker, *Another Gospel*, p. 340, who devotes little more than half a page to this important phenomenon.

45. Steichen, *Ungodly Rage*, p. 64, quotes a feminist witch who emphasizes that Wiccans are not Satanists.

46. Zsuzsanna E. Budapest, *The Grandmother of Time: A Woman's Book of Celebrations, Spells and Sacred Objects for Every Month of the Year* (San Francisco: Harper, 1989), p. 57.

47. Ibid., p. 21.

48. See Hastings, ed., *Encyclopedia of Religion and Ethics*, vol. 7, p. 434.

49. Nelle Morton, "Beloved Image," published as "Deo/Dea immagine dilletta" in *La sfida del femminismo al teologia*, ed. Mary E. Hunt and Rosino Gibellinini (Brescia, Italy: Queriniana, 1981), quoted, with agreement, in Christ, "Symbols of the Goddess," p. 248.

50. David Miller, *The New Polytheism: Rebirth of the Gods and Goddesses* (New York: Harper and Row, 1974), p. vii.

51. Ibid., p. 3.

52. Ibid., p. ix.

53. Ibid., p. 12.

54. "RE-Imagining Conference: A Report," p. 7.

55. Ibid., p. 13.

56. *Good News* (January 1994), p. 8.

57. "RE-Imagining Conference: A Report," p. 6.

58. Miriam Starhawk, "Witchcraft as Goddess Religion," *The Politics of Women's Spirituality: Essays on the Rise of Spiritual Power Within the Feminist Movement*, ed. Charlene Spretnak (Garden City, NY: Anchor Press/Doubleday, 1982), pp. 50-51.

59. Sjoo and Mor, *The Great Cosmic Mother: Discovering the Religions of the Earth* (San Francisco: HarperSanFrancisco, 1987), p. 63.

60. Miller, *The New Polytheism*, p. 74. Scott and Smith, *Trojan Horse*, p. 164, maintain that Madeleine L'Engle was favorable to goddess notions.

61. Elizabeth Cady Stanton, *The Women's Bible* (1895), p. 14.

62. Ibid., p. 13.

63. Mollenkott, *Sensuous Spirituality*, p. 64.

64. Oddie, *What Will Happen to God? Feminism and the Reconstruction of Christian Belief* (San Francisco: Ignatius Press, 1988), p. 87.

65. Stanton, *Women's Bible*, p. 13.

66. Mollenkott, in her speech at the RE-Imagining Conference in Minneapolis. See "RE-Imagining Conference: A Report," p. 5.

67. According to Methodist theologian, Fowler, *Weaving*, p. 105.

68. Ibid., p. 113.

69. Ibid., p. 61.

70. Theosophical Society brochure, quoted in Constance Cumbey, *Hidden Dangers of the Rainbow* (Shreveport, LA: Huntingdon House, 1983), pp. 45-46.

71. See Frederica Halligan, "Keeping Faith with the Future: Towards Final Conscious Unity," *The Fires of Desire* (New York: Crossroads, 1992), p. 192, emphasis added: "The cooperative efforts of humankind will prevail when we are aided in our work by the essential creative action of the Deity, who is beyond all our knowing."

72. Oddie, *What Will Happen To God?* p. 88, emphasis added.

73. Os Guinness, *The Dust of Death: A Critique of the Establishment and the Counter-Culture—and a Proposal for a Third Way* (Downers Grove, IL: Intervarsity Press, 1973), pp. 228-229.

74. Brooke, *When the World Will Be as One: The Coming New World Order in the New Age* (Eugene, OR: Harvest House, 1989), p. 68.

75. Shirley MacLaine, *Going Within: A Guide for Inner Transformation* (New York: Bantam Books, 1989), p. 100.

76. Mollenkott, *Sensuous Spirituality*, p. 63.

77. "The RE-Imagining Conference: A Report," p. 2, emphasis added.

78. See Romans 1:24-25.

79. Description of feminist theater portrayal of Lilith, quoted in Pirani, *The Absent Mother*, p. 149.

80. See Isaiah 34:14.

81. Alicia Suskin Ostriker, *Feminist Revision and the Bible* (Oxford: Blackwell, 1993), p. 99, recounts the Jewish legend. Lilith was Adam's first wife, who refused to submit to him and was banished from the garden. She was found consorting with demons in the Red Sea. Ostriker, professor of English at Rutgers University, takes the Lilith legend as a profound symbol of the modern feminist revision of the Bible and writes poems in praise of her (ibid., pp. 92-98).

82. Ibid., p. 145.

83. Ibid., p. 152.

84. See Judith Plaskow, "The Coming of Lilith: Towards a Feminist Theology," *WomanSpirit Rising*, pp. 198-209.

85. Ibid., p. 156.

86. Ibid.

87. Ibid., p. 160.

88. On this see the fine treatment by Alan Morrison, *The Serpent and the Cross: Religious Corruption in an Evil Age* (Birmingham, UK: K and M Books, 1994), pp. 229ff.

89. See the excellent critical treatment of Process Theology as it relates to feminism, by Steichen, *Ungodly Rage*, pp. 202-206.

90. See chapter 12.

91. See Miller, *The New Polytheism*, p. 4.

92. Ibid., p. 72.

93. See James Lovelock, *Orion Nature Quarterly*, 8 (1989), p. 58.

94. See Miller, *The New Polytheism*, p. 5.

95. See Mollenkott, *Sensuous Spirituality*, pp. 72-73.

96. See Fiorenza, *Miriam's Child, Sophia's Prophet* (New York: Continuum, 1994).

Chapter Eleven

1. *Allogenes* 51:12: the Aeon of Barbelo is revealed as "the Perfect Youth" (51:37). Barbelo is another name for Sophia—see Rudolf, *Gnosis*, p. 80.

2. Cullen Murphy, "Women and the Bible," *The Atlantic Monthly* (August 1993), p. 40, quotes Pagels, *Gnostic Gospels* (New York: Random House, 1979), who shows how the Gnostics invoked the feminine in their prayers.

3. I. P. Couliano, *The Tree of Gnosis* (San Francisco: Harper, 1992), p. 70. Pheme Perkins, "Sophia and the Mother-Father," *The Book of the Goddess, Past and Present: An Introduction to Her Religion*, ed. C. Mackenzie Brown and Carl Olsen (New York: Crossroads, 1983), p. 98.

4. Couliano, *Tree of Gnosis*, p. 76.

5. K. Rudolf, *Gnosis: The Nature and History of an Ancient Religion* (Edinburgh, Scotland: T and T Clark, 1977), p. 11.

6. Ibid., p. 65.

7. Hans Jonas, *The Gnostic Religion: The Message of the Alien God and the Beginnings of Christianity* (Boston, MA: Beacon Press, 1958), p. 26.

8. Asphodel P. Long, *The Absent Mother: Restoring the Goddess to Judaism and Christianity*, edited by Alix Pirani (London: Mandala, 1991), p. 53.

9. In a few Gnostic texts, Christ as the Logos takes the place of Sophia. See *Tripartate Tractate* 100:1ff. The Logos created the various aeons and authorities, over which he placed the Chief

Archon. "When the archon saw that they are great and good and wonderful, he was pleased and rejoiced, (101) as if he himself in his own thought had been the one to say and do them, not knowing that the movement within him is from the spirit who moves him . . . he was thinking that they were elements of his own essence."

10. G. Filoramo, *A History of Gnosticism* (Cambridge, MA: Basil Blackwell, 1990), p. 82, quoting the Valentinian, Ptolemy.
11. *Sophia of Jesus Christ* 112:19, 114:14-15.
12. *Gospel of Thomas* 101, according to the reconstruction of T. Lambdin, *The Nag Hammadi Library in English (NHL)*, pp. 128-129.
13. *On the Origin of the World* 100:5-10, 26-27.
14. *Apocalypse of Adam* 64:14-16.
15. *Apocryphon of John* 15-19 cp., 21:30: "And his (man's) thinking was superior to all those who had made him."
16. See *Prayer of the Apostle Paul* 1 A:26-27, *NHL*, 28.
17. *Apocalypse of James* 34:10, *NHL*, 246.
18. Couliano, *Tree of Gnosis*, p. 96.
19. See *Letter of Peter to Philip* 135:16—God the Creator is called "Authades (Arrogance)." Arrogance became proud and "commissioned the powers within his authority to produce mortal bodies" (136:11-13).
20. See also *Apocryphon of John* 11:15-25.
21. This is the summary of Couliano, *Tree of Gnosis*, 96. For other examples from the Gnostic texts, see *Apocryphon of John* 11:25-35, 13:5; *Gospel of the Egyptians* 58:23-26; *Sophia of Jesus Christ* 108:9-11, 119:9-15; *Gospel of Philip* 75:1-10; *Gospel of Truth* 17:10-19.
22. *Apocryphon of John* 2:15.
23. *Gospel of the Egyptians* 41:7-9. See *Trimorphic Protennoia* 37:20.
24. Filoramo, *Gnosticism*, pp. 77-78.
25. See Isaiah 45:18.
26. A reference to Psalm 8:4.
27. The account of the Naasene Gnostics in Irenaeus (1:30:7), quoted by Hans Jonas, *The Gnostic Religion*, p. 93.
28. *Apocryphon of John* 21:15—22:1.
29. *Apocryphon of John* 10:19, 10:33—11:3.
30. For the text, see *Gospel of the Egyptians* 57:16-20, *NHL*, p. 201.
31. Gnostic text, quoted in Couliano, *Tree of Gnosis*, p. 94.
32. Ephesians 1:3; 2:11-13.
33. *Trimorphic Protennoia* 39:21, 40:23, 43:32, 43:35—44:2. In *Testimony of Truth* 70:1-4.
34. *Apocalypse of Peter* 82:18-25. These texts confirm the accuracy of the Hippolytus account (*Refutation of All Heresies* 1:12), which describes a Gnostic Jesus explaining to the Pharisees that their father, a murderer from the beginning, was the Demiurge and that the "Son is the Serpent."
35. Filoramo, *Gnosticism*, p. 132.
36. *Hypostasis of the Archons* 95:8ff cp., *On the Origin of the World* 103:25ff.
37. For the text, see *On the Origin of the World* 126:20-30, *NHL*, pp. 178, 179.
38. Rudolf, *Gnosis*, p. 50.
39. Irenaeus, *Against All Heresies*, p. 11.
40. *Apocryphon of John* 3:20-25.

41. *Eugnostos the Blessed* 71:14ff, 72:3ff.

42. *Allogenes* 62:28—64:13, 65:33 and 66:26-27.

43. For the text, see *Teaching of Silvanus* 100:13-16, *NHL*, p. 353.

44. *Tripartite Tractate* 85:34.

45. *Allogenes* 48:10-11.

46. See Rudolf, *Gnosis*, p. 59.

47. Pheme Perkins, "Sophia and the Mother-Father," *The Book of the Goddess, Past and Present: An Introduction to Her Religion*, ed. C. Mackenzie Brown and Carl Olsen (New York: Crossroads, 1983), p. 98.

48. For the full text, see *Gospel of Mary* 7:4-9, *NHL*, p. 471.

49. *Gospel of Thomas* 77.

50. See Irenaeus, *Against Heresies* 1:5:3.

51. Perkins, "Sophia and the Mother-Father," p. 107.

52. Turner, *NHL*, p. 461.

53. *Trimorphic Protennoia* 35:9-18.

54. According to George MacRae, who introduces this text in the *NHL*, Thunder is "a revelation discourse delivered by a female revealer in the first person. . . . Antithesis and paradox (are) used to proclaim the absolute transcendence of the revealer whose greatness is incomprehensible" (George W. MacRae, "Introduction," ibid., p. 271). This analysis is possible if Gnosticism is seen simplistically as a dualistic system.

55. See Emily Culpepper, "The Spiritual, Political Journey of a Feminist Freethinker," *After Patriarchy: Feminist Transformations of the World's Religions*, ed. Paula Cooey, et al. (Maryknoll, NY: Orbis, 1991), p. 155. See also the semi-humorous article by Peter Berger, "The Other Face of Gaia," *First Things* (August/September 1994), pp. 15-17, which includes a description of Kali.

56. Pirani, *The Absent Mother*, p. 54.

57. James Preston, "Goddess Worship: An Overview," *The Book of the Goddess, Past and Present: An Introduction to Her Religion*, ed. Carl Olsen, (New York: Beyond Words Publishing Company, 1983), p. 38.

58. See the description of Sophia in the program of the RE-Imagining Conference as "the place where the entire universe resides." "The RE-Imagining Conference: A Report," p. 19.

59. Gnostic text, quoted in Sjoo and Mor, *The Great Cosmic Mother: Discovering the Religions of the Earth* (San Francisco: HarperSanFrancisco, 1987), p. 253, without reference.

60. C. J. Bleeker, "Isis and Hathor, Two Ancient Egyptian Goddesses," in *The Book of the Goddess*, p. 32.

61. Caitlín Matthews, *Sophia, Goddess of Wisdom: The Divine Feminine from Black Goddess to World-Soul* (London: The Aquarian Press/Harper Collins, 1992), p. 67.

62. Ibid., p. 38.

63. Ibid., pp. 33, 35.

64. *Trimorphic Protennoia* 45:2-6. See also *Exegesis of the Soul* and an introductory article by W. C. Robinson, Jr., "The Exegesis of the Soul," *Novum Testamentum*, 12/2 (1970), especially p. 116, who argues that the content of this text is close to that of the Naasenes for whom the mutilation of Attis was a type of the androgynous ideal.

65. *Trimorphic Protennoia* 44:30-33. Filoramo, *Gnosticism*, pp. 61, 63, understands what MacRae seems not to have grasped: "Androgyny is the distinctive trait of this (Gnostic) God." In the Gnostic understanding of god is "the conquest of all duality."

66. Perkins, "Sophia and the Mother-Father," p. 107.

67. See, for example *The New Testament and Psalms: An Inclusive Version* (New York/Oxford: Oxford University Press, 1995), p. 9.
68. Filoramo, *Gnosticism*, p. 58.
69. Genesis 3:5.
70. Irenaeus, *Against Heresies* 1.30.6.
71. *First Apocalypse of James* 27:7-9, emphasis added.

Chapter Twelve

1. Justice Antonin Scalia, quoted in the *San Diego Union-Tribune* (July 4, 1994), p. A-4.
2. Elinor Gadon, *The Once and Future Goddess* (New York: Harper and Row, 1989).
3. See Jeffrey Satinover, *Homosexuality and the Politics of Truth* (Grand Rapids, MI: Baker Books, 1996); and Peter Jones, "Androgyny: The Pagan Sexual Ideal," *Journal of the Evangelical Theological Society,* 43/3 (September 2000), pp. 443-469.
4. Ruether is professor of applied theology at Garrett-Evangelical Seminary, Evanston, Illinois.
5. Rosemary Radford Ruether, *Women-Church: Theology and Practice* (San Francisco: Harper and Row, 1985), p. 57.
6. For a fascinating overview of this modern spirituality, see Jean Houston, *The Passion of Isis and Osiris: A Gateway to Transcendent Love* (New York: Ballantine, 1995); Tony Schwartz, *What Really Matters: Searching for Wisdom in America* (New York: Bantam Books, 1996); Peter Ochiogrosso, *The Joy of Sects* (New York: Doubleday, 1996); Peter H. Van Ness, *Spirituality and the Secular Quest* (New York: Crossroad/Herder, 1996); Lama Syurya Das, *Awakening the Buddha Within: Tibetan Wisdom for the Western World* (New York: Broadway Books, 1997).
7. Ruether,*Women-Church,* pp. 57, 61, 63, 69, 73-74, 125, 131-132, 153, 280-281.
8. Virginia Mollenkott, *Sensuous Spirituality: Out from Fundamentalism* (New York: Crossroads, 1992), p. 73.
9. Ibid., p. 12.
10. Kate Millett, *Sexual Politics* (Garden City, NY: Doubleday, 1970), pp. 250-251.
11. Patricia Beattie Jung and Ralph F. Smith, *Heterosexism: An Ethical Challenge* (New York: State University of New York Press, 1994).
12. Stanley J. Grenz and Roger E. Olsen, *Twentieth Century Theology: God and the World in a Transitional Age* (Downers Grove, IL: InterVarsity, 1992), p. 234.
13. *Christians for Biblical Equality: Books, Reprints and Tapes Catalog,* August 1991. See also Rebecca M. Groothuis, *Women Caught in the Conflict: The Culture War Between Traditionalism and Feminism* (Grand Rapids. MI: Baker, 1994), p. 65.
14. Rebecca M. Groothuis, *Women Caught in the Conflict: The Culture War Between Traditionalism and Feminism* (Grand Rapids, MI: Baker, 1994), p. 122, denies the possibility that patriarchy can be reformed along Christian lines, for she claims their "mutually exclusive features" (the authority of patriarchy and the intimacy of Christian love) make the attempt absurd.
15. See W. C. Roof's sociological study, *A Generation of Seekers: The Spiritual Journeys of the Baby Boom Generation* (San Francisco: Harper, 1993), p. 222. See also Peter Jones, *The Gnostic Empire Strikes Back* (Phillipsburg, NJ: P and R, 1992), pp. 63-64.
16. Naomi Goldenberg, *The Changing of the Gods: Feminism and the End of Traditional Religions* (Boston, MA: Beacon Press, 1979), p. 41, quoted in Mary A. Kassian, *The Feminist Gospel: The Movement to Unite Feminism with the Church* (Wheaton, IL: Crossway Books, 1992), p. 154. See

also Sjoo and Mor, *The Great Cosmic Mother: Discovering the Religions of the Earth* (San Francisco: HarperSanFrancisco, 1987), p. 197.

17. Goldenberg, *Changing of the Gods*, p. 5.

18. Few Christian books on the New Age broach this subject, so that great sections of the church have been swept along by a more modified, sanitized form.

19. Oddie, *What Will Happen to God? Feminism and the Reconstruction of Christian Belief* (San Francisco: Ignatius Press, 1988), p. 11.

20. Andrew Greeley, *Omni* magazine (January 1987), p. 98, quoted in K. B. Welton, *Abortion Is Not a Sin: A New Age Look at an Old-Age Problem* (Costa Mesa, CA: Pandit Press, 1987), p. 163.

21. Elizabeth Schlusler Fiorenza, *In Memory of Her: A Feminist Theological Reconstruction of Christian Origins* (New York: Crossroad, 1988), p. xvii.

22. Mary Daly, *Beyond God the Father: Towards a Philosophy of Women's Liberation* (Boston, MA: Beacon Press, 1973), p. 169.

23. Donna Steichen, *Ungodly Rage: The Hidden Face of Catholic Feminism* (San Francisco: Ignatius Press, 1991), p. 9. See also the incisive article by E. Michael Jones, "What Lesbian Nuns can Teach Us about Vatican II," *Fidelity* (December 1985), pp. 16-26.

24. See chapter 3. New Age liberal spirituality, especially in its feminist form of gender liberation, is bringing people back to church.

25. Goldenberg, *Changing of the Gods*, p. 5.

26. Ibid., p. 2. See also Oddie, *What Will Happen to God?* p. 12.

27. See Naomi Goldenberg, "Feminist Witchcraft and Inner Space," *The Politics of Women's Spirituality*, ed. Charlene Spretnak (New York: Doubleday, 1982), p. 217.

28. Emily Culpepper, "The Spiritual, Political Journey of a Feminist Freethinker," *After Patriarchy: Feminist Transformations of the World's Religions*, ed. Paula Cooey, et al. (Maryknoll, NY: Orbis, 1991), pp. 153-154.

29. A report from Religious News Service appearing in the *Los Angeles Times* (July 24, 1993).

30. Ibid., p. 13. Steichen comes to a similar conclusion concerning the spread of radical feminism in the Catholic church.

31. See Mary Daly and Jane Caputi, *Webster's First New Intergalactic Wickedary of the English Language* (Boston, MA: Beacon Press, 1987), pp. 78, 186.

32. Steichen, *Ungodly Rage*, p. 330, documents that Harvey Cox was one of 300 scholars who signed a petition from the American Academy of Religion pleading that Daly be promoted.

33. See Leila Prelec, "BC Campus Scene of Small Daly Protests," *National Catholic Register* (April 30, 1989), p. 1, quoted in Steichen, *Ungodly Rage*, p. 330.

34. Don Feder, "What's Up at the Harvard Divinity School?" *Conservative Chronicle* (April 1994), p. 28. I believe the accepted plural is "shamans," but I reproduce Feder's original form, "shamen," which he no doubt intended as a pun.

35. A speech by Jeff Levi in 1987 to the National Press Club in Washington, quoted in Joseph P. Gudel, "That Which Is Unnatural: Homosexuality in Society, the Church and Scripture," *Christian Research Journal* (Winter 1993), p. 10.

36. "Gays on the March," *Time* (September 8, 1975), p. 43, quoted in Joseph P. Gudel, "That Which Is Unnatural: Homosexuality in Society, the Church and Scripture," *Christian Research Journal* (Winter 1993).

37. See Peter Jones, *The Gnostic Empire Strikes Back* (Phillipsburg, NJ: P and R, 1992), p. 67.

38. "Gay Rights Moves on Campus," *Los Angeles Times*, January 10, 1994, front page.

39. So writes Larry Kramer, playwright and gay activist in "Film Comment," *Los Angeles Times* (January 9, 1994), p. 30.

40. By Jerry Z. Muller, associate professor of history at the Catholic University of America, in "Coming Out Ahead: The Homosexual Movement in the Academy," *First Things* (August/September 1993), pp. 17-24.

41. Ibid.

42. Nicole Foulke, "Kali Morgan, dominatrix, proprietrix gets medieval on Bryn Mawr's er...," *Bi-College News* (April 25, 2000), p. 12.

43. Robert Muller, *The New Genesis: Shaping a Global Spirituality* (New York: Image Books, 1984), p. 189.

44. Robert Muller, quoted in Constance Cumbey, *Hidden Dangers of the Rainbow* (Shreveport, LA: Huntingdon House, 1983), pp. 111-112.

45. Daly, *Beyond God the Father*, p. 19, emphasis added.

46. G. A. Moloney and B. J. Rogers-Gardner, two Christian psychologists, in their book *Loving the Christ Within You: A Spiritual Guide to Self-Esteem* (New York: Crossroads, 1991), p. 93, call people to spiritual wholeness by "thinking of yourself 'as both male and female.'"

47. Mollenkott, *Sensuous Spirituality*, p. 165. Mollenkott is not sure whether Carl Jung's educated guess is accurate, but she is "certain that healthy les-bi-gay people have a lot to teach society about sex roles."

48. Scott Lively and Kevin Adams, *The Pink Swastika: Homosexuality in the Nazi Party* (Keizer, OR: Founders Publishing Corporation, 1995), p. 46.

49. See Mollenkott, *Sensuous Spirituality*, p. 74.

50. Ibid., p. 16.

51. Mircea Eliade, *Myths, Dreams and Mysteries* (New York: Harper and Row, 1975), pp. 174-175, and *Patterns of Comparative Religion* (New York: New American Library, 1974), pp. 420-421.

52. Matthew Fox, quoted in Steichen, *Ungodly Rage*, p. 230.

53. John Spong, Episcopal Bishop of Newark, quoted in *World* (November 7, 1992), p. 19.

54. Judy Grahn, *Another Mother Tongue: Gay Words, Gay Worlds* (Boston, MA: Beacon Press, 1984), p. 44, quoted in Culpepper, "The Spiritual, Political Journey," p. 158.

55. Robert M. Baum, "Homosexuality and the Traditional Religions of the Americas and Africa," in Arlene Swidler, *Homosexuality and World Religions* (Valley Forge, PA: Trinity Press International, 1993), p. 15.

56. Ibid., pp. 147, 150, 158.

57. Ibid., p. 164, quoting Judy Grahn.

58. Sjoo and Mor, *The Great Cosmic Mother: Discovering the Religions of the Earth* (San Francisco: HarperSanFrancisco, 1987), p. 131.

59. John Ankerberg and John Weldon, *Encyclopedia of New Age Beliefs* (Eugene, OR: Harvest House Publishers, 1996), p. 532ff.

60. Ibid., p. 155.

61. Ibid.

62. Ibid., p. 541.

63. Ibid., p. 543.

64. See Randy P. O'Connor, *Blossom of Bone: Reclaiming the Connections Between Homoeroticism and the Sacred* (San Francisco: Harper, 1994).

65. Mollenkott, *Sensuous Spirituality*, pp. 42, 166.

66. Ibid, pp. 19, 24.

67. "The RE-Imagining Conference: A Report," p. 2.
68. According to Ben MacIntyre, *Forgotten Fatherland: The Search for Elizabeth Nietzsche* (New York: Farrar Straus Giroux, 1992), p. 92, quoting remarks from Sigmund Freud and Carl Jung.
69. Culpepper, "The Spiritual, Political Journey," p. 149, broke with Christianity, in part through her reading of Nietzsche.
70. Chuck and Donna McIlhenny, *When the Wicked Seize a City: A Grim Look at the Future and a Warning to the Church* (Lafayette, LA: Huntington House, 1993), p. 18.
71. Ibid., pp. 85-93.
72. Ibid., p. 16.
73. Mollenkott, *Sensuous Spirituality*, p. 49.
74. K. Rudolf, *Gnosis: The Nature and History of an Ancient Religion* (Edinburgh, Scotland: T and T Clark, 1977), p. 257.
75. John Dart, "First Draft of Lutheran Statement Revises Teaching on Sexuality," *Los Angeles Times* (Saturday, December 4, 1993).
76. Naomi Goldenberg, quoted in Mary A. Kassian, *The Feminist Gospel: The Movement to Unite Feminism with the Church* (Wheaton, IL: Crossway Books, 1992), p. 220.
77. See ibid. for a description of the slide towards paganism in those who began their feminism as a Christian protest movement.
78. "Feminists and pagans are both coming from the same source without realizing it, and are heading toward the same goal without realizing it, and the two are now beginning to interlace," says feminist Margot Adler, *Drawing Down the Moon: Witches, Druids, Goddess-Worshipers and Other Pagans in America Today* (Boston, MA: Beacon Press, 1986), p. 182, quoted in Kassian, *The Feminist Gospel*, p. 219.
79. Patricia Miller, "Leadership at Grailville," *Women of Power*, 24 (1995), p. 76.
80. Source unknown.

Chapter Thirteen

1. Rosemary Radford Ruether, *Women-Church: Theology and Practice* (San Francisco: Harper and Row, 1985), p. 39.
2. See Pagels, *Gnostic Gospels* (New York: Random House, 1979), p. 44, and Peter Jones, *The Gnostic Empire Strikes Back* (Phillipsburg, NJ: P and R, 1992), p. 31. This bridal chamber ceremony is called a sacrament of "redemption," that is, release from the God of Creation and Scripture.
3. *Sophia Jesu Christi* 119:9-15. "Ialdabaoth" is a mixing and punning on the Hebrew names for God. As the Prime Begetter, God is at the source of the evil process of childbirth.
4. Ibid., 118:23–119:8. This is called "the Gospel of God, the eternal, imperishable Spirit," 119:15-16.
5. Wilfred M. McClay, *The Masterless: Self and Society in Modern America* (Chapel Hill, NC: University of North Carolina Press, 1994).
6. *Apocryphon of John* 28:1-5 and 2:20-25. See G. Filoramo, *A History of Gnosticism* (Cambridge, MA: Basil Blackwell, 1990) and K. Rudolf, *Gnosis: The Nature and History of an Ancient Religion* (Edinburgh, Scotland: T and T Clark, 1977), p. 220-221 and 206 where he lists their preferred names.
7. Douglas Parrot, in the introduction to his translation of *Eugnostos the Blessed* (III, 3 and V, 1), and *Sophia Jesu Christi* (III, 4 and BG 8502, 3), *The Nag Hammadi Library in English (NHL)*, p. 206. He refers to *Sophia Jesu Christi* 108:9ff. The text is mysterious, but speaks of the "unclean rub-

bing . . . that came from their fleshly part." Then comes the exhortation: "Tread upon their malicious intent."

8. *Gospel to the Egyptians* 56:5-15, 60:9-18, suggests some form of homosexuality. See also *Paraphrase of Shem* 28:25—29:34.

9. Marvin W. Meyer, *The Ancient Mysteries: A Source Book* (San Francisco: Harper and Row, 1987), ibid., p. 147.

10. Catullus, quoted in Meyer, *Ancient Mysteries*, pp. 126-128.

11. *Metamorphoses*, p. 26, quoted in Meyer, *Ancient Mysteries*, p. 143. Apuleius also describes their transvestite clothing and female cosmetics on their faces (p. 27), as well as a gang-rape scene of a "lusty young rustic, chosen for his goodly proportions," brought in for the occasion (p. 29).

12. See Meyer, *Ancient Mysteries*, pp. 128-130, for a fourth-century A.D. description of this rite.

13. Hippolytus, *The Refutation of All Heresies* 5:9:10.

14. Ibid., 5:7:13-15. This clearly helps explain logion 114 of the *Gospel of Thomas*, which Hippolytus cites as one of their sources a few lines further on (5:7:20).

15. Ibid., 5:9:11.

16. Ibid., 5:21.

17. *Paraphrase of Shem* 28:35—29:33.

18. *Gospel of the Egyptians* 56:4-21. K. Rudolf, *Gnosis: The Nature and History of an Ancient Religion* (Edinburgh, Scotland: T and T Clark, 1977), p. 139, in his discussion of this text, does not mention a possible homosexual reference.

19. Epiphanius, *Panarion* 27:4:5.

20. Ibid., 25:2:5. The Nicolaitans "teach their followers to engage in promiscuous intercourse with women and *unnatural acts of incurable viciousness* (23.22), it is not right to say how." In the light of his vocabulary elsewhere, this is likely to be a reference to homosexuality.

21. Ibid., 26:11:9-11. "These persons who debauch themselves with their own hands . . . finally get their fill of promiscuous relations with women and grow ardent for each other, men for men."

22. At an international conference in 1966, the then-recognized experts on Gnosticism—G. Widengren, C. Colpe, U. Bianchi, H. Jonas and J. Danièlou—produced a "Final Document" which concluded that Gnosticism was a particular expression of the so-called mystery religions—see *Lo Origini dello Gnosticismo: Colloquio di Messina 13-18 Aprile, 1966. Testi e Discussioni* (Studies in the History of Religions, Suppl. Numen 12: Ed., U. Bianchi, et al.; Leiden: Brill, 1977), p. xxvi.

23. Hippolytus, *The Refutation of All Heresies*, 5:8:23.

24. See for instance the statement of L'Engle: "the male chauvinistic pig god of the Old Testament" or Eisler's characterization of the "powerful upstart [male] God Jehovah," to name but two.

25. *Gospel of Thomas*, p. 75, and compare *Dialogue of the Savior* 142:18-19. See J. J. Buckley, "An Interpretation of Logion 114 in the *Gospel of Thomas*," *Novum Testamentum* XXVII, 3 (1985), pp. 261, 266.

26. G. Filoramo, *A History of Gnosticism* (Cambridge, MA: Basil Blackwell, 1990), p. 24, sees the "superman" theme as an element of great attraction.

27. *Apocryphon of John* 15-19.

28. *Gospel of Thomas* 16, commenting on Matt. 10:34-36 and Luke 12:49-53.

29. Marvin W. Meyer, "Male and Female in the Gospel of Thomas," *New Testament Studies*, 31 (1985), p. 556.

30. *Apocryphon of John* 24:26-27.
31. *Book of Thomas the Contender* 139:8-11, 28-29.
32. Ibid., 144:9-11.
33. *Dialogue of the Savior* 144:19-20.
34. *Authoritative Teaching* 23:18-20. See also *Gospel of Philip* 56:25, which teaches that the soul is precious but came in "a contemptible body."
35. *Paraphrase of Shem* 18:34-35, 27:2-3, and 22:34.
36. *Zostrianos* 131:5-8. See also *Testimony of Truth* 68:6-8. Compare *Gospel of Philip* 82:4, which speaks of the "marriage of defilement." On this see Meyer, "Male and Female," p. 565.
37. The texts which mention this bridal sacrament are *Teaching of Silvanus* 94:26-2, *Exegesis of the Soul* 132:12-14, *Gospel of Philip* and *Gospel of Thomas*. On the latter see chapter 15.
38. *Gospel of Philip* 68:24-26.
39. Ibid., 70:13-20.
40. B. Gärtner, *The Theology of the Gospel According to Thomas* (New York: Harper, 1961), p. 256.
41. Pagels, *Gnostic Gospels*, p. 66.
42. For a careful exegesis of Gen 1–3, see Raymond C. Ortland, Jr., "Male-Female Equality and Male Headship: Gen 1–3," *Recovering Biblical Manhood and Womanhood*, John Piper and Wayne Grudem, eds., (Wheaton, IL: Crossway, 1991), pp. 95-112.
43. J. J. Buckley, "A Cult Mystery in the Gospel of Philip," *JBL* 99 (1980), p. 246.
44. Ibid., p. 255.
45. *Gospel of Thomas* 75. See Meyer, "Male and Female," p. 558.
46. Ibid., p. 61.
47. *Zostrianos* 131:5-10.
48. Filoramo, *Gnosticism*.
49. See the Hermetic Gnostic text, Right Ginza III: "When there was no unevenness (or: inequality) (then) we had but one form . . . we were both made as a single mana (spirit). Now, where there is no evenness (or: equality), they made you a man and me a woman."
50. This certainly characterizes the works of Letty Russell, Phyllis Trible and Rita Gross.
51. Clearly a citation of Gen 3:1, referring to the serpent—*On the Origin of the World* 113:30—114:4. *Hypostasis of the Archons* is one of the few (perhaps the only) Gnostic documents that describes the Creator, in demeaning terms, as androgynous—see 94:34.
52. *Thunder, Perfect Mind*, according to George MacRae, *Nag Hammadi Library in English (NHL)*, p. 271, has no distinctively Gnostic themes. He believes the antitheses and paradoxes wish to express the absolute transcendence of the revealer. MacRae surely has not considered the important theme of the monistic joining of opposites, which, according to Filoramo, is essential to Gnosticism. See also Rudolf, *Gnosis*, p. 271, who says that bi-sexuality (androgyny) is an ideal of Gnosticism. See also *Apocalypse of Adam* 81:4-11.
53. John D. Turner, in the introduction to his translation of *Trimorphic Protennoia* [literally "three-formed first thought"], *NHL*, p. 461.
54. *Trimorphic Protennoia* 45:2-6.
55. H. Jonas, *The Gnostic Religion: The Message of the Alien God and the Beginnings of Christianity* (Boston, MA: Beacon Press, 1958), p. 257, asserts that the ascetic tendency of Gnosticism rejected marriage. See Irenaeus, *Against Heresies* 1.24.2 on the followers of Saturnilus: "Marriage and procreation, they maintain, are of Satan." Epiphanius, *Panarion* 45.2.1, quotes Severus, the Marcionite, to the same effect: "Those who consort in marriage fulfill the work of Satan." See also *Dialogue of the Savior* (NHL) 144:15-21: "Judas said . . . 'How shall we pray?' The Lord said,

'He says to us, "Pray in the place where there is no woman," (and) "Destroy [the] works of femaleness."'"

56. Epiphanius, *Panarion* 26:5:5, describes an orgiastic cult as an example of the libertine option- eating sperm and menstrual fluid "immoral unions" by which a man is "made one with Christ." But note that like in the ascetic option, "child-bearing is avoided. If pregnancy ensues, the infant embryo is forcibly removed . . . [and] consumed after being torn apart and duly pre- pared." K. Rudolf, *Gnosis: The Nature and History of an Ancient Religion* (Edinburgh, Scotland: T and T Clark, 1977), pp. 248-249, finds this an example of "perverted phantasy" on the part of Epiphanius. Rudolf (ibid., p. 250) nevertheless gives the theological reason for doing these barbarous acts, found in *Panarion* 26:9, 6-9: "We are doing a kindness to created things, in that we collect the soul from all things and transmit it with ourselves to the heavenly world," find- ing this explanation "more credible." If the theological reason makes sense, why not Epiphanius's description of the practice?

57. *Apocalypse of James* 41:15-18.

58. Genesis 1:27. See Meyer, "Male and Female," p. 560.

59. Epiphanes, *On Righteousness*, preserved in Clement of Alexandria's *Stromateis* 3:6:1-9:3, quoted in K. Rudolf, *Gnosis: The Nature and History of an Ancient Religion* (Edinburgh, Scotland: T and T Clark, 1977), p. 268.

60. See Meeks, "The Image of the Androgyne: Some Uses of a Symbol in Earliest Christinity," *History of Religions*, 13 (1974), p. 185, argues that Galatians 3:28 "presupposes an interpretation of the creation story in which the divine image after which Adam was modeled was mas- culofeminine."

61. Tertullian, *De Praescriptione*, p. 41.

62. K. Rudolf, *Gnosis: The Nature and History of an Ancient Religion* (Edinburgh, Scotland: T and T Clark, 1977), pp. 211, 251, 270.

63. Hippolytus, *Refutation of All Heresies* 6:35, and Irenaeus, *Against Heresies* 1:13:1-2.

64. See my discussion of this in Jones, *Gnostic Empire*, pp. 32-33.

65. See Jones, *Gnostic Empire*, p. 40, note 39 for an extended discussion of this point.

66. For the text, see *Gospel of Mary* 8:17—9:4, *NHL*, p. 472.

67. *Gospel of Mary* 9:20. For the full text see *NHL*, p. 472.

68. *Gospel of Mary* 17:15.

69. Ibid., 17:19.

70. Ibid., 10:7-8, 18:13-14.

71. Pagels, *Gnostic Gospels*, p. 66.

72. Rudolf, *Gnosis*, p. 212.

Chapter Fourteen

1. James Plath, ed., *Conversations with John Updike* (Jackson, MS: University Press of Mississippi, 1994), p. 14. I am grateful to my colleague, Dr. W. Robert Godfrey, for this quotation.

2. Marilyn Ferguson, *The Brain Revolution: Frontiers of Mind Research* (Davis-Poynter, 1974), pp. 111-113, quoted in Alan Morrison, *The Serpent and the Cross: Religious Corruption in an Evil Age* (Birmingham, UK: K and M Books, 1994), p. 128.

3. Betty Eadie, *Embraced by the Light* (Placerville, CA: Goldleaf Press, 1992), pp. 40-41.

4. Donna Steichen, *Ungodly Rage: The Hidden Face of Catholic Feminism* (San Francisco: Ignatius Press, 1991), p. 285.

5. Ibid., p. 309.
6. David F. Wells, *No Place for Truth: Or Whatever Happened to Evangelical Theology?* (Grand Rapids, MI: Eerdmans, 1993), p. 267.
7. Sister Madonna Kolbenschlag, quoted in Steichen, *Ungodly Rage*, p. 93.
8. Steichen, *Ungodly Rage*, p. 60.
9. Sjoo and Mor, *The Great Cosmic Mother: Discovering the Religions of the Earth* (San Francisco: HarperSanFrancisco, 1987), p. 427.
10. Sister Madonna Kolbenschlag, quoted in Steichen, *Ungodly Rage*, p. 93, emphasis added.
11. Steichen, *Ungodly Rage*, p. 150.
12. *Escondido (California) Times Advocate* (June 13, 1994).
13. W. C. Roof's sociological study, *A Generation of Seekers: The Spiritual Journeys of the Baby Boom Generation* (San Francisco: Harper, 1993), pp. 126-127.
14. Donald Capps quoted in Roof, *Seekers*, p. 258. David Wells, *No Place for Truth*, pp. 111-112, sees the evangelical church as deeply influenced by this modern view of the world.
15. Definition of "Hinduism," quoted in Alan Morrison, *The Serpent and the Cross: Religious Corruption in an Evil Age* (Birmingham, UK: K and M Books, 1994), p. 186.
16. Sjoo and Mor, *The Great Cosmic Mother*, p. 420.
17. Sister Elaine Prevallet, S.L., quoted in Donna Steichen, *Ungodly Rage*, p. 291.
18. Sister Madonna Kolbenschlag, *Kiss Sleeping Beauty Goodbye: Breaking the Spell of Feminine Myths and Models* (Garden City, NY: Doubleday, 1979), pp. 184-186, quoted in Steichen, *Ungodly Rage*, p. 92.
19. Scott Peck, *The Road Less Traveled* (New York: Simon and Schuster, 1978), p. 283.
20. Virginia Mollenkott, *Sensuous Spirituality: Out from Fundamentalism* (New York: Crossroads, 1992), p. 17.
21. Peter Russell, *The White Hole in Time: Our Future Evolution and the Meaning of Now* (Wellingborough, Northants, UK: Aquarian Press, 1992), p. 223, quoted in Morrison, *The Serpent*, p. 140.
22. Morrison, *The Serpent*, p. 140, emphasis added.
23. Mollenkott, *Sensuous Spirituality*, p. 98.
24. Lazaris, *Concept: Synergy* (August 1994).
25. Sjoo and Mor, *Great Cosmic Mother*, p. 17.
26. J. Gordon Melton, *New Age Encyclopedia* (Detroit, MI: Gale Research Inc., 1990), p. xiii.
27. See Steichen, *Ungodly Rage*, p. 36.
28. See the whole section, Genesis 3:1-7.
29. See 1 Corinthians 15:26,55.
30. Elizabeth Kübler-Ross, "Death: The Final State of Growth," quoted in Morrison, *The Serpent*, p. 174.
31. See especially Eadie, *Embraced by the Light*.
32. Elizabeth Clare Prophet, *Prayer and Meditation: Jesus and Kuthumi* (Chelsea, MA: Summit Press, 1963), inside cover, quoted in Morrison, *The Serpent*, p. 112.
33. Oddie, *What Will Happen to God? Feminism and the Reconstruction of Christian Belief* (San Francisco: Ignatius Press, 1988), p. 139.
34. Ibid., p. 143.
35. Judith Plaskow, a leading religious feminist and her committee at a 1972 feminist conference at Grailville, Loveland, Ohio—see Steichen, *Ungodly Rage*, p. 94.
36. Steichen, *Ungodly Rage*, p. 81. This program, "The Goddesses and the Wild Woman," was the first in a series presented at Mundelein, a conference center in the Midwest, held in March 1985.

37. A poem "For the Unknown Goddess," by Elizabeth Brewster, for "Christian" feminist liturgies in the UK, quoted in Oddie, *What Will Happen to God?* p. 20.

38. Ibid., p. 21, emphasis added.

39. Rosemary Radford Ruether, quoted in Steichen, *Ungodly Rage*, p. 145.

40. Marjorie Procter-Smith, *Women at Worship: Interpretations of North American Diversity* (Louisville, KY: Westminster/John Knox Press, 1993), on the back cover. This is the second explosive book published by John Knox/Westminster Press, which, at the time, was the official publishing arm of the Presbyterian Church U.S.A. This book contains all the radical notions that were later expressed at the RE-Imagining Conference in the fall of 1993.

41. As Steichen, *Ungodly Rage*, p. 96, sees so well.

42. Samantha Scott and Barbara Smith, *Trojan Horse: How the New Age Movement Infiltrates the Church* (Lafayette, LA.: Huntingdon House Press, 1993), p. 44, show that these same four steps are promoted in Madeleine L'Engle's books.

43. I am following here the account of Steichen, *Ungodly Rage*, p. 72.

44. Procter-Smith, *Women at Worship*, p. 3.

45. Ibid., p. 4.

46. Ibid., p. 145.

47. Ibid., p. 158.

48. Ibid., p. 159.

49. Steichen, *Ungodly Rage*, p. 71.

50. Rosemary Radford Ruether, *Women-Church: Theology and Practice* (San Francisco: Harper and Row, 1985), pp. 162, 175.

51. Ibid., p. 171.

52. Steichen, *Ungodly Rage*, p. 55.

53. Oddie, *What Will Happen to God?* p. 139.

54. Steichen, *Ungodly Rage*, p. 92.

55. Ibid., p. 151.

56. Phil Jackson with Hugh Delehanty, *Sacred Hoops: Spiritual Lessons of a Hardwood Warrior* (New York: Hyperion, 1996), reported via the *Gannett News Service* in the *Montgomery Advertiser* (March 23, 1996).

57. Philip St. Romain, *Kundalini Energy and Christian Spirituality: A Pathway to Growth and Healing* (New York: Crossroads, 1991), pp. 24, 115.

58. Ibid., p. 74.

59. Ibid., p. 129.

60. Ibid., p. 131: "Surrender yourself into the care of Christ, Whose Spirit is capable of guiding your kundalini energies toward a wholesome integration. Trust that a Higher Guidance is at work in the process. Ask for this Guidance when confused."

61. Deepak Chopra, *The Higher Self* tape series, distributed by Conant and Nightingale.

62. Sjoo and Mor, *The Great Cosmic Mother*, p. 432.

63. Ken Carey, *The Starseed Transmissions* (New York: Harper, 1982), quoted in Morrison, *The Serpent*, p. 124.

64. Sjoo and Mor, *The Great Cosmic Mother*, p. 172.

65. Deepak Chopra, *The Higher Self.*

66. *Light Connection* (July 1994), pp. 14-15.

67. Mollenkott, *Sensuous Spirituality*, p. 16.

68. Mollenkott, ibid., p. 107, is a firm believer in this form of meditation.

69. Lazaris, *Concept: Synergy*, emphasis added.
70. A transcript from tapes of the addresses given at the RE-Imagining Conference in Minneapolis, 1993, published by *Good News: A Forum for Scriptural Christianity Within the United Methodist Church* (January 1994), p. 13.
71. In particular, *The Presbyterian Layman* (PCUSA) and *Good News* (United Methodist).
72. Steichen, *Ungodly Rage*.
73. Ibid., pp. 220, 229.
74. Matthew Fox, *The Coming of the Cosmic Christ: The Healing of Mother Earth and the Birth of a Global Renaissance* (San Francisco: Harper, 1988), pp. 170, 180.
75. Miriam Starhawk, quoted in Steichen, *Ungodly Rage*, p. 176, emphasis added.
76. Berit Kjos, "An Unholy Renaissance of Sacred Sexuality," *Southern California Christian Times* (July, 1994), p. 9.
77. Sjoo and Mor, *The Great Cosmic Mother*, p. 75.
78. Ibid., p. 173.
79. Steichen, *Ungodly Rage*, p. 231.
80. "Ouroboros" means literally "devourer of its own tail": compare the Latin term *carni-vorus* which has borrowed from the Greek. See K. Rudolf, *Gnosis: The Nature and History of an Ancient Religion* (Edinburgh, Scotland: T and T Clark, 1977), p. 223.
81. Sjoo and Mor, *The Great Cosmic Mother*, pp. 57-58.
82. Ibid.
83. Ibid., p. 58. "Gliding in and out of holes, it symbolizes the dead awaiting rebirth."
84. Ibid., p. 59.
85. Ibid., p. 277.
86. Ibid., p. 425.
87. 2 Cor. 6:16.
88. St. Romain, *Kundalini Energy*, p. 148.
89. Ibid., p. 130.
90. Ibid., p. 128.
91. David Schnarch, "Joy, with Your Underwear Down," *Psychology Today* (July/August 1994), p. 78.
92. Livy, Book XXXIX, p. xiii:11, in *Livy, with an English Translation in Fourteen Volumes*, trans., Evan T. Sage (Cambridge, MA: Harvard University Press, 1965), p. 255.
93. Mollenkott, *Sensuous Spirituality*, p. 27.
94. Ibid., p. 118. She says on page 100: "I believe that every honest attempt to relate to another human being is a good attempt, including recreational sex or sensuality, if that is all a person can achieve."
95. Ibid., p. 139.
96. Mary Daly and Jane Caputi, *Webster's First New Intergalactic Wickedary of the English Language* (Boston, MA: Beacon Press, 1987), ad loc.
97. Ibid.
98. Jones, "What Lesbian Nuns Can Teach Us About Vatican II," *Fidelity* (December 1985), p. 22.
99. Ibid., p. 20.
100. Good News tape transcripts, p. 7.
101. Nun quoted in E. Michael Jones, "Lesbian Nuns," p. 21.
102. The apostle Paul, Romans 1: 24.
103. 1 Corinthians 6:18.
104. Sjoo and Mor, *The Great Cosmic Mother*, p. 377.

105. Ibid., p. 388.
106. Ruether, *Women-Church*, p. 130.
107. Ibid., p. 145.
108. James R. Edwards, "Earthquake in the Mainline," *Christianity Today* (November 14, 1994), p. 39.
109. Ibid.

Chapter Fifteen

1. *Apocryphon of James* 12:12-16.
2. As opposed to the Christian teaching that death has been vanquished and has no final victory—see 1 Corinthians 15:54-57.
3. K. Rudolf, *Gnosis: The Nature and History of an Ancient Religion* (Edinburgh, Scotland: T and T Clark, 1977), p. 171.
4. Ibid.
5. If you have been pronouncing the *g* up till this point, return to "Go," and read everything again!
6. *Tripartite Tractate* 110:11-23. See Rudolf, *Gnosis*, p. 55.
7. G. Filoramo, *A History of Gnosticism* (Cambridge, MA: Basil Blackwell, 1990), p. 60.
8. Ibid., pp. 38-39 speaks of a "profound transformation the Gnostic brings to the word gnosis."
9. *Gospel of Truth* 22:2-15.
10. For the actual text, see *Apocryphon of James* 12:10ff.
11. *Gospel of Truth* 1:18. G. W. MacRae, "Introduction," *The Nag Hammadi Library in English (NHL)*, p. 37, says that the Gospel of Truth is "about the eternal divine Son, the word who reveals the Father and passes on knowledge, particularly self-knowledge."
12. Aristotle, *Fr.* 15, quoted in Walter Burkert, *Ancient Mystery Cults* (Cambridge, MA: Harvard University Press, 1987), p. 89.
13. Walter Burkert, *Ancient Mystery Cults* (Cambridge, MA: Harvard University Press, 1987), p. 11.
14. *Dio Chrysostom Or.* 12.33, quoted in Burkert, *Ancient Mystery Cults*, p. 90.
15. *Paraphrase of Shem* 34:22-23.
16. Rudolf, *Gnosis*, p. 76.
17. *Gospel of Truth* 1:37-38.
18. *Testimony of Truth* 36.
19. *Gospel of Truth* 25:5-10, 38:1ff, and 42:25.
20. *Tripartite Tractate* 71:8ff.
21. Hans Jonas, "Delimitation of the Gnostic Phenomenon—Typological and Historical," in *Le origini dello gnosticismo*, p. 97, quoted in by Lee, *Against the Protestant Gnostics* (New York: Oxford University Press, 1987).
22. *Gospel of Truth* 25:1-7.
23. In a public address at the Parliament of the World's Religions, at which I was present. J. J. Buckley, "The Cult-Mystery in the Gospel of Philip," *JBL*, 99/4 (1980), p. 581, maintains that the *Gospel of Philip* moves beyond dualism when it describes the Gnostic initiate transcending the creational structures. This entrance into true liberty produces "a collapse of a dualistic worldview."
24. Lee, *Against the Protestant Gnostics* (New York: Oxford University Press, 1987), p. 23, emphasis added.
25. Rudolf, *Gnosis*, pp. 186-187.

26. Lee, *Against the Protestant Gnostics*, p. 44.
27. *Tripartite Tractate* 124.21ff.
28. *Apocryphon of James* 4:19-21. Burkert, *Ancient Mystery Cults*, p. 69, notes the very same tendency in pagan mystery religions. The pagan mysteries were "unspeakable," (*arrheta*) not only in the sense that one was obliged to a vow of secrecy, but also in the sense that "what was central and decisive was not accessible to verbalization."
29. Rudolf, *Gnosis*, p. 117.
30. See 1 Timothy 4:3.
31. This makes for an inevitable overlap in the chapters on Gnostic sexuality and Gnostic spirituality.
32. *Gospel of Truth* 22:3.
33. Lee, *Against the Protestant Gnostics*, p. 26.
34. Filoramo, *Gnosticism*, p. 40.
35. Marvin Meyer and Richard Smith, *Ancient Christian Magic: Coptic Texts of Ritual Power* (San Francisco: Harper, 1994), p. 61. This book is a further project of the Institute for Antiquity and Christianity of Claremont Graduate School, of which the director is James M. Robinson.
36. Burkert, *Ancient Mystery Cults*, p. 8.
37. Irenaeus, *Against Heresies* 21:2.
38. *The Gospel of Philip* 67:25ff.
39. Luke 12:49-50. This is the baptism of His death on the cross.
40. Irenaeus, *Against Heresies* 1:21:2. See Rudolf, *Gnosis*, p. 227.
41. *Gospel of Philip* 76:25ff.
42. See Rudolf, *Gnosis*, p. 229. See *Gospel of Philip* 69:15-25.
43. *Gospel of Philip* 75:15-25.
44. *Acts of Thomas* 50, quoted in Rudolf, *Gnosis*, p. 242.
45. Gnostic text quoted in Rudolf, *Gnosis*, p. 242.
46. Epiphanius, *Panarion* 37:5, 6-8.
47. C. G. Jung, quoted in J. Dart, *The Laughing Savior: The Discovery and the Significance of the Nag Hammadi Gnostic Library* (San Francisco: Harper and Row, 1976), p. 33.
48. This title is meant to recall E. Michael Jones, *Degenerate Moderns: Modernity as Rationalized Sexual Misbehavior* (San Francisco: Ignatius, 1993).
49. This is Rudolf's position, *Gnosis*, p. 250. For defense of Epiphanius, see Robert L. Wilken, *The Christians as the Romans Saw Them* (New Haven and London: Yale University Press, 1984), pp. 17-21.
50. See Rudolf, *Gnosis*, p. 250. Rudolf provides this evidence while still charging Epiphanius with fantasy, etc.
51. Epiphanius, *Panarion* 2:26:4,3-5,9. Dart, *The Laughing Savior*, pp. 33-34, shows that Jung found important and useful "symbolism" in these extreme Gnostic rites.
52. Rudolf, *Gnosis*, p. 245.
53. Ibid., p. 246.
54. Marvin W. Meyer, "Male and Female in the Gospel of Thomas," *New Testament Studies*, 31 (1985), p. 557, sees the solitary ones in the bridal chamber as being joined to their spiritual alter ego.
55. Filoramo, *Gnosticism*, p. 141.
56. *Gospel of Philip* 82:5-10.
57. Ibid., 59:10. Scholars generally believe that there is no reference here to carnal union because Philip is ascetic. See J. J. Buckley, "A Cult Mystery in the Gospel of Philip," *JBL*, 99 (1980), p. 575.

58. Ibid., 70:5-10, cp., *Gospel of Thomas* 37.

59. Rudolf, *Gnosis*, p. 207: "the Gnostics practiced a more or less rigid code of secrecy (the so-called arcane discipline)."

60. These are the words of Burkert, *Ancient Mystery Cults*, p. 90, characterizing Dio's description.

61. Epiphanius, *Panarion* 2:11:9-11. See also the witness of Irenaeus, *Against Heresies* 1:6:3.

62. Ibid., 24:3:2.

63. See Acts 8 and Epiphanius, *Panarion* 2:21:2:2ff, according to whom Simon, "naturally lecherous," went around with a prostitute from Tyre whom he called the Holy Spirit.

64. This library is associated with the St. Pachomius monastery which is close to the site and indicates a strong interest in asceticism. On the other hand, in the Isis initiation, there is an emphasis upon sexual abstinence, while at the same time there is the suggestion that sexual activity is reserved for the final stages of initiation.

65. Burkert, *Ancient Mystery Cults*, p. 3 notes: "Certain Gnostic sects seem to have practiced mystery initiations, imitating or rather outdoing the pagans, and even orthodox Christianity adopted the mystery metaphor." The most explicit testimony is Irenaeus, *Against Heresies* 1:21:3 (1:14:2, p. 185, Harvey): "They prepare a bridal chamber and celebrate mysteries." Clement repeatedly says the Gnostics celebrate sexual intercourse as mysteries, see *Stromata* 3:27:1,5, cp., 3:10:1; 3:30:1. A homosexual encounter is insinuated in the "Secret Gospel of Mark," Smith, (1973), pp. 115-117; 185; 452. See also R. M. Grant, "The Mysteries of Marriage in the Gospel of Philip," *Vig. Christ.* 15 (1961), pp. 129-140.

66. Epiphanius, *Panarion*.

67. Livy, Book 39:13:12.

68. Irenaeus, *Against Heresies* 1.31.2.

69. Ibid., 1.25.4 cp. Eusebius, *Ecclesiastical History* 4:7.

70. 1 John 3:6, emphasis added.

71. 1 John 3:8.

72. Irenaeus, *Against Heresies* 1:21:3.

73. Sometimes even 365. See Epiphanius, *Panarion* 2:10:6-8.

74. Rudolf, *Gnosis*, p. 183.

75. Epiphanius, *Panarion* 2:10:6-8.

76. Irenaeus, *Against Heresies* 1:21:5.

77. Rudolf, *Gnosis*, p. 177, quoting the Left Ginza.

78. Rudolf, *Gnosis*, does not make anything of this aspect of Gnostic spirituality, but it is certainly there.

79. John H. Siebeck, "Introduction," *NHL*, p. 368.

80. Ibid.

81. *Zostrianos* 129:6-12.

82. *Zostrianos* 53:19.

83. All this material is quoted from Pagels, *Gnostic Gospels* (New York: Random House, 1979), p. 165.

84. See Meyer and Smith, *Ancient Christian Magic*, pp. 64-65.

85. See Matthew 6:7.

86. *Apocalypse of Paul* 22:24-30, 23:26-27, goes beyond 2 Corinthians 12 and reveals what the Paul of Scripture said was unlawful to reveal.

87. Dieter Mueller, "Introduction," *NHL*, p. 27, observes that the Prayer of the Apostle Paul "displays a striking resemblance not only to the prayers in the Corpus Hermeticum but also to invocations found in magical texts."

88. Lee, *Against the Protestant Gnostics*, p. 25.

89. Rudolf, *Gnosis*, p. 14, shows that Hippolytus structures his *Refutatio* in such a way that he first presents the Greek heathen ideas, then gives an exposition of the Christian Gnostic heresies, attempting to show thereby that the Gnostics took their doctrines from the "wisdom of the heathen" —which incidentally they (the heretics) even misunderstand and misuse sometimes.

90. Hippolytus, *The Refutation of All Heresies* 5:16.

91. Irenaeus, *Against Heresies* 1:6:3. Irenaeus adds, "they observe other rites that are just like those of the pagans."

92. David Miller, *The New Polytheism: Rebirth of the Gods and Goddesses* (New York: Harper and Row, 1974), p. 36. Interestingly, Virginia Mollenkott has made use of the *I Ching* (a form of Chinese divination) in her exit from "Fundamentalism"—see Virginia Mollenkott, *Sensuous Spirituality: Out from Fundamentalism* (New York: Crossroads, 1992), p. 16.

93. Epiphanius, *Panarion* 11:6:9, speaking of the Carpocratians, and Hippolytus, *Refutation of All Heresies* 6:17-19, who argues that the Simonians and the Valentinians both derive from Pythagoras.

94. Alan Morrison, *The Serpent and the Cross: Religious Corruption in an Evil Age* (Birmingham, UK: K and M Books, 1994), p. 380, quoting, in particular, Eliade, ed., *The Encyclopedia of Religion*, p. 114.

95. Alexander the Great extended the Greek Empire to India.

96. James Preston, "Goddess Worship: An Overview," *The Book of the Goddess, Past and Present: An Introduction to Her Religion*, ed. Carl Olsen, (New York: Beyond Words Publishing Company, 1983), p. 38.

97. C. J. Bleeker, "Isis and Hathor," in *The Book of the Goddess, Past and Present*, p. 32. The wisdom of Isis is recognized when the Egyptians call her "great in magic power."

98. Ibid.

99. Ibid., p. 38.

100. Metamorphoses, quoted in Burkert, *Ancient Mystery Cults*, p. 97.

101. Ibid., p. 91, refers to a text of Plutarch that attempts to describe the presumed process of dying in terms of a mystery initiation.

102. Tertullian, *De Praescriptione* 43.

103. Irenaeus, *Against Heresies* 1:23:4. Filoramo, *Gnosticism*, p. 166, notes that Marcion's disciple, Apelles, wrote down the oracles of a virgin possessed, Philmena (according to Eusebius, *Ecclesiastical History* 5:13:2-4), which is a further witness to the Gnostic use of occult pagan practices.

104. Plotinus, *Enneads* 2:9:14.

105. Rudolf, *Gnosis*, p. 225.

106. Ezekiel 8:1-16.

107. See Walter Zimmerli, *Ezekiel 1: A Commentary on the Book of the Prophet Ezekiel, Chapters 1-24*, Hermeneia Series (Philadelphia: Fortress Press, 1979), p. 243. See also pp. 236-245.

108. See Ezekiel 8:16.

109. Zimmerli, *Ezekiel 1: A Commentary*, p. 245.

110. Ezekiel 9 recounts the physical destruction of the idolaters. In the theocracy of ancient Israel, such punishment was legitimate. In the time of the Church, Jesus says to Peter, "Put your sword back in its place" (Matt. 26:52), and that is where it remains until God's final judgment of sin. The exercise of the "sword" in the Church is limited to spiritual discipline in all its forms, from consultation to confrontation to excommunication (Matt. 18:15-18; 1 Cor. 1:1-5,

14:36-38; 2 Cor. 13:1-10; Gal. 1:9). "'It is mine to avenge; I will repay,' says the Lord," (Rom. 12:19) is the principle which guides the Church in its present pilgrimage.
111. Ezekiel 8:18.

Chapter Sixteen

1. Caitlín Matthews, *Sophia, Goddess of Wisdom: The Divine Feminine from Black Goddess to World-Soul* (London: The Aquarian Press/Harper Collins, 1992), p. 332.
2. Ibid., p. 330.
3. Ibid., pp. 322, 327.
4. Ibid., p. 320.
5. See Nancy Wilson, *A Lesbian Ecu-Terrorist Ousts the Bible for the Queer Millennium* (San Francisco: HarperSanFrancisco, 1996).
6. *Books for the Nineties* (San Francisco: HarperSanFrancisco, 1996), p. 10.
7. Sir Arnold Toynbee, quoted in Herbert J. Pollitt, *The Inter-Faith Movement: The New Age Enters the Church* (Edinburgh: The Banner of Truth Trust, 1996), p. 13.
8. The virtual silence on this issue is surprising in our day when feminism has become a raging forest fire. The well-known statement of Luther applies here: "If I profess with the loudest voice... the truth of God except precisely at that little point which the world and the devil are at that moment attacking, I am not professing Christ."
9. 1 Timothy 2:14 , cp., 2 Corinthians 11:3.
10. See 1 Timothy 2:15.
11. For the global pretensions of this movement and its well-laid plans for planetary "governance," see Nancy Hodes and Michael Hays, eds., *The United Nations and the World's Religions: Prospects for a Global Ethic* (Boston, MA: Boston Researching Center for the 21st Century, 1995); *Buddhist Peacework: Creating Cultures of Peace* (Boston: Wisdom Publications, 2000), and Maurice Strong, *Where on Earth Are We Going?* (New York: Texere, 2001). For a critique of this movement, see Michael S. Coffman, *Saviors of the Earth: The Politics and Religion of the Environmental Movement* (Chicago: Northfield Publishing, 1994), and Lee Penn, "The United Nations: Globalist and New Age Plans," *SCP Journal*, 23/2-23/3 (1999), pp. 36-73 and, by the same author, "Dark Apocalypse: Bloodlust of the Compassionate," *SCP Journal*, 23/4-24/1 (2000), pp. 8-31. For a view of the third millennium from a conservative Roman Catholic point of view, see David Walsh, *The Third Millennium: Reflections on Faith and Reason* (Washington, DC: Georgetown University Press, 1999).
12. Philip E. Johnson, *Reason in the Balance: The Case Against Naturalism in Science, Law and Education* (Downers Grove, IL: InterVarsity Press, 1995), p. 124.
13. Michael Swift, "Gay Revolutionary," *Gay Community News* (February 1987), quoted in Scott Lively and Kevin Abrams, *The Pink Swastika*, p. 199.
14. Peg Thompson, quoted in Sandi Dolbee, *The San Diego Union-Tribune* (September 16, 1994).
15. Mary Daly and Jane Caputi, *Webster's First New Intergalactic Wickedary of the English Language* (Boston, MA: Beacon Press, 1987), p. 133.
16. Guerra, "The Practice of Witchcraft," quoted in Donna Steichen, *Ungodly Rage: The Hidden Face of Catholic Feminism* (San Francisco: Ignatius Press, 1991), pp. 70-71.
17. James Webb, *The Occult Establishment* (Lasalle, IL: Open Court, 1976), p. 161.
18. Malachi Martin, *Windswept House: A Vatican Novel* (New York: Doubleday, 1996).
19. See Jeffrey L. Sheler, "Plotting World Order in Rome," *U. S. News and World Report* (June 10, 1996), p. 66.

20. Abraham Kuyper, *Lectures on Calvinism* (Grand Rapids, MI: Eerdmans, 1931), p. 199.
21. See Revelation 17.
22. I hope to do so in a forthcoming volume.
23. Hippolytus, *The Refutation of All Heresies* 4:45.
24. See Jeremiah 3:9.
25. See Matthew 16:18.
26. Psalm 112:4.
27. See Ezekiel 3:18-19.
28. Christian orthodoxy today seems but a bothersome pimple on the face of liberalism.
29. Philippians 2:11.
30. George W. Kitchin and Michael R. Newbolt, "Lift High the Cross," *Trinity Hymnal* (Atlanta, GA: Great Commissions Publications, 1990), p. 263.

ABOUT THE AUTHOR

Peter Jones was born in Liverpool, England, where he used to buy fish and chips on Penny Lane with John Lennon, a high-school friend with whom he shared a desk for five years. Later, Peter went off to the University of Wales and then to the United States to study theology at Gordon Divinity School. He received a master's degree in New Testament Studies at Harvard and a Ph.D. in the same field at Princeton.

In 1971, Peter married Rebecca Clowney; and in 1973 he, Rebecca and their first two childen moved to France, where they lived until 1991. He taught New Testament at La Faculte Libre de Theologie Reformee d'Aix-en-Provence. In addition to teaching, he helped start a Christian school and a church. During his time in France, he and Rebecca had five more children, bringing the total to seven: five daughters and two sons.

In 1989, Peter received a letter asking him to return to the United States to teach. Upon his return in 1991, he was shocked at the changes that had taken place since he first arrived in America in 1964. The culture shock led Peter to publish *The Gnostic Empire Strikes Back* (1992). He quickly realized that what he had thought of as New Age was more than just a fad. A new spirituality had taken over America. Two years of research led to the publication of *Spirit Wars: Pagan Revival in Christian America* (1997), which has been significantly revised, updated and republished as *Pagans in the Pews*. He is also the author of *Gospel Truth, Pagan Lies: Can You Tell the Difference?* (1999). He is presently finishing two books, one on Paul, *Return of the Rabbi*; and one on sexuality and world view, entitled *God and Sex*.

Since returning to the United States, Peter has been teaching New Testament at Westminster Theological Seminary in California. He also travels widely in the States and abroad, hosting two different seminars: Winning the Spirit Wars, which seeks to explain the religious-pagan nature of the changes taking place in once-Christian America; and a men's retreat: Be the Man: Male Leadership in a Feminized World, which confronts men with the biblical challenge of male leadership in a society that has been profoundly reconfigured by the ideology of feminism.

For more information about Peter Jones's ministry, his seminars and his publications, please check out his website at

www.spirit-wars.com

INDEX

U
Updike, J., 188

V
Valentius, 151
Veith, G., 242
Vivekananda, 29, 243
von Harnack, A., 65, 248

W
Walton, J., 200
Watson, F., 113, 258
Weaver, M., 255
Webb, J., 280
Weldon, J., 268
Wells, D., 100-101, 189, 243, 254

Wenham, J., 84, 252
Wildavsky, B., 256
Wilken, R., 39, 244
Willeford, L., 46-47, 245
Williams, T., 246
Williamson, M., 23-24
Wilson, L., 136
Wilson, N., 232, 280
Wintermute, O., 256
Woodward, B., 241
Woolf, V., 259

Z
Zappone, K., 56, 246
Zimmerli, W., 229-230, 279